WRITERS AND THEIR WORK

ISOBEL ARMSTRONG
General Editor

BRYAN LOUGHREY
Advisory Editor

Please return on or before
the last date stamped below.
Contact: 01603 773 114
or 01603 773 224

0 4 DEC 2012

D1374751

ROBERT TRESSELL

A photograph of the author of THE RAGGED TROUSERED PHILANTHROPISTS
taken at Old Roar near Hastings (circa 1908),
by kind permission of his grand-daughter, Joan Johnson

WV

Working-class Fiction

from Chartism to *Trainspotting*

Ian Haywood

First published in 1997 by Northcote House Publishers Ltd, Plymbridge House, Estover Road, Plymouth PL6 7PY, United Kingdom.
Tel: +44 (01752) 202368   Fax: +44 (01752) 202330.

British Library Cataloguing-in-Publication Data
A catalogue record for this book is available from the British Library

ISBN 0-7463-0780-2

Typeset by PDQ Typesetting, Newcastle-under-Lyme
Printed and bound in the United Kingdom

To my father

Contents

Acknowledgements

Thanks are due to Roehampton Institute London, the staff of the British Library and Marx Memorial Library, and to all those colleagues and students who encouraged me to undertake this study. I owe a particular debt of gratitude to Northcote House for their patience and flexibility with deadlines. Very special thanks to Joan Johnson, Robert Tressell's grand-daughter, and her husband Reg, for their hospitality, and their generosity in granting access to their collection of photographs, letters and other Tressell papers. Last but never least, thanks to Theresa for her unfailing support.

A Chronology

1832	Reform Bill disenfranchises the working class.
1834	The Tolpuddle 'martyrs' transported for establishing a trade union.
1839–48	Chartist agitation for universal male suffrage and electoral reform.
1845	Thomas Cooper, 'Merrie England – No More!'
1848	Revolutions in France, Germany, Italy and Austro-Hungary.
1849–50	Thomas Martin Wheeler's Chartist novel *Sunshine and Shadow* appears in the *Northern Star*.
1867	Enfranchisement of urban working-class men (extended in 1885 to rural areas).
1870	Elementary education becomes compulsory.
1873–96	The 'Great Depression' leads to renewed imperialism and a revival of socialism.
1884	Foundation of Social Democratic Federation, Socialist League and Fabian Society.
1885	Emile Zola, *Germinal*.
1888–89	The Liverpool 'match girls' and the London dockworkers' strikes.
1893	Independent Labour Party founded.
1894	Arthur Morrison, *Tales of Mean Streets*.
1898	Allen Clarke, *The Daughter of the Factory*.
1903–14	Women's suffrage movement enters a militant phase.
1906	The Labour Party is founded.
1906–14	Period of Liberal social reforms includes rudimentary welfare state.
1910–12	Waves of strikes in key industries; troops sent to Rhondda valley.

1911	Robert Tressell dies in Liverpool.
1913	D. H. Lawrence, *Sons and Lovers*.
1914	Publication of first, abridged edition of *The Ragged Trousered Philanthropists*.
1914–18	First World War.
1916	Easter rebellion in Dublin.
1917	Russian revolution.
1918	Enfranchisement of women over 30 (extended to all women over 21 in 1929).
1918–39	Economic recession hits 'old' industries (coal, steel, shipbuilding, textiles) and their regions badly; the north, north-east, Scotland and South Wales suffer high levels of unemployment. Meanwhile 'new' industries (cars, chemicals, food processing) in midlands and southern England prosper, leading to a 'boom' in private house building.
1919	'Red' Clydeside disturbances; government sends in troops and tanks.
1920	Trade Union 'Councils of Action' block military supplies bound for counter-revolutionary forces in Russia. James Welsh, *The Underworld*.
1922	Partition of Ireland.
1925	Ethel Carnie Holdsworth, *This Slavery*.
1924	First Labour government.
1926	The General Strike (3–12 May).
1929	The Wall Street Crash. Ellen Wilkinson, *Clash*. Harold Heslop, *The Gate of a Strange Field*.
1929–31	Second Labour government.
1931	Election of the 'National' government; dole cut from 17s to 15s 3d; introduction of the Means Test. James Hanley, *Boy*.
1932–3	Unemployment reaches 3.75 million.
1932–4	Lewis Grassic Gibbon, *A Scots Quair*.
1933	Hitler elected Chancellor of Germany. Walter Greenwood, *Love on the Dole*. Frank Tilsley, *The Plebeian's Progress*.
1934	Ralph Bates, *Lean Men*.
1935	Walter Brierley, *Means Test Man*. James Hanley, *The Furys*. Simon Blumenfeld, *Jew Boy*. Harold Heslop, *Last Cage Down*.

1936	The Left Book Club established; Cable Street riots; Jarrow March. John Sommerfield, *May Day*. James Barke, *Major Operation*. Leslie Halward, *To Tea on Sunday*.
1936–9	The Spanish Civil War leads to defeat of Republican government by fascist General Franco.
1937	George Orwell, *The Road to Wigan Pier*. Lewis Jones, *Cwmardy*. Walter Brierley, *Sandwichman*.
1938	Football pools attract ten million customers.
1939	Lewis Jones, *We Live*.
1939–45	Second World War.
1940	Willy Goldman, *East End My Cradle*.
1942	Beveridge Report sells 630,000 copies.
1944	Butler Education Act gives free access to secondary and higher education.
1945	Third Labour government elected on a landslide.
1945–51	Creation of the welfare state and the National Health Service; nationalization of electricity, mines, railways, steel industry, Bank of England; rationing of food and clothes lasts into mid-1950s.
1947	End of British rule in India marks beginning of decolonization struggles in British Empire.
1948	The *Empire Windrush* brings Caribbean immigrant workers to Britain. The Berlin airlift marks beginning of the 'Cold' War.
1950	The Korean War. Sid Chaplin, *The Thin Seam*.
1951–64	Election of Tory government committed to the welfare state, nationalized industries and co-operation with trade unions; period of 'consensus' politics begins.
1955	The restored text of *The Ragged Trousered Philanthropists* published. Len Doherty, *A Miner's Sons*.
1956	Suez canal conflict; invasion of Hungary by Russian troops. John Osborne's *Look Back in Anger* plays at the Royal Court theatre. Twenty-year period of economic prosperity begins; standard of living rises; the onset of 'teenage' culture in music (rock and roll) and fashion.
1957	John Braine, *Room at the Top*. Richard Hoggart, *The Uses of Literacy*. Sam Selvon, *Ways of Sunlight*.
1958	Alan Sillitoe, *Saturday Night and Sunday Morning*.
1959	Alan Sillitoe, *The Loneliness of the Long Distance Runner*.

1960	First episode of *Coronation Street* broadcast. Stan Barstow, *A Kind of Loving*. David Storey, *This Sporting Life*. Raymond Williams, *Border Country*.
1961	Sid Chaplin, *The Day of the Sardine*. David Storey, *Flight into Camden*.
1963	Nell Dunn, *Up the Junction*. E. P. Thompson, *The Making of the English Working Class*.
1960s	Period of permissiveness and protest in politics, social and sexual life.
1967	Abortion made legal; homosexuality decriminalized; divorce laws liberalized; contraception widely available. Jeremy Sandford, *Cathy Come Home*.
1968	Student riots in Paris; Tet offensive in Vietnam war; Soviet troops quash democratic uprising in Czechoslovakia. 'Dialectics of Liberation' conference held at the Roundhouse, London. Barry Hines, *A Kestrel for a Knave*.
1970	Germaine Greer, *The Female Eunuch*.
1971	Troops sent to Northern Ireland.
1973–4	Huge rise in price of crude oil.
1974	Miners' strike leads to power cuts and defeat of Tory government. Buchi Emecheta, *Second Class Citizen*.
1976	International Monetary Fund imposes public spending cuts on Labour government.
1979	Plans for Scottish devolution fail. Election of Margaret Thatcher.
1979–97	Period of New Right government reverses many postwar reforms: privatization of infrastructure (mines, railways, electricity, gas, water), restrictions on trade union power, cuts in public spending, centralization of power, high levels of unemployment, job insecurity and deskilling; in electoral and economic terms Britain becomes again 'two nations' of the north (Labour) and south (Tory).
1981	Youth riots in many inner cities.
1982	The Falklands War. Pat Barker, *Union Street*.
1984–5	Miners' strike.
1984	Beatrix Campbell, *Wigan Pier Revisited*. James Kelman, *The Busconductor Hines*.
1985	Jeanette Winterson, *Oranges are not the only fruit*.

William McIlvanney, *The Big Man*.
1990   The Gulf War.
1992   Livi Michael, *Under a Thin Moon*. Jeff Torrington, *Swing Hammer Swing!*
1994   Irvine Welsh, *Trainspotting*.
1996   Agnes Owens, *People Like That*.
1997   Election of New Labour government.

There ought to be a Radical Literary Reform. The virtues of the masses ought to be sought out and extolled...

(*Chartist Circular*, 1840)

The proletariat must face the problem of winning intellectual power...

(Antonio Gramsci, *Avanti!*, 1920)

Take away all that the working class has given to English literature and that literature would scarcely suffer.

(Virginia Woolf, 'The Leaning Tower', 1940)

Language ought to be the joint creation of poets and manual workers, and in modern England it is difficult for these two classes to meet.

(George Orwell, *The English People*, 1944)

...it will be useful to see how far competitors can do the best sort of propaganda: that which does not simply state facts and arguments, but drives facts and arguments into readers' minds, rouses their feelings, excites them, by showing the human tension, the clash of drama in the struggle of the working class.

(*Left Review* competition, 1935)

Literature had made the working class a convention – literature, which needs leisure, and therefore has been written for the leisured classes, with always – irrespective of the merits of the author – a standpoint above five hundred a year. Or nearly always. One hardly knows how to write simply and straightforwardly, now, about the normal circumstances of ninety per cent of humanity. God, what a decadence!

(Dan Billany, *The Trap*, 1950)

1

From Chartism to Socialism

It is fitting that the first attempt to produce working-class fiction should arise from Britain's (possibly the world's) earliest mass political movement. Chartism derived its name from the six-point 'Charter' drawn up in 1837 by the London Working Men's Association to demand the inclusion of working-class men in the franchise. The Charter was the working-class response to the Whig Reform Bill of 1832 which had betrayed its initial promise of delivering universal suffrage and given the vote only to the middle classes. While we must always be sceptical of placing too much historical meaning on one single event, there is a compelling case for seeing 1832 as the year in which the British working class were (in E. P. Thompson's famous description) 'made' – that is, born out of exclusion, absence, and denial of fundamental rights. To be working class was to be unrepresented, yet the classical political economy which underpinned the industrial revolution decreed that a country's wealth originated in the labour process. In Marx's terms, it was this economic 'base' that constituted a society's 'real foundation' – a claim strikingly at odds with the observable social reality. If the working class were now the acknowledged producers of wealth, they were not its consumers.

For the majority of the population, the 1830s and 1840s must have felt like a downward spiral into poverty, disease, misery and alienation. Much of this suffering was attributed to the *laissez-faire* and repressive policies of a government which preached individual freedoms while imposing or supporting vicious new social and economic controls on the mass of the population. To name but a few of the upheavals and regimes

1

that were transforming the lives of the British proletariat: urbanization and slum housing; the factory system with its shift-work, child labour and rigid supervisory culture; the new Poor Law of 1834 which created a national network of workhouses – emblems of pauperism, failure and the breaking-up of families; victimization of trade unions, symbolized by the persecution of the Tolpuddle 'martyrs' in 1834; a tougher colonial regime in Ireland, which culminated in the great famine of 1846–8, in which more than a million died or emigrated.

The Chartist movement was born out of the simple belief that a more democratic political system would deliver a just and equitable society. Both the 'Old Corruption' of the landowning aristocracy and the 'New Corruption' of the bourgeoisie would give way to a truly representative constitution, not the half-way house of 1832. Chartism harnessed the grievances of the working class against their deteriorating condition and grew quickly into a mass movement. Founded on strong local groups, it established a national organization based around its news-paper the *Northern Star*. Parliament was petitioned three times: 1839, 1842 and 1848. Although the Charter was rejected on each occasion, there is no doubt that Chartism represented a major threat to the structures of power. In each of those three key years, the potential for revolutionary action was strong. In 1839 the Chartists passed a number of 'ulterior measures' to be implemented if their petition was rejected. These included a consumer boycott and a general strike – the latter was rescinded only at the last moment. However, in 1842 a severe recession led to a massive confrontation between northern factory workers and owners. As the unrest spread to the midlands, the Chartists moved quickly to provide political leadership. Orators were despatched to strike areas, and a special convention met at Manchester, scene of numerous pitched battles between workers and the authorities. It was too late. The resolve of the workers crumbled, and the Chartists had to wait six years to be reinvigorated. The source of inspiration this time was inter-national. In 1848 a breathtaking outbreak of revolutionary fervour swept across Europe from France to Germany, Hungary and Italy. As the old regimes toppled, Chartism responded with a renewed campaign. To coincide with the petitioning of Parliament, a 'monster' meeting was planned for 10 April, on

Kennington Common, London. The government's response showed its genuine fear of a revolution. London was effectively put under martial law. Some 80,000 special constables were sworn in, including some press-ganged workers. The day ended with only a few skirmishes, an anti-climax that was soon mythologized as Chartism's swansong (for example in chapter 34 of Charles Kingsley's *Alton Locke* (1850), entitled 'The Tenth of April'). In fact there were disturbances, conspiracies, and mass arrests well into 1849. Though Chartism undoubtedly declined as a mass movement, it survived for several more years under a more radical, socialist leadership.

I have outlined this history not only to illuminate the background to Chartist fiction but to establish one of the premisses of this book, that the most productive context for enjoying and interpreting working-class fiction is within a labour movement and political tradition: the collective struggle for equal representation in the political, social, and literary spheres. This does not mean that a working-class novel or short story must always reveal a high degree of class-consciousness, but class factors will always be a material influence on a working-class text's production and reception, and therefore, ultimately, on its aesthetic dimensions. That crucial dual meaning of the word 'representation' – it can refer to both politics and aesthetics – has particular relevance to literary realism, a mode developed in the eighteenth and nineteenth centuries to express the outlook of the middle classes. By the time Chartist authors turned their hands to fiction, the British novel was deeply biased against reflecting a working-class perspective on society. The prevalence of plots relying on inheritance and the property stakes of marriage is one obvious signifier of the ideological persuasion of mainstream fiction. The working-class author existed in an alien culture, so it is not surprising that Chartist authors harnessed, modified and challenged the established conventions of realism. As this book will show, not all working-class texts are as clearly oppositional in form and content as those of the Chartists. But it is hard to imagine how, in a class society, the experience of the working class can ever be fully assimilated into a literary tradition which still continues to be unrepresentative. The relation of the working class to literary production has always been more decentred and insecure than the classes above it. The material obstacles blocking access to literary production have been and remain formidable, from the availability of good education to having the time and resources to write and seek publication. The working class is not the only section of society to have suffered these disadvantages, of course, but while gender, race and sexuality have moved to the centre of the critical debate, the importance of class as a cultural signifier has diminished in recent years. The causes and symptoms of this decline are discussed towards the end of this study.

Though Chartist authors could not inherit a working-class novelistic tradition which reflected their history and language, they were fortunate to be part of a highly literate movement which could sustain its own intelligentsia.[1] Thomas Cooper and Thomas Martin Wheeler can be singled out for attention here, as they both came from humble backgrounds (unlike, for example, Ernest Jones and George W. M. Reynolds, two major Chartist writers who were middle class) to take up careers as organic intellectuals of Chartism. They performed a range of duties, including journalism, speaking tours, and administrative work.

Thomas Cooper was a midlands shoemaker, preacher and phenomenal autodidact (by the age of 24 he claimed to have known by heart seven Shakespeare plays and the whole of *Paradise Lost*). Poverty cut short a promising academic career and forced him into an apprenticeship, a classic example of the material obstacles in the way of working-class intellectual and social mobility. Cooper's literary skills eventually found fruition in provincial journalism, and his conversion to Chartism took place when he was assigned to do a report on a Chartist meeting. What happened next is both fascinating and resonant. Uninspired by the meeting's political ideas, which he dismissed as derivative (this was partly the point, of course – demands for universal suffrage were not new, but the mass following of Chartism was), Cooper left the meeting hall and discovered that local 'stockingers' (hosiery-makers) were still hard at work in their cottages and workshops. A few enquiries revealed the desperate poverty of the community, far worse than Cooper remembered from his own artisan days. Cooper dramatizes this moment in his 1892 autobiography with the consummate skill of a practised fiction-writer. On asking how much these workers earned, he was told, 'four and sixpence':

> 'Four and sixpence,' I said, 'well, six fours are twenty-four, and six sixpences are three shillings; that's seven-and-twenty shillings a week. The wages are not so bad when you are in work.'
>
> 'What are you talking about?' said they. 'You mean four and sixpence a day; but we mean four and sixpence a week.'
>
> 'Four and sixpence a week!' I exclaimed. 'You don't mean that men have to work in these stocking frames that I hear going now, a whole week for four and sixpence. How can they maintain their wives and children?'
>
> 'Ay, you may well ask that,' said one of them sadly.[2]

Cooper's conversion only occurred when he stumbled on the vital connection between Chartism's political aims (inside the hall) and its real social foundations (the starving workers outside the hall). Despatched to write about Chartism, he could only find a means to represent it in words when he located both the real body politic which Chartism represented, and his own representative role. Cooper's conversion re-invented his discursive identity. He would now turn his authorial skills to championing the 'real' England. This reconfiguration of intersecting discourses of representation differentiates Cooper from those upper- and middle-class 'condition of England' novelists of the 1840s (Disraeli, Dickens, Gaskell, Kingsley, the Brontës) who brought the working class into mainstream fiction. For Cooper and other Chartist authors, writing was political practice, not its antithesis. Writing was not a transcendent imaginative act. One illustration of this materialist aesthetics is that the Chartists admired the Romantic poets primarily for their democratic passions, not their formal innovations.

Of course the need to earn a living and the demands of activism made it very difficult for Chartist authors to produce prose narratives. Hence the dubious blessing of periods of unemployment or, as in Cooper's case, imprisonment. Cooper was jailed for two years for making an inflammatory speech to striking Staffordshire miners in the disturbances of 1842. While incarcerated, he followed in the footsteps of Bunyan and other radicals and wrote imaginatively about the themes of oppression and emancipation. He produced a long satirical poem *The Purgatory of Suicides* and a series of short stories about the disappearance of the artisan life he had known as a child, and whose devastation had played such a key role in his conversion to Chartism. The proletarianization of the skilled worker and his lifestyle represented for Cooper the cutting edge of the social vandalism of capitalism. Once out of jail, Cooper's journalistic background helped him in his quest for a publisher. Eventually the small publisher Jeremiah How brought out the poem and the stories in 1845. The stories volume had the nugatory title *Wise Saws and Modern Instances*, which concealed its critical attitude. The intention of the collection is made much clearer by the title of the best story: '"Merrie England" – No More!' The title harks back to a mythic golden age of artisan splendour, while also debunking patriotic loyalties. Like Cobbett, Cooper mobilizes a radical nostalgia.

This iconoclasm extends to the content and form of the story, which deals with a group of unemployed stockingers in Hinckley, near Leicester, during the recession of 1842 (the fact that much working-class fiction is regional or provincial is an obvious but important feature, as it adds to the decentred values of the fiction, distanced from the political and cultural power of London; the relationship between working-class heroes and heroines and London is usually an anxious one). In the barest of plots, the workers save one of their sons from a recruiting sergeant. This proto-insurrection occupies only a small part of the story. Most of the narrative is taken up with conversation. With little else to do, the men gather in groups and talk: they debunk the political and religious establishment, pin hopes on the Charter's second presentation, and try to keep up their spirits. Cooper's reveals to the reader that the point of this approach to his material is to demonstrate the intelligence of these self-educated workers. Their conversation is oral proof of their right to be the equals of their social superiors. Cooper challenges doubting readers to venture into any typical working-class town and check the veracity of these characterizations (an indication that he expected a middle-class readership for his book, which few working-class readers would be able to buy or borrow). Cooper knows his story is breaking new ground in politicizing the issue of literary verisimilitude, but his most impressive innovations are at the level of form. In order to create a sense of community, he sets the action entirely in non-domestic space (though this marginalizes the role of women), and does not allow any single character to monopolize the narrative: both features which run against the grain of mainstream Victorian realism. Even more striking, however, is the story's open ending:

> There is no 'tale' to finish about John or his lad, or Rem and his wife. They went on starving, begging, receiving threats of imprisonment, tried the 'Bastille' for a few weeks, came out and had a little work, starved again; and they are still going the same miserable round, like thousands in 'merrie England'. What are your thoughts, reader?[3]

This must be one of the most original endings in Victorian fiction. Cooper challenges both literary decorum and the 'naturalized' relation between narrative and history. Until the working class is emancipated, there can be no termination of this 'miserable round'. Resistance to narrative closure is therefore the only 'realistic' option. Like other Chartist writers, Cooper understood that nineteenth-century realism reflected a bourgeois view of the world, with property and marriage the driving force of most storylines. In one of his newspapers he called on the working class to 'join hands and heads to create a literature of your own'.

Cooper claimed to have written a full-length novel about Chartism which he then lost. If this claim is true, it is a severe blow to working-class literary heritage. Fortunately, its absence is partially compensated for by Thomas Martin Wheeler's serialized novel *Sunshine and Shadow* (1849–50), which appeared in weekly instalments in the *Northern Star*.

Wheeler's novel has not received the critical attention it deserves for two main reasons: its inaccessibility and its form. Those left-wing critics who have sought it out tend to dismiss it as a thinly veiled piece of propaganda or journalistic reportage, lacking rounded characters and a coherent plot.[4] If those are the agreed requirements for good fiction then *Sunshine and Shadow* will certainly be deemed to be of low-grade quality. But the narrative requires a different set of reading principles, as Wheeler was writing for a Chartist audience.

Wheeler was trained as a woolcomber, but like Cooper he achieved a measure of social mobility through self-education. He became a schoolteacher, secretary to the Chartist Land Company, and a member of the Chartist Executive committee.

The Land Company was an initiative aimed at resettling poor, urban labourers on the land. The company purchased land out of weekly subscriptions and built fine cottages in generous allotments (many of these buildings survive to the present day). As a reward for his administrative work, Wheeler was provided with a cottage in the settlement called O'Connorville (now part of Rickmansworth, near London). It was there that he wrote *Sunshine and Shadow* in thirty-seven weekly 'communions' from March 1849 to January 1850.[5]

The date of composition is the first clue to the story's purpose, which is to take stock of Chartism after the turbulence of 1848. This does not mean Wheeler wrote an elegy for a defeated cause, as some critics claim. Indeed, Wheeler makes impassioned pleas for renewed effort and remobilization. But equally important was to find a narrative method that would allow him to both present and assess the movement as a historical event. As he declared at the opening of the first instalment, the 'fiction department of literature has hitherto been neglected by the scribes of our body, and the opponents of our principles have been allowed to wield the power of imagination over the youth of our party, without any effort on our part to occupy that wide and fruitful field.' In order to 'wield the power of imagination' successfully Wheeler decided to focalize a 'History of Chartism' through the depiction of 'one of yourselves struggling against the power of adverse circumstances.' In other words Wheeler proletarianized the *Bildungsroman*, not only in placing a working-class hero at the centre of the story, but in opening up realism to social and political analysis, and using the story to mobilize the reader. Moreover, he constructs his hero's destiny out of the key moments in Chartism's development. Arthur Morton does not stand apart from history but is woven into its texture, personifying its contradictions and uneven progress. Arthur's immediate relevance is to show Chartism's 'high and generous inspirations' in a climate of counter-revolutionary smears and misrepresentation.

Arthur conforms to the conventions of *Bildungsroman* heroism in being an orphan and underdog. His uncle is a crass south of England woolmerchant, who lazily despatches his nephew to a second-rate boarding school. The one ray of sunshine in this experience is the friendship of Walter North, son of a wine merchant and school boxing champ (any resemblance to David Copperfield and Steerforth must be coincidental, as Dickens's novel did not commence serialization until May 1849). The North family take Arthur in, where he falls in love with Julia North, who is both educated and a 'lover of liberty'. Class forces soon assert themselves, and Arthur is separated from the Norths geographically and socially. While he is apprenticed to a printer, Walter goes to Liverpool to take over the expanding family business. Wheeler transforms the traditional device of the wresting apart of two childhood 'brothers' into a model of the class structure after 1832. As Arthur tramps for work in London, Walter becomes a merchant prince, 'a specimen of that large and influential class' set to 'dethrone the feudal aristocracy of the realm, and monopolize the political and social power of the empire' (ch. 6). Talent and prosperity are inversely related. Arthur has a 'cultivated intellect' and a Shelleyan imagination. Walter is a philistine and so corrupted that he plots the seduction of Julia and her marriage to a West Indian island governor. Julia's Clarissa-like treatment provokes one of several outbursts in the story against Victorian sexual morality. Marriages of convenience are merely 'legalized prostitution' (ch. 7), a feminist statement owing much to Wollstonecraft and Godwin. As the plot unfolds, it is clear that Julia has more in common with the exploited working class than her own exploiting class which betrays her.

The class polarization of Arthur and Walter gathers pace as Arthur tramps to Birmingham and arrives in the middle of the Chartist ferment of 1839. Chartism provides his grievances with a voice and he becomes an activist and speaker. After the Bull Ring riots, which Wheeler attributes to *agents provocateurs*, Arthur is wrongly accused of arson and flees to Liverpool to take a boat to America. He almost seeks refuge at the house of Walter, who is now a ruthless class enemy and would have certainly turned him in to the authorities. His sexual *rite de passage* begins appropriately at sea. His boat sinks in a storm and he and other survivors are picked up by a ship coincidentally carrying Julia to her new estate in the Caribbean. They embark on a doomed liaison. While Wheeler does not allow adultery to happen, he defends the lovers' feelings, and refutes the convention of the fallen woman:

Love in her was no crime, albeit she was the bride of another – it was the result of feelings as pure as nature ever implanted in human breast...we produce human nature as it is – veritable flesh and blood, – glowing with warm and ardent feelings. (ch. 12)

Almost half a century before Tess Durbeyfield, Julia is victimized by 'a false and slavish code of morals [which] still reigns in all its pristine barbarity' (ch. 14). Although Arthur manages to secure employment on her husband's estate, she dies of a broken heart (not guilt), surrounded by 'luxury and power' (ch. 17). While there are echoes here of Heathcliff and Cathy Earnshaw, Wheeler's method of disturbing moral orthodoxies is very different from Emily Brontë's ironizing tiers of first-person narratives. While Brontë's approach removes narrative authority, Wheeler uses the discourse of direct address he has inherited from radical journalism to defend the 'sins' of his characters with an evangelical fervour.

Arthur is now gloomier if wiser, and his reflections on his experience begin to merge with Wheeler's. He works in America for a while, depressed by slavery, but hopeful it will not be succeeded by the 'white slavery' of industrial capitalism. He then takes a gamble and returns to England, arriving during the 1842 disturbances. Once again his fortunes are revived by collective struggle and he is swept into a leadership position (one of the tale's weaknesses is in not providing us with any examples of Arthur's oratory). Despite the failures of 1842, Arthur is now rejuvenated and a period of 'sunshine' ensues with romance and marriage. He and wife Mary (whom he meets at a Chartist rally) settle into a respectable life until unemployment blights Arthur's life for the second time – this time more ferociously as he is the 'breadwinner'. His spirits deteriorate rapidly. Like John Barton in Gaskell's *Mary Barton* (1848), he personifies the tragic insecurity and precarious civility of life under *laissez-faire*. In a desperate last act to prevent descent into the workhouse (in working-class demonology this is hell-on-earth), Arthur robs a stranger. Wheeler again stretches the moral conventions of fiction by allowing Arthur to get away with this crime, which redeems his family from destitution. Arthur has to live with his own guilt, but for the reader's benefit Wheeler uses the artifice of plot-making to ameliorate the offence. The stranger Arthur robs turns out to be Walter North, newly knighted, and returning from a visit to a brothel. If Arthur cannot quite cleanse his conscience by applying a class-conscious analysis to his situation, Wheeler does it for him. On the other hand, this is the only occasion Walter is punished. As the villain of the narrative, we might expect further horrors to be in store for him, but it is clear that until the working class can arrest the tide of history, Walter's class is in the ascendant.

Despite his moral lapse, Walter is renewed for a third time in the Chartist revival of 1848. Wheeler's analysis of the failure of this campaign is to identify the same pattern of state provocation and belated leadership that undermined 1839 and 1842. As the mass arrests begin, Arthur has to flee the country again. The story ends in a state of asymmetry, suspension and expectation. Arthur joins the flow of European political exiles like Mazzini and Kossuth. Arthur still believes that one day 'the glorious red banner, the emblem of unity and freedom, shall proudly float on the highest pinnacle of St. Stephen's' (ch. 36). Only when that 'national jubilee' (ch. 37) takes place will Arthur be reunited with Mary. Private and public history are not separable.

While *Sunshine and Shadow* undoubtedly has its callow aspects, Wheeler's achievement is all the more impressive when we consider he constructed the narrative out of very small units: a weekly 'communion' of a few thousand words. Though we can only speculate about the influence of the story on future working-class readers and writers, Wheeler must be credited with producing the first truly working-class novel.[6] His materialist aesthetics and unorthodox techniques established a precedent for innovative proletarian realism that would find its fullest expression in Robert Tressell's famous *The Ragged Trousered Philanthropists* (1914). As Louis James has remarked, the way in which Chartist fiction fused political vision and didactic narrative method represented a 'possible turning point in the emergence of the English working classes.'[7]

There were stories in between Wheeler and Tressell, of course. In the 1880s and 1890s there was a revival of literary interest in the working class not seen since the 1840s. This renewed focus reflected some wider social and political shifts. The impetus of Victorian social reforms suffered a setback with the 'rediscovery' of urban poverty and slum life, particularly in the East End of London. A rash of investigations of 'darkest' London picked up what Henry Mayhew had begun in the 1840s. These studies included Mearns and Preston's *The Bitter Cry of Outcast London* (1883), George Sims's *How the Poor Live* (1883) and Charles Booth's monumental *Life and Labour of the People in London* (begun in 1886). Walter Besant's novel *All Sorts and Conditions of Men* (1882) was a thinly fictionalized argument for the establishment of a People's Palace in the East End, which actually came about only five years later.

But novelists were also attracted to this social and literary terrain under the aesthetic influence of continental naturalism, which applied a new objectivity and particularity to 'low' subjects, and developed new standards of unpatronizing realistic detail. In George Gissing's *The Nether World* (1889) and George Moore's *Esther Waters* (1894), for example, the narrative focus rarely departs from the working-class community (this distinguishes naturalism from the 'social problem' novel of the 1840s). This innovation in realism also applied to a rich crop of short fiction which involved the fledgling talents of middle-class authors such as Somerset Maugham and Rudyard Kipling, as well as the innovations of Arthur Morrison, son of an engine-fitter, ex-clerk and journalist, who administered the People's Palace in its early years.[8] The emphasis of this 'tough' new approach was on the brutal and brutalizing aspects of working-class life: a combination of deprivation, social entrapment, poor education and lax morals that found its typical expression in bad language, crime, sexual irregularity and domestic violence against women and children. The *frisson* for the middle-class reader was to feel a sensationalist thrill at the 'darkest' details while also fearing that the working class were beyond redemption, impenetrable to the language of reason and progress.

Arthur Morrison's *Tales of Mean Streets* (1892–4) established a Darwinian *mise-en-scène* of graphically represented images of social debasement and impoverishment that has been influential to the present day.[9] In 'Lizierunt' the heroine is beaten so badly by her husband that she has a miscarriage. When he sees the battered foetus emerge, 'a blind, hairless homunculus, short of a foot long' all he can remark is, ' "Well, it is a measly snipe" ' (p. 36). But just as important as the shocking, Zolaesque subject matter is Morrison's 'flat, terse style' as Peter Keating calls it, a 'stark immediacy' which gives the working-class environment an authenticity 'unlike anything earlier in Victorian fiction'.[10] For instance, in the opening story, 'The Street', the typical monotony of working-class domestic life is echoed in the photographic impressions of the prose: 'the scrubbing, and the squalling, and the barren flower pot; the end of the sooty day's work, the last homecoming; nightfall; sleep' (p. 5).

Yet, while the shedding of Dickensian sentimentalism and melodrama was a step forward in the literary representation of the working class, it could not happen without the pendulum of realism swinging back towards melodrama's successor, sensationalism. The 'rediscovered' working class of the late nineteenth century are too often portrayed as a pseudo-anthropological Other world, whose primitivist freedoms from moral restraint make them objects of repressed fear and desire to bourgeois culture. The new realism did not automatically steer class consciousness in a progressive direction, even if it retained what Keating identifies as a stubbornly British sociological bias.[11] It reminded readers that Disraeli's two nations were more polarized than ever (most notably in the two halves of the metropolis) but its focus on squalid brutality and dehumanized, 'determined' subjects detracted from the laying bare of the history surrounding this graphically realized canvas of working-class experience.

So it would be very misleading to take the generally gloomy, disempowering proletarian naturalism of the *fin de siècle* as totally representative of the social and political condition of the working class at this time. There had been considerable progress since the days of Chartism. The state gradually realized that it needed to invest in its workforce to safeguard the economic future. Improvements to the infrastructure were paralleled by political reforms: the Reform Bills of 1867 and 1885 enfranchised most working-class men over 21 (women of all classes had to wait until 1918 and 1929); and the Forster Education Act of 1870 began a rudimentary system of universal elementary education. While the 'slum' fiction of the eighties and nineties could be read as a salutary reminder of how little impact these state reforms had made on the average working-class community, there is no mention in this fiction of the important self-help measures that probably did the most to define working-class culture in this period.

Unable to control economic slump and boom through the democratic process, the working class built the best defences it could: trade unions, co-operatives, Friendly Societies. The limited security provided by these institutions aided the evolution of amenities, leisure pursuits and cultural activities that gradually emerged into a distinct way of life. The historian Gareth Stedman-Jones refers to this process as the 'remaking' of the working class: the creation of a 'classic' social imagery that persists until the next great transformation in the late 1950s (also a fertile period of working-class fiction).[12] Conspicuous icons of this way of life are the extended family, the terraced street, the local factory, the pub, football match, sporting paper, race track, music hall, Sunday stroll and holiday excursion. This is both a real and a mythic working class (note how some of these images are still recycled in television adverts for their nostalgic value). According to Stedman-Jones, it is also a conservative class formation, highly class-conscious but also 'enclosed and defensive' (p. 238). For example, the separation of leisure and politics, best seen in the splitting of the tavern or coffee-house (once a major venue of radical meetings) into the pub (for drinking) and the Working Men's Club (for drinking and meetings), was a major loss. Put starkly, then, cultural difference was bought at the expense of depoliticization and insularity, a 'decay in indigenous metropolitan radical traditions' (p. 211).

Yet this is still not the complete picture. The Great Depression of the 1870s did not simply dehumanize the working class still further. It led to the greatest revival of socialism this country has ever known. The intellectual and political dimensions of this resurgence can be seen in the prolific spawning of new political movements and groups: the Fabian Society (1884), the Social Democratic Federation (1884), the Socialist League (1884) and the Independent Labour Party (1893) – the Labour Party followed in 1906. An English translation of *Das Kapital* in 1886 made Marx's economic ideas more widely available. The practical impact of this wave of opposition to *laissez-faire* was seen in the rise of 'new' (unskilled) unions, who won significant victories in strikes by London dockers and the Liverpool Bryant and May matchgirls (both in 1888). On the streets a new calendar of radical martyrology began with the Bloody Sunday riots of 1887. The Utopian socialists William Morris and Edward

Bellamy offered powerful and enticing visions of a future cleansed of industrial pollution and capitalist division in their novels *News from Nowhere* (1890) and *Looking Backward* (1888). These stories drew inspiration from the earlier communitarian socialism of Robert Owen and the artisan nostalgia of Cobbett, but now the role of a powerful state was central to the vision. The subordinate feminist element in British radicalism also burgeoned as agitation for women's social and political rights found expression in the New Woman and Suffragette movements.

Increased literacy and cheap mass publishing methods gave the working class unprecedented print access to this renewed, combative radicalism and class consciousness (this was not their only access, of course – working-class culture was primarily oral in nature, and much political education occurred in the course of activism, but we should not marginalize the importance of print and its dissemination). The reading habits of the working class had been an object of official interest since the counter-revolutionary 1790s, when the state tried to suppress the availability of cheap reprints of radical texts such as Paine's *The Rights of Man* (1791–3). By the latter part of the nineteenth century there had been a number of laments over the mass consumption of trashy fiction such as 'penny dreadfuls' and other one-penny serials. These did not all originate in the do-gooding middle class. A tradition of working-class jeremiads about the impending demise of self-improving working-class culture can be traced from the Chartist journalist Thomas Frost, through the 'journeyman engineer' and novelist Thomas Wright, to Richard Hoggart's *The Uses of Literacy*. But if the working class continued to consume large quantities of popular 'pulp' literature, it was not all they consumed. Reading habits are complex and heterogeneous. If creative literature did not figure on the syllabuses of Mechanics Institutes (as it was not regarded as 'useful knowledge'), and if fiction did not find a theoretical justification or encouragement in radical cultural circles until the 1930s, this does not mean there was no appetite or demand amongst the working class for both bourgeois classics and working-class fiction. The case of the Lancashire writer Allen Clarke shows very clearly that outspokenly political fiction could also be popular.[13]

Allen Clarke was the son of a Bolton mill-worker, who became

15

a factory 'piecer' (cleaning the machines while still in motion), a pupil teacher, and a journalist. His political activities began as a member of the Social Democratic Federation, an organization which promoted some important and impressive publications, including Robert Blatchford's *Merrie England* (1891–2), a popular introduction to 'practical socialism', which sold 700,000 one-penny copies by 1894.[14] It was first published in Blatchford's paper the *Clarion*, which was at the centre of a network of SDF cultural and political pursuits such as the cycling clubs and the famous socialist van. Another SDF venture was Twentieth Century Press, which occupied the site in Clerkenwell Green which is now the home of the Marx Memorial Library. Twentieth Century Press published Allen Clarke's *The Red Flag: A Tale of the People's Woe* in 1908. By this time Clarke had stood as a parliamentary candidate for the Independent Labour Party. But his literary career began much earlier, in the 1890s, and extended throughout the Edwardian period.

The Edwardian years are mythically remembered as a quintessential English idyll shattered by the First World War. As Philip Larkin puts it in his poem 'MCMXIV', 'never before such innocence'. Clarke's fiction looks at the Edwardian 'twilight' rather differently. His aim is to expose the grim reality beneath the imperial splendour: the familiar litany of deprivation, class exploitation, injustice and insecurity which determines the daily experience of the working class. However, unlike the 'slum' fiction of his contemporaries, Clarke is not a naturalist. His origins lie equally in popular narrative forms and the realist tradition. Most of his stories first appeared in his Lancashire newspaper the *Northern Weekly*. which ran for many years and published stories by other 'Lancashire school' socialists Arthur Laycock, John Tamlyn and Fred Plant. Much of his fiction has an industrial setting, which contradicts Peter Keating's view that in this period 'the industrial working class was entirely absent from fiction'.[15] For his local audience Clarke wrote in an unashamedly populist vein, combining romance devices, melodrama, sentimentality and slapstick with reportage, social and political comment, and investigative journalism. These forms are fused together with unwavering class-consciousness. For as Blatchford said in *Merrie England*, 'the best way to realise socialism is – to make socialists' (p. 91). Both Clarke and, later,

Tressell answered this call-to-arms by making conversion to socialism and the cause of the working class the aim and the substance of their fiction. They were not worried about transgressing the new standards of modernist impersonality.

Clarke's most interesting and engaging story is 'The Daughter of the Factory', first published in 1898 in the *Northern Weekly* (also called *Teddy Ashton's Journal*).[16] Clarke's heroine Rose Hilton is a sparky and vivacious portrait of a proletarian New Woman. The struggle for women's political equality entered a new and more militant phase at this time with the burgeoning of the Suffragette movement and the creation in 1903 of the Women's Social and Political Union. Like many working-class writers Clarke sees women's 'hideous slavery' as the essence of class oppression. While there has been a revival of critical interest in New Woman novelists such as Ella Hepworth Dixon, Sarah Grand and Clementina Black, Clarke's portrayal of a working-class woman radical has gone unnoticed.[17]

Rose Hilton is made even more memorable by her passionate and fiery temperament which stems from her gypsy blood – she is a foundling, the illegitimate daughter of a caddish, libertine factory owner Benjamin Crosswaite (Clarke is fond of recycling the seduction plot – here with a eugenist twist – but as in Chartist fiction the rakish villain belongs firmly to the bourgeoisie). Brought up by a respectable working-class couple, Rose learns quickly about the 'sickening struggle for life' around her (ch. 19). Her indignation is matched by her courage. She stands up to bullying teachers and licks Crosswaite's Blifil-like son in a straight fight. Clarke makes sure she is not merely an instinctual class warrior. She has to leave a promising career as a pupil teacher to work in her father's cotton factory so as to earn money for her family. While there she is inspired by a visiting 'female agitator' into becoming a feminist and trade union leader (in an industry with a hardened sexist union structure). She believes in equality in love and vigorously defends the sexual virtue of working-class women; her view is that because these women are vulnerable to predatorial middle-class men, that does not make the women more sinful. On the other hand (and this is a cross many enlightened working-class heroes and heroines have to bear), she is frustrated by her women workmates' lack of consciousness about sexual and class politics. Rose's bottomless talents are thrown into overcoming this ignorance. Under the pseudonym 'daughter of Demos', she writes a weekly column about the conditions in the factory for a local paper. She rebuffs an attempted seduction by Crosswaite's son and publishes it as an exposé of sexual harassment (ch. 35). In one delightful scene she goes a step further and horsewhips an overseer who has seduced one of her workmates (ch. 38). Her passions also find a creative outlet as an accomplished singer. In the calamitous final scene, which is reminiscent of the 'industrial' novels of the 1840s, Rose unintentionally sparks a riot when she sings the Marseillaise at a rally. During the clash of workers and the military her father is killed, but not before he leaves his fortune to Rose in a death-bed reconciliation. However, this time-honoured device for rewarding the heroine does not pacify her. Refusing to desert her adopted class, she gives her fortune to the labour movement. Rose's true identity is determined by her class allegiance not her blood. Nor will that other conventional ending of English fiction satisfy her. She accepts an offer of marriage only on the basis that she and her husband 'go forward side by side'. Rose is a triumphalist fantasy, bristling with the aspirations of contemporary radicalism, and marching off into a future where much work still needs to be done.

In his other important fiction Clarke uses the more familiar figure of the tramp as a means to traverse and illuminate the landscapes of Edwardian poverty. In *The Red Flag* Clarke extends his feminist project by exposing the abuses of women in workhouses – his women tramps (though in fact they are social reformers incognito) represent a rich vein of social protest which, regrettably, remains undeveloped in later fiction. The central theme of the novel is the conversion of the tramping hero Jim Campbell to socialism. Jim has a vision of the red flag and its curative social powers while taking refuge in a socialist club house. He meets his wife at a political meeting and at the end of the novel the newly wed couple celebrate by speaking to a May Day rally – perhaps the ultimate sanctification of their union. To quote Blatchford again, there is 'no such thing as personal independence in human affairs' and everyone is a 'unit of society' (p. 32).

In this early phase of working-class fiction the characteristic trajectory of the hero is often an anxious movement towards rather than away from class solidarity. It is only in the 1950s and 1960s, when social mobility through education becomes a more feasible goal for the working class, that the emphasis changes to separation and anxious return, and aesthetic and erotic goals become dominant aspirations. The isolated working-class hero is often a tragic figure in earlier fiction; an outcast by circumstance not by choice. For example, there is no romantic glamour attached to Jos Coney in Margaret Harkness's *Out of Work* (1888). He is the dehumanized personification of the destructive 'laws' of capitalism, whose ultimate value is to be found only in a pitifully ironic image of martyrdom. Compare this fate with that of Belton, the tramping hero of Allen Clarke's *The Knobstick* (1893) – the word means a scab or strikebreaker. Belton is rescued from despair and destitution by the family of a trade union leader. Whether or not this seems a blatant partisanship, it reminds us that working-class safety nets did exist, and that realist conventions of defeat and dehumanization were not the only ways to represent working-class experience in fiction.

Of course the benevolent intervention of the state into working-class life began in the Edwardian period. The British male working class did not use their votes to elect a socialist government. Instead they installed a Liberal regime which swept to power in 1906 and began a series of social reforms (inspired in part by Bismarck's Germany) that laid the foundations of the welfare state: old age pensions, unemployment benefit and health insurance, labour exchanges and wages councils. It is significant that Robert Tressell makes a 1907 by-election one of the set-pieces of *The Ragged Trousered Philanthropists*. By 1914, however, the 'liberal experiment' had run out of steam, and the years immediately preceding the First World War saw a massive upsurge of industrial and social unrest. The formation of a 'triple alliance' of miners, steelworkers and railway workers seemed to herald a syndicalist threat to the state. The Suffragette movement deployed spectacular acts of direct action, including the suicide of Emily Davidson, who threw herself under the King's horse at the Derby in 1913, hunger strikes, and incendiarism. In Ireland, British army officers threatened to mutiny if the government pressed ahead with plans for Home Rule. Far from seeing the outbreak of war as a national calamity which obliterated a country at peace with itself and basking in imperial greatness, the war may well have saved the state from this multiple attack on its legitimacy. Even the militant Welsh miners flocked to volunteer for Flanders (this topic is dramatized in Lewis Jones's novel *Cwmardy* (1935), looked at in chapter 2). So the war postponed the revolutionary moment for at least five years (the Dublin rising of Easter 1916 excepted), while the experience of centralized state control gained during the course of the war gave the government a renewed confidence in implementing 'emergency' powers in peacetime.

It is against this momentous background that I want to compare four working-class novels published in 1913–14: D. H. Lawrence's *Sons and Lovers* (1913), Allen Clarke's *The Men who Fought for us* (1914), Robert Tressell's *The Ragged Trousered Philanthropists* (1914), and Patrick MacGill's *Children of the Dead End* (1914).[18] The aim of the comparison is not to judge which is the best novel (conventionally the laurels would go immediately to Lawrence), but to investigate which novel is most representative of working-class life in the years immediately preceding the First World War.

There is no doubting the pioneering achievement of *Sons and Lovers*. No previous novel about working-class life had given its characters such psychological, emotional and sexual depth. Paul Morel is the first post-Freudian proletarian hero. His Oedipally smothering mother represents the claustrophobic restrictions of a mining community that Paul must reject if he is to become a creative individual. Lawrence's portrayal of the Morel family has traces of the degraded and brutalized working class of slum fiction of the 1880s and 1890s: Morel both drinks and beats his wife. But the narrative lens is not sociological. The novel is a *Künstler-Bildungsroman*, a subset of the *Bildungsroman* in which the hero is destined to become an artist or writer. Despite the wonderful particularity of some of the novel's domestic realism, the narrative dominance of Paul's development means that there is a corresponding loss of social detail. The material conditions of the Morels' life are rarely foregrounded. We are told that in their 'early married life' the Morels were very poor (victims both of the cycle of poverty first identified by the Rowntrees, and of Morel's cavalier approach to budgeting), but little attempt is made to visualize this deprivation. On a wider scale, the evocation of a working, evolving community which informs the novel's opening pages quickly fades away. This loss of historical context means that it is quite difficult to date the action. There is no reference to the industrial struggles that were shaping working-class history as Lawrence wrote the book. The ideological affiliation of the novel is with bourgeois individualism, just as the literary affiliation is with the *Bildungsroman*. Of course Paul (like Lawrence) is sufficiently gifted to merit this special attention. His destiny lies with the bohemian middle class who can appreciate his talents (there is a hint of eugenist logic here in that Paul seems to have inherited his mother's intelligence and not his father's morally degenerative failings; considering that Mrs Morel originated in the lower middle class, this seems to consign working-class intelligence to a subnormality, as shown in Lawrence's next novel *Women in Love* (1921); see particularly the market scene in chapter 26, where a proletarian with rat-like features appears). At the end of the novel, Paul vanishes over the horizon to join his readers' class. In the process, he establishes a new kind of working-class hero (based on Lawrence's own social trajectory), who becomes upwardly mobile through a combination of bracing intelligence and vigorous sexuality – the latter is the result of growing up in an 'earthy', less regulated moral culture, but also a feature of the newly acquired bohemian lifestyle. The capacity of the novel to offend its contemporary readers' sensibilities arises from Paul's sexual irregularity (his affairs with Miriam and Clara) and his religious heterodoxy, but not his class-consciousness. Paul flirts with the idea of class solidarity. He tells his mother:

'You know...I don't want to belong to the well-to-do middle class. I like my common people best. I belong to the common people...from the middle classes one gets ideas, and from the common people – life itself, warmth.' (p. 313)

When pressed by his mother, he has to admit that he only mixes with working-class intellectuals (none of whom appear in the story).

Allen Clarke's *The Men who Fought for us in the 'Hungry Forties': A Tale of Pioneers and Beginnings* (1914) is a fictional tribute to the co-operative movement first established in Rochdale. At the side of Lawrence's incipient modernism, Clarke's writing seems unremarkable, but the novel becomes more resonant when we realize it was published by the Manchester Co-Operative Newspaper Society, and therefore spoke directly to its readers. Also it is feasible that Clarke was displacing contemporary unrest onto a founding moment of working-class history (it has to be said that historical topics have insufficiently preoccupied working-class authors – the claiming and reclaiming of the past remains a vital project). Clarke's heroes are models of self-education, self-improvement and public spiritedness. Their radicalism stems from their Owenite vision of a better collective existence. They are not attracted to individualist solutions to social ills. This does not mean Clarke's novel is artistically better than Lawrence's, but Clarke may better reflect working-class consciousness – in Engels's famous terms, Clarke's characters behave 'typically'. At one point in the story one of the heroes emerges from the Staffordshire disturbances of 1842 (in which Thomas Cooper was arrested) in a state of despair. His thoughts can almost be read as a pastiche of the ending of *Sons and Lovers*:

> The years were before him. What did the future hold for him?
> Not possibly anything gloomier or ghastlier than the past. Life, as far as he was concerned, was all over. His sweetheart dead, and he an outcast.
> Well, at least he could do some work for the world – he could help the suffering, fight for the oppressed.
> He strode towards Rochdale. (p. 41)

For Paul Morel, the city (Nottingham) offers renewal through individual self-realization, the classic expression of the liberal notion of the self. For Clarke's hero, Salford is the collective site of working-class self-help.

Robert Tressell's masterpiece *The Ragged Trousered Philanthropists* (1914) is a complete antitype of *Sons and Lovers*.[19] It is a remarkable novel in many ways: not just in its experimental juxtaposition of styles ranging from allegorical satire to long disquisitions on socialist economic theory, nor in its scathing condemnation of working-class servility and benightedness, but in its sheer bulk. The fact that Tressell, a downwardly mobile Hastings signwriter, who died of pneumonia aged 40 in 1911 and was buried in a pauper's grave in Liverpool, could produce 1,700 pages of handwritten manuscript over the course of several years is a heroic feature in itself. The mythic status of the novel has been preserved by generations of leftwing readers, for whom it is a socialist classic. This canonization runs counter to the book's absence from mainstream and academic literary tradition. The mystique of the novel was further enhanced when the story of the text's ritualistic slaughter by publishers came to light in the 1950s (a story I return to below). Hence the novel has acquired among its followers an iconic value as a precious object and a source of inspiration. Pamela Fox in a recent study refers to the novel as a 'master-narrative'.[20] This is more true of the book's influence over readers than writers, however. Few working-class novels have attempted anything so ambitious as to combine lectures in 'practical socialism' with a tragicomic study of provincial working-class life and municipal corruption. Peter Keating regards the novel as the 'one major exception' to the surprising dearth of impressive socialist and working-class fiction in an era of 'unprecedented' radicalism.[21] Yet Tressell's narrative craft also looks back to the non-realist elements of *Sunshine and Shadow*.[22]

The story follows the lives of a group of painters and decorators in the seaside resort of Mugsborough (Hastings) in that notable year 1906–7, just after a Liberal government swept into power and began the construction of a welfare state. As Tressell explains in his preface, in order to provide a 'complete' picture of 'how the workers are circumstanced at all periods of their lives', he had to abandon the traditional narrative structure of the dominant hero. Instead he constructed a form of montage or collective *Bildungsroman*, comprising representative characters (Engels's 'types') 'from cradle to grave': women, children, an apprentice, mature workers, and 'wornout old men'. Despite this important innovation in decentredness, however, there is an identifiable hero in Frank Owen, who true to his surname is a socialist (Robert Owen, 1771–1858, was a pioneer of factory reform, co-operatives and Utopian communes, who had a huge influence on the development of the labour movement and socialist thinking from the 1820s onwards). Owen spends much of the novel trying to enlighten his workmates about the myths and iniquities of capitalism. It is an uphill task – the other workers are mistrustful, complacent, defensive and downright hostile. As Jack Mitchell notes in his full-length study of the novel, Owen is the 'revolutionary germ' in a 'sluggish mass'.[23] On several occasions Owen uses lunchbreaks to give impromptu tutorials on socialist economics – these often occupy near whole chapters, and stretch the limits of realism to the extent that they almost become autonomous discourses (see chapters 15, 21 and 25 in particular). Owen's wary audience provides a subject position for the unconverted reader, whose patience may well be sorely tested by Owen's sometimes tetchy delivery. There is a welcome moment of light relief in chapter 21, when after a demonstration of the 'great money trick' with a piece of bread and the use of role-play, the workers erupt into what Pamela Fox calls spontaneous 'mimicry and drama',[24] including a threatened rebellion by those workers (Philpott, Harlowe and Easton) representing the unemployed. Fox claims that these antics ironically expose the workers' condition as a construct, while self-mocking their revolutionary potentiality, and it is certainly true that the scene shows that comedy can be both a consolation and a weapon. The novel resolutely refuses to show anyone converted to socialism. The three 'rebels' soon lapse back into unthinking acceptance of their condition.

So Owen's aim is not merely to create class-consciousness – he must inspire a revolutionary social outlook. He must move the workers beyond defensive 'trade union consciousness', Lenin's term in *What is to be Done?* (1905) for the limits of awareness that can be achieved by the working class without the input of a revolutionary party. There is a grim irony in the fact that the nearest thing to a union meeting in the story is the organization of the annual 'beano'. But Mugsborough is a deeply conservative community, a long way from large industrial urban centres. Unions are basically a 'dead letter' (p. 387). Mugsborough citizens are easily stirred into rioting against socialist speakers (ch. 43), and like all true martyrs Owen himself is beaten up by a reactionary mob (p. 546; note that he is also, like Tressell, a consumptive – his walk in the rain to tell his sacked workmate Linden about a possible job is an act of pure self-sacrifice). Mugsborough's working class is dependent for work on public amenities (hence the power of local officials in the novel) or the middle-class luxury economy, still at this historical juncture the staple market for artisan skills, and which must not be antagonized. Raymond Williams has remarked that this is an unlikely, 'marginal' setting for a socialist narrative, yet it is also perfect for showing 'acutely visible' class polarization.[25] The reader coming to the novel for the first time may be surprised to find it is not peppered with class warriors. There is no celebration of organized labour in Mugsborough's social backwater. Skilled workers scapegoat unskilled workers for undermining their rates of pay (p. 332). Even Owen is kept on by his firm when most others are laid off, implying he is not perceived as a threat (ch. 28).

Tressell's novel is a salutary exercise in deromanticizing and deheroicizing the working class. We are reminded that many working-class communities bear little resemblance to Marx's historic proletariat (when Engels catalogued different strata of the working class in his seminal study *The Condition of the Working Class in England* (1845; first English translation 1892), he identified the factory communities, the rural workers, the slums of the great towns, and the 'savage' mining areas, but he omitted the provincial backwater). While the triple alliance and the Labour Party were forming in the industrial and metropolitan heartlands, quasi-feudal social relations between employers and workers persist in Mugsborough's 'whited sepulchre': 'wages were low, and the level of servility high'.[26] Owen sometimes feels sheer hatred at the 'colossal imbecility' (p. 365) of his workmates, who cannot see that capitalism has proletarianized their artisan heritage and left them denuded of social protection: 'They were the enemy; they abased themselves, and grovelled before their oppressors' (p. 46). To choose merely one narrative strand which rubs this point in, the old Tory Jack Linden is sacked for smoking, quickly becomes a lost soul, and dies a pauper in the workhouse. To remind us that capitalist transformation of social relations is a continuing process, an element of Taylorism is introduced into Rushton and Co. in the form of a timesheet (p. 393). Though these workers are not subjected to machinery, they are inexorably annexed to new, deskilling, rationalized forms of work discipline and the alienating 'solitary system' (p. 405).

So Owen's pedagogic task is to try to convert the workers' lived experience into a theoretical and analytical awareness of a corrupt system. The twin poles of this mission are reflected in the narrative's oscillation between the two themes identified in Tressell's preface: his first aim is to 'paint a faithful picture of working-class life in a small town in the south of England', emphasizing 'the conditions resulting from poverty and unemployment' (p. 13); his second aim is to present 'what I believe to be the only real remedy, namely – Socialism'. These aims are not readily compatible within traditional fictional genres. If the British novel by this stage in its development had evolved prodigious means to represent individual experience, there was no place within realism for the explicitly theoretical and political (even Engels preferred the naturalization of the author's political message). Hence Tressell borrows heavily from a non-realist genre, the Utopian novel, in which exposition is foregrounded. This form had already attracted socialist writers like Morris and Bellamy, whose work also influences Tressell's programme for reform (Owen's 'oblong' lecture in chapter 25 owes much to Morris's essay 'Useful work versus useless toil' (1885); Barrington's 'great oration' in chapter 45 is modelled closely on the nationalization of the retail sector imagined in *Looking Backward*). The apparent incongruity between the novel's two dominant discourses – the realistic and the expository – is only reconcilable as a dialectical relationship. As the novel unfolds, the empirical and the abstract interact in a series of contradictions and revelations which lead to a higher level of understanding. If the workers' experience is the 'problem', Owen's lectures, and some of the narrator's comments, present the 'cure'. The novel's aim, in George Lukács's terms, is to 'ascribe' class-consciousness, fusing the practical and theoretical; only through this means can the working class overcome the mystification of 'the devastating and degrading effects of the capitalist system'.[27]

But in order to achieve a totalizing understanding of capitalist illusions, the material facts of oppression must be revisited and analysed constantly. Owen is often the device for promoting analysis and debate. For him it is a mental reflex, as in the scene in chapter 27 where he tries to get Cross and Slyme to interpret correctly the significance of a march by unemployed labourers. While his two workmates are contemptuous and defensive, Owen asserts the need for class solidarity and attacks Slyme's 'silly' superiority complex (p. 288). But Owen can never become complacent or self-righteous. He may believe socialist truths to be self-evident, but his version of reality is constantly refuted by the 'common sense' of the workers.

The novel is neither a treatise nor a social satire but a dynamic combination of both genres. In its creative deformation of nineteenth-century realism, the novel actually has something in common with its more famous modernist counterparts, though its aims and many of its techniques are antagonistic to the modernist focus on fragmentation, psychological isolation, and authorial impersonality. Interestingly, an early review in the *Times Literary Supplement* (23 April 1914) took in its stride the fact that 'there is very little attempt at anything like conventional form' and claimed Owen's lectures 'take us, if anything, a step nearer reality' (p. 199).

But this is still to simplify the novel's polyphonic richness. Like most writers, Tressell is pragmatic enough to borrow from literary tradition whatever is most useful. Whereas Morrison and the naturalists of the late nineteenth century rejected the comic and Gothic extravagance of Dickens's fiction, Tressell embraces comic allegory to lampoon Mugsborough's petty bourgeois mandarins and bigwigs. The inflated self-regard and blatant corruption of the 'Brigands' is ripe for such classic debunking. The emblematic names (Graball, Didlum, Starvem), the philistine use of local dialect which aligns its users (for example Didlum the housefurnisher, p. 308, and Grinder the greengrocer, ch. 30) with workers not masters (Owen's self-educated impeccable English excepted), the conspiracies and skulduggery (buying the Electric Light Company out of local rates, for instance), the religious hypocrisy of the Strong Light Chapel (in which Slyme the seducer is a leading 'light'), combine to give the effect of the social system as one huge swindle. The readers of the novel are invited to revel in the comedy of this personified, grasping exploitation and political chicanery, while also being asked to make the leap to an understanding of the systemic abuses of capitalism. The tensions between these two modes of reading can be disconcerting. Tressell reminds us (taking his cue from Marx) that it is misguided to blame individual capitalists for only doing what the system demands of them, as in Rushton's need to drive down wages in order to undercut competitors (pp. 120–1, 201, 394). But in novelistic terms it is much easier to pillory conspicuous villains than it is to lay bare the economic 'laws' of modern society, and to propose generalized solutions. On occasions, Tressell's satirical imagination solves this problem brilliantly. Making Rushton an actual thief rather than a purely economic thief (a representative of the appropriation of his workers' surplus value) is an example of the analytical and comic discourses finding a common artistic expression.

The novel's ridiculing of Hunter, Rushton, Graball, Mrs Starvem and the other local tyrants does yield much readerly pleasure. After all, they represent institutional corruption, particularly in the collusion between municipal authority and local business (a timely reminder that the 'free' market is often a front for élite power-broking), and in the hypocrisy of the church's attitude towards poverty (there is a strong vein of anti-clericism in much working-class writing). Nor is this comic technique the only populist appeal of the narrative. In order to 'tell an interesting story', Tressell recycles the seduction plot in the story of Ruth Easton, who has an affair with Slyme, one of her husband's workmates who is lodging in their house. Tressell's fallen woman is not the melodramatic or sentimental figure of Victorian fiction, however. The collapse of her marriage has its roots in economic deprivation. While the teetotaller Owen disapproves of her husband's lapse into drunkenness, the novel steers clear of becoming a temperance tract, as Slyme the seducer is also a teetotaller.

Tressell also indulges in the rather shakier device of Barrington, who is the novel's least successful characterization. Barrington has two generic origins: the myth of the hero of noble birth who finds himself (by accident or misfortune) displaced into the lower classes; and the god or king who visits his people in disguise. In the latter part of the nineteenth century this persona was sociologically transformed into the social investigator operating incognito. The best example of this 'undercover' narrative genre is Jack London's *The People of the Abyss* (1903). Even though Barrington's *deus ex machina* role carries some of this realist weight, his sudden blossoming into a tour de force orator seems indulgent on Tressell's part: Barrington's 'great oration' outlining the virtues of 'practical' socialism is longer than any of Owen's tutorials. It is also a more confident performance than any of Owen's. When this fact is added to Barrington's superior physique, there seems to be a tinge of hero-worship about the characterization. It is difficult not to read Barrington as an idealized socialist figure. Barrington's departure from the story can barely avoid being tainted with the stigma of social slumming, however 'interesting' it may be. One justification for the inclusion of Barrington in the story may be to emphasize that socialism does not derive solely, or even preferably, from the working class, even if it is primarily for them. On the other hand we should not overestimate Barrington's role in the novel. Jack Mitchell notes with obvious pleasure that the novel marginalizes Barrington for most of the narrative, refusing to give him authority over the story. Mitchell criticizes a BBC adaptation of the book for giving Barrington a more central role as a voice-over narrator.

Tressell's achievements are not limited to this unique blending of comedy, decentred sentimentalism and pedagogic abstraction. At one moment the novel rises to bizarre heights of surreal satire. In chapter 44 the four brakes (carriages), which are taking home all the novel's main characters from the beano, begin an inebriated race. Each brake is described as a 'travelling lunatic asylum' (p. 455) containing a category of madness: bosses (who injure others and themselves), demoralized workers (driven to drink by circumstances), religious workers (cunning yet ignorant) and respectable workers (including those receptive to socialism, who are mad to believe in the redemptive power of reason). The chariot race is a satirical image of a crazily divided society heading for self-destruction. The scene includes some of the novel's most excoriating invective and, like the brakes, seems to be barely under control. The writing reminds us that Tressell had at his disposal violently non-realist modes of representation.

On the other hand, seen purely as a 'faithful picture of working-class life', the novel also broke new ground. Most conspicuously, much of the action takes place at work. This innovation immediately inverted the spatial and ideological priorities of the English novel, which had focused mainly on the leisure time of the leisured classes. By making productive work invisible, the novel had colluded with a bourgeois view of the world which repressed its reliance on the 'labouring' class. As a materialist, Tressell wanted to foreground the economic 'base' and show its determining power over people's lives. But as a novelist, he could draw on the metaphoric richness of textuality to achieve this end.

Consider, for example, 'the cave', the name given to Sweater's large house which Owen and his team are renovating at the opening of the novel. The ironic reference to Plato sets the tone for Owen's attempts to make his fellow workers understand the real meaning of their experience. Additionally, the setting reverses the usual narrative perspective from which large houses are seen in fiction. Normally the mansion is a signifier of class privilege and implicit social power. In this novel the house is explicitly a place where class forces collide and the hidden processes of production are exposed in all their threadbare grandeur. The 'cave' also has connotations of burial and entrapment. Tressell's subtitle for the novel on his hand-drawn title page is revealing in this context: 'Being the story of twelve months in Hell, told by one of the damned'. This is not an entirely accurate indication of the comic procedures of the text, but it does capture the story's relentless reversion back to the tyrannical workplace. A brilliantly naturalistic example can be found in chapter 25, where the 'hands' are painting outdoors in freezing weather: 'their hands, of course, suffered the most, becoming so numbed that they were unable to feel the brushes they held' (p. 253). The power of this scene (made even more poignant by the fact that this is the last remaining work before the annual 'slaughter' of seasonal unemployment) makes Tressell's decision to employ other discourses all the more impressive. But his main target in the workplace scenes is the social relations that work generates. In Foucauldian terms the employers operate a 'panoptic' or surveillance regime, constantly spying on the workers to spot the most minor infringement of the rules (there is a biting use of poetic justice in the suicide of Hunter the foreman (ch. 52), who dies closeted in his office). Yet the production of beauty (the 'cave') is a deliberate swindle. In order to undercut their competitors, Rushton and Co. jerry-build, cut corners, use cheap materials, steal, skimp on health and safety, and hire and fire on the slightest pretext. Philpott's fatal accident leads to a macabre comic squabble between Rushton and a rival undertaker for Philpott's corpse (it is not too far-fetched to see this scene as an extreme parody of the contest for the armour of the epic hero

Patroclus in *The Iliad*).

Tressell's imagination is consistently iconoclastic. By focusing on material production, he debunks the bourgeois respectability of architectural splendour. This fine house cannot transcend the real economy of jerry-built niggardliness and exploitation. On the other hand, it is a place protected by the production of false consciousness. Even Owen is not completely immunized against the 'degrading' influence of the work ethic. There is a particularly poignant narrative strand in which Owen is given a special assignment to make an ornate interior screen (chs. 11, 14 and 22). He is so thrilled to be doing truly creative work (it was a socialist orthodoxy that art can be defined as non-alienated labour) that he overlooks the extent to which Rushton is cheating him. Owen's status as a superior skilled worker is also problematic when we discover he lives in 'Lord Street', though he was not welcomed by his well-to-do neighbours. He does not have the mettle of a workers' leader. The only time Owen confronts his employers directly arises from a barely controlled explosion of anger at the callous treatment of the apprentice Bert White (ch. 51). The scene is highly melodramatic (even to the extent that Owen bursts in on a tableau of Rushton and his secretary *in flagrante*) and is a very high-risk strategy for Owen. Its successful outcome is a surprise to both Owen and the reader.

But if Owen has all-too-human faults, the novel never wavers in referring experience back to its economic motivation. We learn little about characters' backgrounds and psychological chemistry, and there is no naturalist 'growth' or major plot revelations. Ruth Easton's affair with Slyme can be traced to the desperate need to take in a lodger. The scene in chapter 3 (given the ironic title 'The Financiers') in which Ruth and Easton pore over their domestic budget is one of the most moving and memorable in the novel. The power of the scene derives partly from its originality – such details are not the usual stock of fiction – but primarily from the formal device of presenting the Eastons' bills on the page. In these columns of relatively minor sums of money lies the Eastons' future; these paltry figures represent the line between respectability and the decline into poverty and pauperdom. The Eastons' balance sheet is both metonymic and metaphorical: a failure to 'add up' will literally ruin their lives, and the dramatic stakes of the failure to 'balance' the books symbolizes the crisis in their fortunes and, later, their marriage. By putting the budget on the page, Tressell emblematizes the reification of working-class life, and the social power given to inanimate objects, in this case items of furniture from Didlum's store. A similar point could be made about Rushton's time-sheet (also represented on the page), which heralds a new regime of factory-style work discipline.

Life is not always miserable for Owen's community. Frankie Owen's Pandorama entertainment, and the annual excursions and binges, are definitive moments of working-class leisure time, part of a fully formed working-class culture. While the beano is deeply infiltrated by the discourse of the employers, who use it as an occasion to preach deference to capitalism, the workers have a rare opportunity to be gluttons: '"Chuck us over another dollop of that there white stuff" shouts the semi-drunk' (p. 437), only to find Crass 'demolishes' it himself, certain that there is plenty more. The scene invokes both an earthy, carnivalesque Cockayne, and the feast of pastoral tradition.

Debunking humour is the workers' instinctive response to a threat, including that posed by Owen. The arch-wag Philpott has many of the best lines (Owen, notably, is not a punster). As the lecture on the Oblong gathers momentum, Easton rises to a 'pint of order' (p. 264): '"And I rise to order a pint", cried Philpott'. Even Barrington's great oration is given a mock-formal staging by Philpott, including putting up a poster (p. 464). But as in most working-class writing, pleasure is an insecure and transitory escape from the brutal cycles of economic life (sunshine and shadows, to recall Wheeler's trope). The iron laws of slump and boom function like the industrialized equivalent of ancient fertility myths of death and rebirth, and they are deeply ingrained in working-class consciousness, and perhaps nowadays in general consciousness. The message of *The Ragged Trousered Philanthropists* is that the only permanent solution to this situation lies in socialism. Owen's concluding Utopian vision is both a symbol of hope and a measure of the task ahead.

Tressell's achievement becomes more remarkable when we look at the story of the novel's publication. This narrative is symptomatic of the unstable foundations of working-class literary production. Tressell died in 1911, bequeathing the handwritten manuscript, which had failed to find a publisher, to his daughter, a servant. She brought it to the attention of her mistress's friend Jessie Pope, who worked for *Punch*. She read the manuscript and was sufficiently impressed to pass it on to her friend, the publisher Grant Richards. Though he found the novel 'damnably subversive, but extraordinarily real',[28] he agreed to publish it subject to Jessie Pope making substantial revisions. Pope carried out this task conscientiously, and reduced the text by almost a half, excising Ruth Easton's affair and Barrington's character, and moving other parts around so that the novel ended with Owen's suicidal thoughts in chapter 34 (this process also involved some scissors-and-paste alterations to the manuscript). The extent to which this textual violence damaged the book's appeal is hard to judge, as early reviews were favourable, praising the novel's authenticity and insight into working-class life. Grant Richards planned a cheap edition, which was delayed by the war for four years, otherwise who knows what impact it would have made on Edwardian England. When this version appeared in 1918 it sold 100,000 copies. The abridged text was reprinted often during the next twenty years, including an edition by Penguin, but there was still no access to the original, complete narrative. Fortunately the manuscript, which had been missing for years, having been sold by Richards to his secretary for £10, was discovered by F. C. Ball in 1946. He restored it and persuaded the communist publishers Lawrence and Wishart to bring out the first unabridged version of the novel in 1955. The manuscript found a fitting home when it was donated to the Trades Union Congress in 1959 – it is currently in the library of Congress House in London.

Compared to *Sons and Lovers*, *The Ragged Trousered Philanthropists* seems a less forward-looking text. It is not interested in exploring modern subjectivity and its primary determinants, sexuality and the unconscious. These absences could easily alienate the non-socialist reader. On the other hand, Tressell embraces a proto-modernist aesthetic of decentred characterization and the incorporation into the text of non-literary discourses. Yet he does this to service a didactic political aim. If John Carey is correct in his theory that modernism developed out of a need for high culture to distance itself from the semi-educated masses, then

Tressell can be credited with the only major attempt by a working-class author to produce what Wim Neetens worthily but rather rosily calls a 'democratic Modernism'.[29]

Patrick MacGill's *Children of the Dead End: The Autobiography of a Navvy*, on the other hand, combines elements of fictionalized working-class autobiography, tramp fiction, the Romantic outsider and the *Künstler-Bildungsroman* to produce a less didactic but still incisive condemnation of Edwardian capitalism, 'a great fraud' (p. 257). MacGill, the son of an illiterate Irish farmer, had experienced as a boy the humiliation of the 'hiring fair' (a 'slave market') where he was bought by a local farmer: 'I was an article of exchange' (p. 37). As soon as he can he heads for Scotland with a squad of potato-diggers, but conditions are still 'brutal and almost unfit for animals' (p. 81). Given the total impossibility of achieving any 'respectable' goals in life, the hero Dermod Flynn prefers a life on the tramp. The narrative mode is therefore not predicated on a tragic fall from grace (the fate of the struggling artisan or skilled worker) but epitomizes the disaffiliated, rootless existence of the migrant unskilled worker and the lumpenproletariat (a group Marx was keen to label as 'scum' and reactionary). Flynn can only survive so long as he has no responsibilities, and it is easy to see how the artisan backbone of socialism would view this outlook – indeed, Tressell's Owen calls an unmarried man 'unnatural'. Nevertheless, it is important to recognize the establishment of a narrative form for this maligned stratum of the working class, particularly as the figure of the 'drifter' has been more usually associated with modernism (Beckett) or bohemianism (the Beats).

Flynn has no plan, no self-improving goal, but his possible salvation commences when he discovers literature. Such a moment of near-religious 'conversion' was a hallmark of nineteenth-century working-class autobiography. Flynn's first contact with books is both magical and embarrassing, as his hands are so dirty he is not allowed to touch them – this emphasizes his social status (he is a 'hand') and his separation from learning. But he is a 'natural' storyteller and soon he is being published in a London daily newspaper. He becomes a journalist, at which point the reader might think Flynn's progress is complete. However, he soon becomes disillusioned with commercial writing and returns to the road. There is no linear plot development, and no closure. The hero reverts to a decentred, marginalized, fluctuating position; an unfixed, floating social signifier. He has neither the resources nor the inclination to become bohemian. He is sometimes a worker and sometimes a writer. He is unplaceable, economically and aesthetically. His relation to property and marriage, those twin pillars of classic realism, is completely antithetical.

So MacGill constructed a different type of autodidact to the heroic or tragic figure of the *Bildungsroman*. His brand of alienated hero has not been a dominant influence on subsequent working-class writers, but it does find an echo in the 'expressionist' fiction of James Hanley in the 1930s (see chapter 2), and some Scottish stories in the present day (see chapter 4).

It is hoped that this comparison of four working-class novels has shown a number of things. First, that historical conditions do not determine literary form. Second, that by 1914 working-class fiction had made significant inroads into literary tradition, while preserving its own distinct character. Third, that the working-class writer has never been chained to a narrow form of realism. Finally, it is now clear that while Tressell may have been the most remarkable working-class writer at this time, he was not the only one of interest. The job of excavating and re-examining neglected working-class texts needs to continue, not least to establish the fullest possible picture of our cultural heritage.

2

Black Earth:
The Interwar Years

There are two periods when working-class fiction achieves a cult status and popular mystique in British culture: the time of rising affluence in the 1950s and 1960s (see chapter 3), and the 1930s. If the motives behind the attentions of the later period are primarily socially and culturally based, the imperatives of the interwar years are economic and political. Britain entered the post-First World War era in a far from triumphalist mood. Over a million casualties had been inflicted (there are few English villages which do not have a war memorial inscribed with the names of the dead). As was the case after previous major wars, the British economy was weakened by debt. Demobbed soldiers, even if they displaced wartime women workers, faced the continuing depredations of mass unemployment and economic insecurity. The numbers out of work never fell below a million in the 1920s, and rose to a staggering peak of over three million in the famous 'Depression' of the 1930s. The fragile wartime pact between the state and the labour movement collapsed as workers demanded due rewards for having won the war (they could take some heart from the granting of the vote to married women in 1919). The Triple Alliance launched a series of major disputes aimed in part at achieving the long-awaited nationalization of the staple industries. Worker confidence was boosted by the Bolshevik revolution of 1917. The crests of this potentially revolutionary surge of militancy included the railway workers' successful dispute for the eight-hour working day, the uprising in 'Red' Clydeside in 1919, the formation of Councils of Action to co-ordinate the opposition to Britain's support for the counter-revolutionary White armies in Russia (including the refusal of

London dockers to load the munitions ship the *Jolly George*), and the TUC-sponsored General Strike of 1926.[1] The state responded with the Emergency Powers Act and the mobilization of troops, volunteer workers and repressive legislation – a situation evoking strong echoes of the 1840s, and similarly successful in inflicting a series of defeats on organized labour.

Despite the election of two minority Labour governments in 1924 and 1929–31, the economy slumped further after the Wall Street Crash of 1929. The Labour government led by Ramsay MacDonald abandoned any attempt to resist the capitalist demands for yet more economic austerity and abdicated power to make way for a 'national' government (soon to be Tory-dominated), which ruled in various guises until 1945. One of the first measures of this regime was to introduce cuts in dole money through the infamous Means Test. This law meant that before a family could receive benefit its total income from all sources had to be assessed. Though the male 'breadwinner' might be out of work, benefits would be reduced if any other member of the family had an income. This could include wives, children and parents with pensions – all 'dependent' groups according to traditional patriarchal values. To the respectable working-class family the Means Test was an unprecedented intrusion into their privacy, as well as the symbol of a mean-spirited and vindictive state. The Means Test was tantamount to a new Poor Law in working-class demonology, and is an abiding image of the period.

Faced with a conservative consensus, many people turned to other sources of political opposition – the newly formed Communist Party, the Independent Labour Party, the National Unemployed Workers Movement – and to that miscellaneous alliance of intellectuals, activists and working people we can think of as an unofficial Popular Front. The most famous cultural expression of this network was probably the Left Book Club, formed in 1936. One of its more famous Book of the Month choices in 1937 was Orwell's *The Road to Wigan Pier*. But the Left Book Club focused not only on domestic mass unemployment but on opposition to fascism both in Europe and in Britain. The Spanish Civil War (1936–9) recruited thousands of volunteers anxious to put their political principles into military service, while in England Oswald Mosley's Blackshirts were rebuffed in the Cable Street clash of 1936. Despite being given police protection for their planned march through a Jewish quarter of the East End, the Blackshirts were driven back by protesters. The inevitability of another major European war invested such struggles with a highly charged apocalyptic intensity. Unemployment and fascism were seen as demonic twins of a failed capitalist system, reducing the working class to either the dehumanized victims of economic blight or the barbaric helots of conquest. On either count, the fate of mass democracy was in the balance, so it is unsurprising to find working-class writing being valued and sought out by the literary establishment.

But before we look at some of the texts produced in this prolific period, it is necessary again to point out that the state of the nation was not as uniformly desperate as many of the abiding media images and literary records would suggest.[2] While it is true that the older 'dirty' industries and their communities concentrated in the north of Britain were particularly badly hit by the Depression (Ellen Wilkinson's 1939 book about Jarrow – origin of the famous march in 1936 – was titled *The Town That Was Murdered*), newer industries based mainly in the midlands and south of Britain experienced something of a boom. The classic illustration of this is the car industry and the new factories using assembly line or Fordist production methods, but there was also an expansion in the production of electrical goods, chemicals and food, as well as a massive programme of house-building. This began with the implementation of the wartime promise of 'homes fit for heroes', but the 1930s switched the emphasis from public to private housing, and thus from working-class to middle-class provision. The state also invested heavily in modernizing the infrastructure, including the electrification of the National Grid and road-building. In overall terms the disposable income and living standards of the average family rose in this period, enabled largely by the cheapness of mass-produced commodities. If the economy could not always provide jobs, it could relieve some of the anxieties of life with forms of cheap mass leisure and entertainment: the new palatial cinemas, radio broadcasting, and sporting extravaganzas such as the FA cup final at Wembley. For some sections of the working class, life was more prosperous and pleasurable than ever before. It seems as if the old two-nation split of 'backward' north and 'enlightened' south had re-emerged, but we must not paint too rosy a picture of the 'haves', as some of the texts below will testify. Also, most commentators agreed that economic blight was a national problem, even if its worst effects varied regionally. While some working-class communities suffered a living death, new ones were created out of job mobility and migration. Though there was no New Deal as in the USA, the government took an active role in the relocation of almost 200,000 workers and their families: unemployed South Wales miners, for instance, were moved to Kent. Their descendants took a prominent role in the great miners' strike of 1984–5.

So the reality is more fluid than media images of the period might suggest, and the social development of working-class communities was not uniformly arrested by the Depression. This knowledge ought to prevent us over-romanticizing working-class writing in the interwar years, and encourage us to search out literary narratives of that 'other' less victimized class of white-collar workers, who are under-represented in working-class writing. Although the majority of working-class children still left school at 14, there was a small but significant increase in the numbers progressing to secondary education and obtaining paper qualifications. This was at best a piecemeal achievement enabled by local authorities, as there was no major educational reform between the wars. It was certainly not government policy to regard investment in education as one solution to economic stagnation, as is the case today. In 1926 the Hadow Report recommended the creation of universal 'primary' and 'secondary' education and the raising of the school leaving age to 15, but the implementation of these initiatives had to wait until the great Education Act of 1944.

So the most valued literary response to the contemporary situation was one that was antagonistic to capitalism and its social evils, that would both expose and challenge its hegemony. Working-class authors continued to explore a range of fictional genres, reworking established forms such as the *Bildungsroman*, the family epic and the love story, while drawing on other influences such as the modernist techniques of stream-of-consciousness and montage, Tressell's disjunctive didacticism, or recent cultural innovations such as the documentary movement and Mass Observation. There was also a flourishing proletarian theatre movement.[3] The adversarial circumstances of the interwar years had the beneficial effect of plugging working-class writers into local, national and international networks of cultural resistance and political organization. This sense of being part of a collective cultural struggle may have been in itself an antidote to the forces of alienation, repression and barbarism.

THE DECADE OF THE GENERAL STRIKE

Considering that the 1920s was responsible for the greatest collective challenge to capitalism mounted by organized labour this century (the General Strike of May 1926), the decade has not been remembered for its working-class writing. The mainstream literary canon has predictably focused on the achievements of high modernism (Eliot, Joyce, Woolf), but even the literary Left has failed to find texts worthy of reprinting. Fortunately, there are two exceptions to this rule: the 1989 Virago reprint of Ellen Wilkinson's novel about the General Strike, *Clash* (1929), and Gustav Klaus's anthology of short fiction from the period, *Tramps, Workmates and Revolutionaries* (1993). Before looking at these texts and others, it is worth drawing attention to Klaus's salutary reminder that finding a publisher in the 1920s was still a precarious business. Many working-class writers relied on the patronage and support of socialist publishers, booksellers and newspapers to launch if not sustain their careers. While this network was never a full-blown alternative public sphere, it did offer the basis for a career as a writer, and some authors went on to find respectable commercial publishers. Klaus also warns us against romanticizing the working-class author as a modern noble savage rooted in a primitive 'simple' community. He points out that mobility, migration and flux has long been an economic and social fact for significant sections of the working class. This perspective will be of particular value when we look at the fiction of the ex-Liverpool seaman James Hanley, but it reminds us again that we should not automatically conflate an author with his or her main characters. Robert Tressell, after all, came from Ireland and spent years in South Africa – neither experience features in *The Ragged Trousered Philanthropists*.

Though the 1920s is not as prolific as the subsequent decade in its production of working-class fiction, three authors collected in Klaus's book did produce full-length texts which are worthy of some attention: James Welsh's *The Underworld* (1920) and *The Morlocks* (1924); Ethel Carnie Holdsworth's *This Slavery* (1925) and Harold Heslop's *The Gate of a Strange Field* (1929). Ellen Wilkinson's *Clash* recreates the General Strike from a woman's perspective, which makes the novel particularly valuable. In their different ways these texts reflect the hopes and fears, the passions and conflicts, the aspirations and betrayals which characterized the turning point of May 1926.

By the time James Welsh published his first novel he was well on the way to becoming a Labour MP. Welsh grew up in the Scottish coalfields in the late nineteenth century, and despite his father being killed in a mining accident Welsh went down the mine aged 11. Welsh is the first of a rich crop of mining novelists active in the interwar period, so *The Underworld* established an important precedent.[4] Some of its appeal can be gleaned from a publisher's advert for the novel. The advert is worth quoting in full as it combines literary, social and political judgements (I have added some comments after each statement):

1. It is a book about mining life by a working miner [authenticity];
2. It tells of the every-day life of the men who supply the motive power of civilization [the labour theory of value; coal is the basic industry of the country];
3. The men and women are alive and their sufferings and hardships cry aloud for Nationalization of the coal-mines [the book has a clear political message – the Sankey Commission recommended public ownership of the mines];
4. There is in *The Underworld* humour and pathos, but above all heroism [the characters are not mere stereotypes of class warriors, though they have an essential epic quality];
5. It is written by a working man who has seen and lived all he depicts in words of intense realism and rare gripping power [the writing, like mining, is elemental and impassioned];
6. Above all it is a story, thrilling and enthralling, and shows by its mastery of incident and character the genius that is in the working man today [there are many others like Welsh];
7. It is full of truths – truths that every man and woman who lives by the work of their head and hands should read [the appeal of the book is to all classes].[5]

Beneath the publisher's puff is the clear message that working-class fiction is vital, mature, and uniquely different.

There is more 'pathos' than humour in *The Underworld*. It tells the sad story of a young Scottish miner, Robert Sinclair. During his first day down the mine, his father and brother are killed in a roof-fall. He is inspired to become an activist by hearing Keir Hardie and Bob Smillie speak, rises to national prominence in the labour movement, and dies trying to rescue some trapped miners. His final thoughts are that workers must 'stand firm together', a robust message in the context of the industrial disputes of the early postwar years. Indeed, the novel's class-conscious assertiveness was enthusiastically received by the reading public, as it sold 32,000 copies in its first year. The novel also points out the sexual indignities suffered by miners' wives. In his youth, Robert is disgusted by the way in which colliery overmen dispense work for sexual favours.

The title of Welsh's second and more ambitious novel *The Morlocks* (1924) reflects the growing confidence of working-class writing: the title is an allusion to the underground workers of H. G. Wells's science-fiction novel *The Time Machine* (1895). Welsh's dystopian dramatization of the apocalyptic struggle between capital and labour is an imaginative intensification of the contemporary industrial strife. The 'Morlocks' are a Trotskyist group who have infiltrated the trade union movement, awaiting their chance to ignite the coalfields and wider labour movement into an insurrection, and make the country ungovernable. 'We are going to create Hell, to try and establish heaven', says one Morlock (p. 294), with a characteristic blend of idealism and callousness. The novel presents 1920s Britain as ripe for revolution; the potent sense of betrayal felt by the millions of demobbed soldiers now facing wage cuts is a 'volcano' (p. 57) waiting to erupt. Welsh's reformist instincts become clear in the blame he places on an irresponsible ruling class, who encourage the Morlocks to unleash their chaos. Once the uprising is crushed, the coalfields are left in a far worse condition than ever before, and the country is in the iron grip of repression and reaction. Rather like the 'moral force' Chartists before him, Welsh implies that violent action by the workers is both futile and out of character, though this leaves open the question of the appropriate response to economic blight and vindictive employers.

The vague reformism of the political vision may account for the awkward development of the plot and the role of the hero. The novel opens with the hero Sydney Barron stumbling into a bleak mining community; he is a lower-middle-class orphan in search of work and succour, and gladly accepts a job down a local mine. This enables Welsh to introduce the seminal device of the hero's first day at work, where the 'epic' quality of mining reveals itself. To this novice and outsider the mine is an 'inferno' of 'hard, brutalizing work' (pp. 38, 40). Barron's decision to stay in the community once his immediate straitened circumstances are relieved seems odd. It transpires that he is a Morlock agent, but it is difficult to reconcile this revelation with his earlier hard-luck story. To keep step with this revelation, the novel's generic affiliation switches from the *Bildungsroman* to a dystopian adventure story, as arson and destruction reduce the coalfields to a state of appalling misery. Outbreaks of pestilence and disease give the conflict a biblical resonance. Other mythic dimensions include the fate of the pacifist miner Alan Rennie, who becomes a Robin-Hood-style Morlock, and the sacrificial entombing of Barron by his own side when the Morlocks torch his pit. The novel's unresolved ending is a classic dystopian image of national desolation and political tyranny. Published in the year of the first Labour government, the novel is a powerful argument for a constitutional settlement to the crisis of capitalism, though it cannot find the language or imagery for such a resolution.

Harold Heslop's *The Gate of a Strange Field* (1929), published in the year of the Wall Street Crash and the election of the second Labour government, uses hindsight to take a more conclusive look at the postwar years, including the General Strike.[6] Heslop is another socialist ex-miner who was educated at a Labour College, the Marxist alternative to the Workers' Education Association. He already had a reputation as a radical writer, as his first novel was published in the Soviet Union in 1926, and reissued in Britain in 1934 as *Goaf*. He also attended the Conference of the International Union of Revolutionary Writers in Kharkov in 1929, where he made a speech denouncing other British working-class authors, including Welsh: 'proletarian art in Great Britain is in a very backward condition – it is in fact hardly begun'.[7]

In order to make *The Gate of a Strange Field* a partial chronicle of the 1920s, Heslop uses slices of reportage which punctuate the story of the hero Joe Tarrant, a miner and rising union activist. Key moments in the build-up to the General Strike include: the collapse of the Triple Alliance on 'Black Friday' in 1921; the triumph of 'Red Friday' on 25 July 1925, when the government granted a nine-month subsidy to the mine-owners to prevent wage reductions; and the passing of the Order for the Maintenance of Supplies in 1925. Once Joe has become a local official of the Miners Federation he is able to play a small part in the making of history, though he is fairly cynical about union careerism, its 'clique manufacturing' and 'masquerades' (p. 183). As a Communist, Heslop could be expected to show some disdain for the leadership of the labour movement, and his political views could also explain the absence of any attempt to narrate the General Strike, which features in the background as a huge anticlimax. Heslop seems more at ease with the early *Bildungsroman* sections of the narrative, including Joe's first day at work, and his first acquaintance with a fatal accident. The novel ends conventionally with a pit disaster – in this case a flood caused by working an old, unsafe seam. The accident is directly attributable to the grasping policies of the pit management, flushed with new power from the victory of 1926. Beginning with Zola's novel *Germinal* (1885), the set-piece of the mining disaster has produced much fine if predictable writing: graphic, thrilling, the sublime expression of the elemental mystique of mining. After being trapped for seventeen days, Joe miraculously survives, though his future is uncertain, another reminder of the basic insecurity of working-class life.

The most interesting feature of the novel is not the study of the labour movement but the exploration of the hero's sexual repression. Heslop gives this Lawrentian theme a non-Lawrentian sociological gloss, making it clear that the problem stems from a working-class culture ruled by the 'taints and traits of patriarchy' (p. 159). Though Joe's masculinity is created primarily out of his identity as a miner (he 'suddenly became a man', p. 19, on his first day at work) his male ego is not intact until 'predatory sin-gratification' has been satisfied. But lacking his peers' 'sexual ferocity' Joe blunders into premarital sex with

44

his girlfriend. When Molly becomes pregnant, the couple enter into an unhappy marriage. Both of them suffer, though Joe has more opportunity to rebel. When he begins an affair with another activist, Molly leaves him. At this point the novel takes a nosedive into melodrama, as Molly resurfaces later in the novel as a prostitute and kept woman. But though her 'fallen' story is backward-looking, her lack of guilt and remorse is not. She speaks like a contemporary feminist (1929, it is worth recalling, was also the year in which unmarried women were given the vote):

> I wonder who's most unfortunate, the woman that has a good time in Piccadilly, or the woman up North who slaves twenty-five hours out of thirty. No, they're not unfortunate. I never met a girl in Piccadilly who didn't think she was working. (pp. 209–10)

While we may query the 'good time' to be had on the streets, Molly's escape from 'Northern' morals is paralleled by Joe's lover Emily, who departs for a job as a lecturer in industrial relations. Her parting comments are bitter: 'It's only you men who are allowed to grumble, leaving it all to us while you run about the country shouting' (p. 246). While Joe ends the novel immobilized, the two 'fallen' women are in command of their own destinies, rejecting a future of domestic drudgery and child-bearing. The narrator remarks that the average body of a working-class mother soon becomes 'distended, marred and spoiled' (p. 84) through her root function of reproducing labour. Although contraception had long been in use by the middle classes, birth control is absent from working-class texts until the 1960s.

It is a pity Heslop did not go one stage further and make a woman the hero of the novel. Fortunately, we can turn to Ethel Carnie Holdsworth's *This Slavery* (1925) and Ellen Wilkinson's *Clash* (1929) to remedy this situation.[8] Ethel Carnie began life as a mill-girl, a fact her publishers exploited to the full, as this detail was usually inserted under her name. She was advised by Robert Blatchford to become a labour journalist, began to write for the *Woman Worker*, and moved up the social ladder. One of her early works is a socialist children's story, *The Lamp Girl* (1913), in which a conventional regime of order is not restored at the end of the tale. When the prince is asked to take the place of his wicked father the King, he astonishes the populace by renouncing the throne: 'We will have no more masters and slaves, but dwell together as friends'. Instead of serving him, the people are told to 'serve ye each other'.[9]

This Slavery follows the parallel fortunes of two Lancashire working-class sisters Rachel and Hester Martin. Rachel is the radical autodidact who spends her spare time away from the mill reading Marx, Paine and Morris. Hester is a consumptive with an aesthetic sensibility. She is happier with a violin than a loom, and faints of exhaustion on her first day at work. These effete and over-refined attributes lead her into the arms of a local yarn agent. Her marriage to him is presented as naked class betrayal – she is now an 'ambassadress of Capital' (p. 139). But Hester keeps some of the reader's sympathies, as it is clear she has exchanged one form of servitude for another, more genteel version, and her motives for marrying were swayed by wanting to provide for her mother. The contradictions of her position become so intolerable that she becomes an informer for striking mill-workers, thus betraying her husband and her new class. In a finale which has echoes of the 1840s 'industrial novels' and Allen Clarke's *Daughter of the Factory*, Hester is shot by riot police while trying to pacify an angry crowd. Meanwhile, in a melodramatic subplot, Rachel discovers that she is the daughter of the local factory owner, who seduced her mother. This *anagnorisis* may be archaic, but Rachel's forgiveness of her mother's 'fall' is modern:

> 'I believe our morals are determined by our necessity an' the economic conditions we live under. After all, I don't see that sex is any more sacred than genius, and to sell one has no more effect than to sell the other.' (p. 59)

Just as important as the Marxist and feminist consciousness in this speech is the tell-tale 'an'' – a working-class tagging of language that differentiates Rachel from her middle-class predecessors in the novels of Wells, Lawrence, Forster or Woolf. Rachel becomes a leading local activist, and at one rally makes a speech proposing a Godwinian solution to the problem of unemployment, that everyone should do a small amount of manual labour each day.

This Slavery is important as it is one of those rare novels which is both by and about a working-class woman. Yet for all its strident politics, the novel lacks a defined historical sense. Its action could take place at any time from the late nineteenth century onwards. Mary Ashraf reckons Carnie wrote the novel well before its publication date.[10] Given the rarity of the novel, the modern reader feels some frustration that an opportunity was lost to engage more fully with contemporary events.

That is not the case in Wilkinson's *Clash*. Wilkinson was another daughter of the factory who became a labour journalist and MP. During the General Strike she worked for the Plebs League, the organization which supported the National Labour Colleges.[11] She collaborated with Oliver Postgate on *A Workers' History of the Great Strike* in 1927, and in 1929 revisited the strike in fictional terms, and with a strong feminocentric emphasis. The story is told from the point of view of Joan Craig, a trade union organizer and fledgling author. Joan is constructed as a career woman. Her class origins are obscure, and she views 'grim industrial towns' (p. 35) in the language of an outsider. But her career brings about a choice of two lovers which will test her class loyalties and her understanding of gender. One lover is a bohemian who asks her to give up working, the other is a socialist who wants to marry her. The narrator poses the problem,

> whether we can stretch the old Victorian codes to fit, or whether we should throw codes over altogether, or whether the modern woman can evolve a new code. (pp. 97–8)

This dilemma is hardly typical of the plight of most working-class women at this time, but it parallels the strike's challenge to the 'old codes' of capitalism, while undermining traditional labourist chauvinism. In the end, Joan chooses the 'new code' of marriage and a career, though this triumphalism contrasts with the fate of the strike. *Clash*'s decentred account of the strike repositions a key moment in labour movement history as a stepping stone in the forward march of middle-class women's emancipation. Wilkinson inverts the usual priority of male-centred narrative; in her history, male agency is in the background. On the other hand, the novel has no answer to the capitalist oppression of the working class.

Turning briefly to Klaus's anthology, the stories have a range of forms and themes. Harold Heslop and Joe Corrie use mining accidents as the dramatic essence of exploitation by a ruthless employing class. James Hanley pushes this theme to a grotesque extreme in 'The Last Voyage'. Rather than face retirement, an ageing seaman commits suicide by leaping into the boiler of his ship – a terrifying image of dehumanization and waste. The tale is also a critique of the dominant role of work in the construction of masculine identity. As we shall see, this is an area Hanley explores with great intensity in his cycle of novels about the Fury family. On the other hand, not all Klaus's stories are tragic in tone. Allen Clarke's 'The Great Chowbent Football Match' is a comic sketch of an improvised match between two pubs. The slapstick action (including one player wearing clogs, and the referee using a bicycle whistle) reminds us of the pleasures of mass spectatorship sports in the lives of the interwar working class, and the enduring importance of humour in working-class culture. In this sense the literary record is probably misrepresentative. It is not until the 1960s that bawdiness, for instance, becomes a central trope in working-class fiction, whereas it had flourished in the music hall for decades.

THE THIRTIES

Compared to the 1920s, the number of working-class authors who published novels in the 1930s is impressively large: any survey must include James Hanley, Joe Corrie, Harold Heslop, Walter Greenwood, John Sommerfield, Lewis Jones, Walter Brierley, Frederick Boden, Jim Phelan, Lewis Grassic Gibbon, Simon Blumenfeld, Willy Goldman, Leslie Halward, Ralph Bates, Jack Hilton, B. L. Coombes, James Barke and Frank Tilsley.[12] In addition to their novels, we can also note the substantial numbers of short stories published in liberal-left and socialist periodicals such as *Left Review* and *New Writing*. These publications encouraged and patronized working-class writers, and launched some, if not all, on successful careers. Most of these authors still relied for their literary training on the time-honoured route of self-education, extra-mural classes and courses at labour colleges. Though some were Communists, it would be a great mistake to assume that all working-class writers at this time looked to Moscow for salvation. While there are some examples of what might be termed socialist realism in the texts that follow, by no means all the heroes of these stories are class warriors. The types of hero range from the apolitical and respectable (Brierley), through the criminal (Phelan) to the tortured and self-destructive (Hanley). Generic influences include documentary realism and the modernist montage (Sommerfield), while there are further variations on the *Bildungsroman*.

Probably the most famous working-class novel of the period, and one which has contributed to our popular memory of the 1930s, is Walter Greenwood's *Love on the Dole* (1933).[13] Greenwood drew on his own upbringing to portray the community of Hankey Park (based on Salford), a *déclassé* suburb of Manchester now suffering the full ravages of economic blight and state intrusion: unemployment, the dreaded Means Test, and the added evils of 'speed-up' and planned obsolescence in the workplace. Out of this uncompromising milieu Greenwood constructs his version of the 'slum' novel. The echoes of nineteenth-century precursors are quite intentional: at one level the novel is a reworking of Gaskell's *Mary Barton*. But though there are some elements of melodrama (such as the Sally–Grundy subplot) and naturalism (Harry's doomed progress and entrapment within Hankey Park), Greenwood's approach is more varied and interesting than has been acknowledged by those critics who have attacked the novel for its lack of political engagement and historical clarity, and for its literary pretensions.[14] The debunking tone of the title (an implicit oxymoron) is more reminiscent of Tressell than Morrison, and points to the novel's central trope: the narrative presents an antitype of conventional fictional romance, in which erotic desire confronts the obstacles of property relations. There are two elements to Greenwood's ironic reworking of the romance plot, shared between the two main characters Harry and Sally Hardcastle. Both are *Bildungsroman* heroes *manqué* – their development is attenuated; their destinies primarily dependent on the iron laws of slump and boom, not individualized choice.

Harry's bathetic trajectory centres on the shattering of the conventional ideals of masculine pride. At the opening of the novel, Harry has just left school and is working as a clerk for the allegorically named pawnbroker Mr Price. He is pushed into doing the job by his mother while he was still at school (under the half-time system), clerical work representing her respectable aspirations. Harry, on the other hand, despises the work for its tedium and low pay, but above all its effeminacy. Being a 'mere pusher of pens' for Mr Price (p. 21) cannot compare with the real, masculine work performed by those 'gods of the machine' in the local engineering plant. Needless to say, he is delighted to be given a place at Marlowe's, the huge engineering factory which dominates the community. Harry's over-romanticization of industrial labour is both understandable and dangerous. Greenwood provides clear signals that he is only partially in sympathy with Harry's point of view. Firstly, the language used to describe Harry's jubilation at becoming the latest recruit to Marlowe's 'army' of workers is deeply ironic. In an apparent reversal of Marx's theory of alienation, Harry is glad to serve as a 'necessary cog in the great organization' (pp. 19–20). Greenwood's ironic detachment prevents us from reading Harry's rejection of clerical work as a completely valid act of heroic class-consciousness. Harry is as romantically self-deluded about his destiny as any of the women characters in the novel, to the extent that he ignores Larry Meath's warning that at the end of his apprenticeship he will be sacked. On the other hand, the novel is in sympathy with Harry's rejection of the pressure from his mother and his girlfriend Helen to be a 'cut above' his peers by choosing 'pen-pushing' above skilled manual labour.

The second major challenge to Harry's control over the narrative point of view comes from within the feminized space of Price's shop. Harry projects his anger and social claustrophobia onto the women customers. He sees them sourly as faded victims of the treacheries of working-class marriage, 'simple natures all, prey to romantic notions' (p. 31) who now find solace in gossip, rumour, scandal and mass consumption of the right-wing press and its myths (particularly court news). Collectively, if we extrapolate from Harry's response, these wives and grandmothers are the reactionary bedrock of working-class culture, easy fodder for capitalist manipulation. Yet this is not how the narrative actually presents them. For the women who make a weekly visit to the pawnbroker, the facility is a vital centre of a local economy of survival which also includes the bookmaker Sam Grundy, the beerhouse and the church. Their discourse dominates the scenes in Price's shop, and does not consist solely of gossip. Mrs Nattle and Mrs Doorbell, two leading lights in a vivacious circle of elder crones, have a shady 'business' relationship with Price which lifts them well out of the category of mindless, conforming victims and into the Dickensian realm of comic villainesses (Mrs Nattle pawns other people's goods at a commission, and Mrs Doorbell trades in old age pension books) – in a flourish reminiscent of Tressell, Greenwood compares their activities to the Bank of England (p. 107). The women of Hankey Park have to compromise economically with Price and Grundy, so they cannot afford the luxury of dismissing the novel's two capitalists as mere villains. Grundy is actually a popular figure with the whole community, for all the wrong reasons. As he dispenses winnings to an eager crowd we are told 'Sam was popular', while there are 'roars of obsequious laughter from all sides' (p. 113). Grundy is structurally a villain in his designs on Sally Hardcastle, but, as we shall see, he is not allowed to have a conventional seducer's triumph over Sally.

So from the outset the novel challenges the dominant masculine ideology that positions women in the role of submissively servicing men's needs. The novel's various plot lines attempt to negotiate the massive faultline of oppressive gender roles. Harry's doomed aspiration to be the masculine breadwinner is cast into a dialectical moral perspective by the novel's foregrounding of the atavistic, resourceful culture of survival of Mrs Nattle and her circle. While they bemoan Hankey Park's decline from the days of elegant 'kerridges', they do not straightforwardly personify an ossified past of Victorian values, as their support for Sally's elopement with Grundy shows. At that point in the novel, gender solidarity overrides traditional sexual morality. While Harry looks ahead to a cruelly blighted, unproductive future, these women keep the social fabric of the community intact – they are choric, comic and convivial. Likewise, the novel lays bare the pain of Mrs Hardcastle's decision to pawn her wedding ring, and the pain of her husband's discovery. As Tressell might say, the fault lies not in the individual but the 'system' which is ultimately, in the absence of collective struggle, the more powerful.

Harry's first day at Marlowe's anticipates all his future disappointments. Instead of the eagerly awaited initiation into the 'mysteries' of the trade 'as had been promised in the extravagant language of the indentures' (p. 46), he runs errands for his seniors. So desperate is Harry to demonstrate his initiation into a man's world that he resorts to the pathetic desperate measure of faking the dirt on his hands. When another apprentice discovers him in the act, Harry is subjected to the real thing: the blacking of his testicles. But at least he is now accepted as a 'man', and his happiest times are the years of his apprenticeship. Earning power brings him status and self-esteem. He conveniently forgets Larry Meath's warnings that the factory system is one huge swindle. Harry's long-awaited purchase of a Sunday suit echoes his earlier fetishistic worship of the boilersuit or factory 'overall', showing that work and home are two sides of the same coin. As he begins to prepare for marriage to his girlfriend Helen Hawkins, the Nemesis of the dole looms ever larger. An omen of this fate occurs after he wins £22 from Sam Grundy and takes Helen on a 'spree' to a seaside resort. This excursion is one of several blighted pastoral moments in the novel, where the chance of even a temporary escape from the 'stinking carcass' of industrialism proves futile. Firstly, the sight of unemployed workers in the resort devastates Harry: 'Unemployed, here, though! Did its stinking carcass foul the air everywhere? Was there no place where it did not lie in wait for your coming?' (p. 123). Secondly, the sexual pleasure that accompanies pastoral escape turns bitter: Helen reveals her deep loathing of sex brought about by witnessing her parents making love (there is also a hint of incestuous goings-on); and she becomes pregnant. The whole episode is intensely mock-romantic, especially the allusion to Keats in the chapter title 'Magic Casements'. The scene is also paradigmatic of those numerous moments in working-class fiction where conspicuous consumption is the prelude to something dire – as if a culture forged in deprivation has developed an innate mistrust of commodities and material success.

Shortly after their return, Harry is sacked. While this disaster is a key moment in much working-class fiction, Greenwood introduces a twist by showing that the employers are conducting a deliberate policy of sacking newly qualified workers, ensuring a cheap supply of labour. They are able to do this because the newly installed machinery is largely automated, so the workforce can be deskilled and casualized under the guise of a conventional apprenticeship. Harry feels an almost sexual thrill at his first contact with these futuristic machines, which only makes his subsequent disenchantment more poignant and profound: 'MACHINES! Lovely, beautiful word!' (p. 69); 'He regarded [the lathe] with pride of possession, ran his hand along it caressingly...' (p. 71). But the customary route to manhood is short-circuited when younger boys are put in charge of larger machines. The productive basis of masculine identity is shattered, and Harry makes a telling comparison between his plight and the 'lost generation' of the war: 'Why, those soldiers had only been three years older than he...Did he lack some masculine quality which others possessed?' (p. 75). It would be no consolation to Harry to be told he had hit upon a critique of the essentialism of gender identity. Even had he listened to Larry Meath's warning, the reader wonders what Harry's options would have been apart from joining Larry in his socialist quest to overthrow the system. The real benefit of Harry's disenchantment is for the reader, who is given an insight into phoney capitalist ideologies. The 'new industrial revolution' (p. 132) is Greenwood's ironic language for capitalism's response to recession (speed-up, deskilling), in a country without a New Deal.

When Helen becomes pregnant, the trashing of Harry's dreams is complete, though his misery is not. A succession of humiliating blows follows: a shotgun wedding, fruitless quests for work as a 'man of leisure', expulsion from his home (the conflict with his father is an Oedipal subplot), the Means Test, resort to the workhouse, and having to take lodgings with Mrs Bull. Harry is the classic emasculated male worker, although he has youth on his side (unlike his father, who is reduced to infantilist dependency on Sally's earnings – 'his brain retarded, bewildered' (p. 251) – and self-destructive attempts to exert his patriarchal authority). In reality, Harry would probably have remained in this obscure, lumpen existence (like Thomas Cooper's stockingers) until rearmament revived the economy, but Greenwood bows to popular convention by redeeming his hero at his lowest ebb. While the *deus ex machina* which provides him with a job is a populist and sentimental touch, it is given a characteristic ironic and bitter twist. In order to understand how this is done, we have to turn to the parallel fortunes of Harry's sister, Sally.

Sally is also a victim of patriarchal conditioning. Romance looms large in her life. Though she works at a factory (and is never on the dole), she associates femininity with marriage and motherhood. Like Mary Barton before her, we never see Sally at work (an absence which shows the limit of Greenwood's critique of the masculine culture of labour). She is also intellectually incurious and inclined to be susceptible to the myths and seductions of popular culture, though she becomes aware that a reality lies beyond the 'trumpery gaiety of a dance room' (p. 142). Her attraction to Larry Meath, the novel's consumptive socialist hero (an effete version of Tressell's Frank Owen), has more to do with his glamorous status as a 'cut above' the average Hankey Park male than his political views. Her fate is heavily dependent on his. Meath's rival for Sally's affections is the brutish Ned Narkey, a war veteran and epitome of debased masculinity. His viciousness towards women is both a legacy of the war's dehumanization, and a barrier to class consciousness. Narkey's reactionary credentials are most fully realized in his recruitment into the police force. The two men finally clash in a melodramatic encounter. Narkey coshes Meath over the head when a demonstration against benefit cuts develops into a riot (this chapter has the revealing title 'Historical Narrative', indicating that private destinies are determined by public events). Narkey is a proto-fascist, though it is also the case that the police are stock figures of class oppression and betrayal in working-class demonology. To her credit, Sally chooses the better of the two men, though the intellectual gap between her and Meath is cruelly highlighted by the narrator. After she has accompanied Meath on one of his socialist hiking trips, she tells her family about listening to discussions of 'Marks', 'Bark' and 'Baytoven' (p. 97). These puns can only be made in writing, of course, and they alert us to the tension between literary narrative and working-class speech, a tension which is foregrounded at other moments in the novel.

If a union between Sally and Larry seems unlikely, it is made more possible by Larry's deep-seated conservatism about gender roles in marriage – beneath his bohemian exterior, he aspires to be the breadwinner as much as Harry. This makes him vulnerable to despair when he loses his job, though it is clear to the reader that his dismissal has been engineered by Sam Grundy, the third of Sally's suitors. Larry would never 'sponge' off Sally (p. 193). But as love and the dole are incompatible, Sally's fate is effectively sealed. Once Larry is wounded by Narkey at the rally, and dies of a weak heart (Greenwood draws back from a full-blooded image of state murder), Sally is spiritually dead. She falls back on her major resource, her beauty, and takes up Sam Grundy's offer.

Sally's tragedy, then, is that she cannot escape convention. By this stage in the novel, she has served her function of satirizing the possibility of a proletarian romance. But Greenwood introduces two twists into this resolution of her story. The first is Sally's defiant refusal to see herself as sinful, wicked and sexually depraved. Normally, her 'fall' would signify the shameful decline of the moral standards of respectable working-class culture. The moment where Sally harangues her parents for condemning her is one of the novel's most original, moving and ironic scenes. Instead of uniting the family against the common enemy of the post-1931 capitalist state, Sally's tirade confirms the gulf between herself and her parents. Her rebellion against their narrow attitudes is both heroic and feminist, yet is also an imploded and isolating protest against destructive social forces: 'There's none Ah know as wouldn't swap places wi' me if they'd chance...You'd have me like all rest o' the women, workin' 'emselves t' death an' gettin' nowt for it' (p. 246). Yet she finds unexpected support in Mrs Bull and her circle. Despite their lingering nostalgia for Hanky Park's genteel Victorian past, they have few illusions about sexual morality, and advise Sally to extract a settlement out of Grundy: 'Marriage, eh? Yaaa. Y' get wed for love an' find y've let y'sel' in for a seven day a week job where y' get no pay. An' y' don't find it out till it's too late' (p. 244). After Sally has acted on this advice there is a second plot twist in her story, as she becomes a fairy-godmother to her forsaken family. Now she is in command of property and influence, she finds jobs for Harry and her father at the local bus depot. While this flagrant *deus ex machina* is deeply sentimental, it also completes the novel's satirical purpose by parodying the conventional property plot of English fiction. Sally is both the ministering fallen angel of nineteenth-century tradition (like Hester Barton), and a critique of that convention in her defiant voice and her inversion of the power relations of seduction.

Another area where the novel engages with the problems of its literary inheritance is the vexed question of standard English. Like most working-class and middle-class authors, Greenwood chooses standard English for the narrator and dialect for the working-class characters. While this technique ensures the middle-class reader will not be alienated, it also enforces a class division between the author and the community represented in the narrative. One scene brings out this tension very strongly. When Harry and Helen are relaxing on Dawney's Hill, a favourite haunt of lovers, the narrator reports to us that Harry feels 'lulled into a state of harmonious quiescence, of peace and quiet breathing' (p. 80), whereas Harry struggles to find words for his Keatsian, pastoral bliss: 'Ah'd such a lovely feelin'... it was all nice' (p. 81). Greenwood makes no attempt to resolve this tension. As Roger Webster has argued, such discrepancies in discursive register expose rather than reinforce the oppressive gap between 'lettered' bourgeois culture and 'unlettered' working-class culture.[15] This post-Althusserian analysis also sheds light on the novel's epigraphs, which display Greenwood's intellectual credentials, and imply that the novel must be interpreted in apocalyptic terms, the 'whole old world sinking', in the words of Rosa Luxemburg. There is further textual evidence that Greenwood consciously exploits the tension between literary tradition and working-class culture, notably in those key mock-pastoral moments, where the novel's satirical message is most trenchant. The love/dole antithesis modulates in various scenes into related binary oppositions: love/squalor and sex/dirt. When Sally invites Larry 'round the back', for example, Larry's revulsion is expressed in literary terms: 'His spirits contracted on the instant; the magic trickled away. A back entry for a love bower!' (p. 149). Harry and Helen's relationship can only be a 'travesty of romantic love' so long as they live in 'eternal shabbiness' (p. 176).

So the novel's aesthetic composition is richer than its surface realism might suggest. Another of its striking formal features is its use of circularity. The novel ends almost exactly where it began, with a description of a typical Hankey Park street in the very early hours. The telling differences are the presence of Ned Narkey, now a policeman, and the 'slumbering' of the unemployed. This circular or cyclical movement is a reflection of some crucial features of working-class life and culture in its 'classic' phase. The material basis of the trope is the nature of working-class work, which for manual workers in particular was repetitive, relentless, and held out little hope of career advancement. As Raymond Williams has remarked, work figures as a 'primary consciousness' in working-class fiction.[16] The sense of time this condition promotes is therefore circular and repetitive, rather than progressive, linear and developmental (the shape of most realistic narratives). The focus in working-class narratives on the start of a new day conveys the dominance of production in working-class life. The workers are rising so early that it is still night-time and an 'unnatural' hour (so the ironic detail of the 'incongruous' slumbering of the unemployed is poignant, in that it is perfectly natural to be asleep at such a time). It is unsurprising that many working-class writers are drawn to this moment, which I would like to call the 'proletarian dawn', as an opening for their narratives. Yet circularity is not always a signifier of entrapment; it can also define secure limits and boundaries, and define time according to cultural traditions and customs. In hard times, however, there are few consolations to the miserable round.

A final tribute to *Love on the Dole* is to note that even if we disregard its more challenging artistic features, its grim revelations of the waste and indignities of capitalism carried enough of a documentary charge in the 1930s to make the government proscribe a film version of the novel until 1941. The novel's basic appeal may well have been its irresistible but unstated case for more state intervention in the economy – a literary advocate for the 'road to 1945'.

If asked, Greenwood would probably have agreed with Engels's recommendation that realism should not 'glorify the author's opinions'. But even when working-class authors of this period are drawn towards more didactic socialist fiction, the result is rarely an untroubled triumphalism. This chariness applies even to those authors associated with the Communist Party.

Take the rich vein of mining fiction. While Harold Heslop and Lewis Jones used their fiction to put the case for a Communist solution to current ills, Walter Brierley and Joe Corrie are best described as 'apolitical' in terms of the explicit alignment of their fiction. But in Engels's terms the latter approach could qualify as 'realism', in that it shows the structural decline of capitalism through the intimate details of personal life. On the other hand, most Marxist critics in the 1930s agreed that progressive fiction must show a grasp of 'the real forces at work beneath the surface of life' (Rex Warner) and a 'steady vision of the whole' (Ralph Fox), while not prescribing the formal means of carrying this out.[17]

Harold Heslop waited until *Last Cage Down* (1935), his third novel, before attempting a portrayal of 'epic' class struggle. The core of the narrative is a locked encounter between hero and villain that he first used in *Goaf* (1934), originally published in the Soviet Union in 1926.[18] As in his other novels, the hero of *Goaf* is a non-Communist lodge secretary of the miners' union who develops major flaws and weaknesses. Tom Drury's problem is that he bears a personal grudge against the turncoat overman John Hartley. After a roof-fall traps the two men underground, Tom escapes through the sinister 'goaf' (the north-eastern dialect term for the area of previous coal cutting where the roof is unsupported), while Hartley breaks down and commits suicide. In an original if far-fetched innovation on the persecution-of-the-hero motif, Tom is put on trial for Hartley's murder. The final chapters are a classic courtroom scene in which the meticulous expertise of Tom's socialist supporters swings justice in his favour. The forces of reaction are narrowly defeated, though Drury's future is uncertain.

In *Last Cage Down* this plot is reworked into a substantial revenge tragedy. Tom Drury becomes James Cameron, a traditional union leader who personifies the fatal errors of a non-revolutionary class consciousness (or what Lenin called 'trade union consciousness'). This is dramatized in his conflict with Tate, the colliery agent whom Cameron blames for the accident that killed his father. When Tate introduces new machinery in order to work an unsafe seam (the familiar bogies of deskilling and speed-up), Cameron knows there will be another disaster (indeed, it kills his brother). He threatens to kill Tate, who brings charges against him. Cameron is thrown in jail, an ironic echo of the colliery 'cage' that has ruled his life and his passions. For the correct class-conscious position, we have to turn to the Communist agitator Joe Frost, a 'new breed' (p. 42) of self-educated, intellectually disciplined and disinterested activist, who finds Cameron's threats against Tate 'melodramatic' (p. 39). Frost's rationality is the correct counter to the harsh new industrial regime of rationalization and modernization. His analysis of the 'decline' of capitalism is at odds with Cameron's intuitive resistance. Frost's point is that it is not the 'wonderful' machines but their ownership and control which are the problem. Hence he calls for a political strike to help the cause of nationalization, an option dismissed by Cameron, who only later realizes that Frost was right all along (even so, the novel does not go so far as to give Frost his strike). But Frost is also perceptive enough to see that Cameron wants to be a martyr, which is a distortion and mystification of his leadership role. Eventually, Cameron recaptures some of his 'Herculean' qualities when an underground explosion traps Frost and Tate (a re-run of an episode in *Goaf*) and Cameron rescues both of them. Even so, the pit will close, and both heroes (old and new) face a bleak, if resolute, future.

Despite its occasional didactic flourishes, passages of hero-worship and moments of crude class triumph (such as Mrs O'Toole's violently abusive encounter with Tate), the novel is more than a mere Communist fable. Like Greenwood, Heslop is fascinated by the faultline of gender roles and their internal contradictions. Cameron, for example, has an unstable masculine identity. He is too 'sensitive' to be a true miner, despite his physical prowess. He feels restored by having sex with his lover Betty, but his most intense relationship is with his mother. This post-Lawrentian taboo is made explicit when Tate goads Mrs Cameron with the salacious suggestion that she 'knows' her son, but there is compelling evidence in the text for this view: 'He kissed her ... the first kiss of his mature years' (p. 169); 'A woman, his mother ... Where the blazes could he sleep?' (p. 171). Heslop's point may be that an incestuous passion is the logical result of Cameron over-identifying with his father, itself a symptom of his failure to see that the class struggle cannot be conducted as a personal mission.

Any attempt to assess *Last Cage Down*'s success as a socialist novel has to confront the rather cruel irony that by the time it was published the Comintern cultural line had changed. The emphasis of 'class against class' underwent a U-turn at the Soviet Writers' Congress in 1934; the new policy was to establish a common front against fascism with other political persuasions. According to the new edict, the novel's critique of flawed working-class leadership, and its less subtle caricatures of class enemies (such as Oxley) became instantly redundant. Whatever the rights and wrongs of this debate, its most important feature is to remind us that working-class fiction of the 1930s needs to be seen in an internationalist context. The teleology of the Communist vision is not only the domestic triumph of the working class against the British state but the apocalyptic struggle against European fascism, that hideous mutation of capitalist decline.

Of course regionality is still a vitally important material and cultural factor in these texts. Lewis Jones's *Cwmardy* (1937) and its sequel *We Live* (1939) have the same subtitle, 'The Story of a Welsh Mining Valley'.[19] The echo of *Middlemarch*'s 'A Study in Provincial Life' may well be intentional, as Jones politicizes a number of nineteenth-century genres: the 'microscopic' study of a non-metropolitan community (Cwmardy), its family life (seen primarily through the Roberts and Jones families) and social issues (all revolving around mining); the epic sweep of the historical novel (the chronology of the two novels runs from the Edwardian 'boom' through the Tonypandy riots, the First World War, the General Strike and the unemployment and anti-fascist campaigns of the thirties). The novels structure historical development primarily as war: this incorporates class, imperialist and gender conflict, and affects formatively the *Bildungsroman* hero Len Roberts's passage through key sexual, psychological, educational, and social stages. Jones was well qualified to write this history from within. As a boy in the Rhondda he witnessed pitched battles between the community and the police. He attended a London Labour College, joined the fledgling Communist Party, and was imprisoned during the General Strike for making seditious speeches to midlands miners. He went on to become an organizer of the National Unemployed Workers Union, leading several hunger marches to London, and in 1936 was elected as one of only two Communist councillors on Glamorgan County Council. He entered fully into the spirit of the Popular Front, working with Labour Party councillors and union leaders to organize support for anti-fascism (much of this work carried out in long spells of unemployment). Unlike his hero Len Roberts, he did not fight in Spain, as his talents were reckoned by his political masters to be more useful on the domestic front. In fact this work proved equally perilous, as he died of exhaustion a few days before the fascist victory in Spain, having just completed *We Live*. In the Foreword to *Cwmardy*, Jones makes the radical claim that his book is effectively a product of collective authorship, in that he has always been a representative of the community. He is merely the conduit of determining forces, not a transcendent, prophetic or inspired exile from his class. The aesthetic flaws in the novel, he states, particularly its 'jumpy' structure, are symptomatic of the material factors of its production, 'written during odd moments stolen from mass meetings'. The decision to 'novelise' history, as he puts it, is an attempt to write the formation of the working class into the literary record, to 'steal' this narrative into culture, and to historicize and denaturalize the perilous contemporary situation Jones gave his life trying to reform.

Cwmardy uses hindsight to explore the contradictions of industrial working-class experience in the Edwardian period. The strongly class-conscious spirit of Cwmardy is personified by Len's father 'Big' Jim Roberts, who like James Cameron is a Herculean figure, renowned for his superior Darwinian physique and prowess. He traces his spiritual descent to the ancient Welsh kings who fought the English: 'An awful lot of blood was spilt that day and the grass have been red with it ever since' (p. 3), he tells the impressionable young Len. But this romanticized nationalism jars with Jim's flagrant jingoism, his constant harking back to his service in the Boer War, and his eagerness to volunteer for Flanders. Jim, like the majority of his class, does not see his willingness to fight and die for his community and for the British state as incompatible. The novel's structure is organized dialectically to highlight this glaring inconsistency. The community bonds together in set-piece confrontations with the authorities: an underground explosion which kills over 150 miners, which the owners blame on workers' negligence; the Zola-esque riots and triumphant pitched battles which lead to a minimum wage; even the death of Len's sister Jane in childbirth is converted into a 'class' event in that her lover is the son of the hated pit 'overman' (who prostituted his wife to the pit boss to gain promotion and who is later paraded around the village by rioters). By two-thirds of the way through the novel, the community (the collective hero of the novel) seem largely in control of their destiny, as the pit 'throbs' with success (ch. 13), and Len and his lover Mary Jones (daughter of the local trade union leader) are busy organizing a political education circle, capitalizing on the recent gains.

But the last quarter of the novel shows the impact of the First World War in reversing this Hegelian trajectory, and exposing its illusions and fragility. Despite having major misgivings, the combination of government propaganda and local guilt-tripping leads even Len to volunteer, though his lack of robust health disqualifies him. From this low ebb, Len begins to organize a fight-back in the form of a campaign for higher wages, despite being accused of treachery. Once the war ends, the picture is mixed. The response of the mine-owners is to introduce new machinery and speed-up (the destructiveness of this new regime is exemplified by a worker having his arm torn off, a clear echo of wartime carnage). Big Jim has not been radicalized by the war, but the Russian Revolution of October 1917 makes Len and Mary cautiously optimistic. Clearly, Len is the personification of the likely dialectical solution to these glaring contradictions, as the novel ends historically poised on the eve of the creation of the Communist Party. It is a pity that Jones could not have done more to bring this tempestuous moment alive.

If Len's characterization bears the burden of the novel's dialectical method, it is closely shadowed by that of Mary Jones, who becomes a major force in *We Live*. However, Mary's advance to consciousness is more complex and compromised than Len's. Mary is the locus of *Cwmardy*'s disturbing treatment of sexuality. As Pamela Fox has shown, heroes and heroines in working-class fiction of this period are often haunted by the spectre of Oedipal and sibling incest. From the novels looked at so far in this chapter, examples include Helen Hawkins in *Love on the Dole* and James Cameron in *Last Cage Down*. Overcrowded housing may be the material basis for this predicament, but in the novels the theme often leads to a crisis of personal and class identity. The intense relationship between Mary Jones and her father is an extension of her role as a substitute for her dead mother. In a classic example of a blighted pastoral interlude (in this case an excursion to Blackpool), Mary refuses to have sex with Len, citing her 'belonging' to her father (p. 250), and her wasting, tubercular body (as if her soul is indeed in her father's possession). As we shall see, these tensions come to a head in *We Live*, but Mary's refusal only shows how well matched she and Len are. His poor health is also associated with his sensitivity and intelligence. His lack of orthodox masculine values is shown by Big Jim's comment on his son: he is a 'queer lad' (p. 14). Len's breast-fixated desires for his sister Jane resurface in a number of later scenes. The abortive sex at Blackpool (where Mary's exposed breast 'taunts' him) recalls a childhood seaside excursion where Len is devastated to find Jane having sex with the colliery overman's son. This incident functions like a primal scene: its outcome (Jane's death in childbirth) marks the end of Len's boyhood, his exit from Lacan's 'Imaginary' state by the removal of the incest threat, but it also leaves Len with an inchoate feminist association of sex with exploitation: 'The boys in work talk of girls as the owners talk of us... If that is love, I don't want it' (p. 202). Male violence does indeed hover over both seaside scenes. In the earlier episode, Len, the disgraced Jane and their mother return to the beach to find Big Jim recovering from a fight, 'his mouth wide open and his legs spread loosely in an obscene sprawl' (p. 38) as if mocking what has just occurred. The corpse-like image also anticipates the conclusion of the later scene when Len and Mary return home from Blackpool to hear the news that war has been declared. The incest theme mediates contradictions of gender and class, and counters any notion that male working-class writing must simply reproduce patriarchal attitudes and stereotypes, rather than exposing the damage inflicted by these codes.

We Live can be compared to *Cwmardy* both horizontally and vertically – it is a chronological continuation of the story, but it shows many of the same battles having to be fought. Big Jim is still the most colourful character, Len and Mary (now married) are the ascendant stars, while Mary's father Ezra suffers a classically tragic fall from grace, going over to the management side, and dying shortly after. This finally releases Mary, although she has already sided with Len against Ezra, as much out of political as conjugal loyalty. Ezra must give way to the Communist interpretation of reality, though in the course of a continental-style sit-in at the mine, even the party line is shown to be vulnerable to the will of people. Len is ordered to persuade the men to call off the action, but not only do they persist in their action, they escalate the militancy by holding Hicks the under-manager hostage until their demands are met. There is more than one comic moment in this episode, including holding a mock-Eisteddfod in complete darkness. Meanwhile on the surface the women, led by Mary, inflict major defeats on the backsliding local Labour-run council, forcing it to retract benefit cuts. For just as the Communist Party offers salvation, the Labour Party is a false god. Like Ezra, it has joined the forces of reaction.

Jones portrays the state apparatus as an unremitting caricature of proto-fascist repression and viciousness (as in *Last Cage Down*, such a portrayal was out of step with Comintern cultural policy). The phoney charges brought against Len during the General Strike produce a show-trial complete with insidious judges and depraved, bloodthirsty policemen. Len is happy to become a class martyr, while Mary takes his place in his absence, joins the party, is elected a Communist councillor, and revitalizes her saint-like flagging body. Though it may have more direct relevance to its contemporary context than its prequel, *We Live* is in some ways less satisfactory as its structure is virtually cleansed of contradiction. The aim of the narrative is to transform Len and Mary into local legends. Len is sent to fight in Spain, which converts him quickly into a 'thrilling' romantic figure, a 'chivalrous crusader' (p. 326). His death puts the seal on this apotheosis. His one letter home evokes Big Jim's breezy and unpolitical letter from Flanders in the earlier novel. This time, however, Len offers a poignant celebration of the fight against fascism in specifically internationalist terms, transforming his father's jingoism into an apocalyptic encounter between democracy and reaction, not nation against nation. Most movingly, he sees the battlefield as an extension of the Welsh valleys: 'those are not strangers who are dying. They are our butties' (p. 331). The future lies with Mary, who is carried off over the horizon at the head of a local procession, a revolutionary icon of liberty. This feminized closure of the story reflects Mary's gradual dominance over Len. This process is illustrated at the level of private experience in a scene where she asks him if he could bear to 'lose' her. While she refers to her poor health, he interprets her word sexually, accusing her of having an affair. In the purified world of class struggle, language must also be purged of bourgeois prejudice and decadence. That does not mean there is no room for metaphors, however, as Jones's frequent literary flourishes attest, but all such moments are reminders of the overwhelming forces of oppression.

Frederick Boden's two novels *Miner* (1932) and *A Derbyshire Tragedy* (1935) are a curious combination of didacticism, documentary realism, and melodramatic class-consciousness.[20] In *Miner*, the hero Danny Handby is a Chesterfield miner who experiences the conventional *rites de passages* of an appalling first day at work, an underground explosion, and unemployment. His inner life oscillates between existential despair, 'the great empty ache inside him' (p. 96) and violent protest at his condition. The latter emotion is triggered by an encounter with a member of the local gentry, who accuses Danny of trespassing on his land. This scene of nostalgic class conflict provokes a livid intervention by the narrator: 'The beauty of the world had been marred by an undersized creature, who got pleasure from mangling rabbits with a shot-gun' (p. 84). In *A Derbyshire Tragedy* decadent bourgeois genes also have an effect on the hero's destiny, as he is the illegitimate son of the local rent-collector. When an act of carelessness in his job as colliery cage operator leads to several deaths, he commits suicide.

Other mining fiction of the 1930s chooses less overtly political ways of dramatizing the waste and tragedy of capitalism. Walter Brierley's *Means Test Man* (1935) and *Sandwichman* (1937), and Joe Corrie's *The Black Earth* (1939) focus on the emasculation of the male worker in order to make a protest against unemployment and capitalist exploitation, and to develop a critique of patriarchal attitudes.[21]

Means Test Man has a strikingly original form. It is a day-by-day account of one week in the life of an unemployed Derbyshire miner Jack Cook, his wife Jane and their son John. The family have been surviving on a 'mere feeding level' (p. 68) for three years, and have exhausted their savings. The title of the novel refers to the monthly visit of the benefits inspector, who assesses the family's income and assets. Cook is based partly on Brierley himself, who used long periods of redundancy from the mines to write his fiction. Brierley's first break came when he wrote a short sketch about the psychological stresses placed on his marriage by long periods on the dole. The experience 'of living on the edge of domestic upheaval... has made me creep within myself'.[22] This atmosphere pervades the novel. However, the hero Jack Cook has no ambitions to become a writer, and seems a paragon of 'coping'. Far from being vigorous, he has adapted to a decent, domesticated routine of helping out with the housework and shopping, claiming his benefit, and looking after his son. Planning a daily round of chores, the 'programme of the day' (p. 7), is a means of imposing some order on an amorphous and meaningless existence. Jack can only fend off the 'brink of ruin' (p. 66) by desperately trying each day to 'tune himself wholly to this lower level' (p. 4). This step down the evolutionary ladder is clearly an emasculation, a reversion to an inferior feminized lifestyle. His trained, masculine habits die hard. Jack still awakes at 5.30, to hear other villagers going to work. The vignette which opens the novel is a bitterly ironic proletarian dawn scene, as the beauty of the piercing sunlight into Jack's bedroom (the aubade) is contrasted with Jack's struggle to remember 'what day it was' (p. l) – hence the title of this section, 'Prologue', is deeply ironic, as time has little meaning. Jack is only too conscious of his feminization. His movements now have 'the gentleness of a woman' (p. 9) and he avoids ex-workmates who reckon he has 'become a woman' (p. 23). Although it is not said explicitly, there is a strong hint that the marriage has become sexless and devitalized (p. 139). Moreover, the goals Jack now sets himself, to 'keep the home at the top level of domestic efficiency' (p. 7) threaten to dilute his wife's identity, so there is constant tension generated by Jack's adoption of the world she traditionally 'rules'. All her genteel aspirations are now transferred to her son, whom she instructs to learn standard English, 'another language' (p. 22). John is potentially a scholarship boy, the figure Brierley went on to explore in *Sandwichman*. Jack has the problem of being a negative role-model for his son.

One of Jack's lowest moments is his failure to stand up to a neighbour who has cuffed John. Only when Jack becomes angry with John does Jane feel a glimmer of her old respect for him. Neither of them can find the language to appropriately realign their roles, as such discourse is not available. They can only revisit their pain. In the novel's deepest moments of interior monologue, Brierley weighs up their relative suffering. Jane thinks about leaving, but confesses 'there was only horror waiting if she went into the world and left him' (p. 107). Her nadir is the visit of the Means Test officer, which exposes the fragility of the protective shell the Cooks have built up. His invasion of their privacy, the enforced revelation of their most intimate financial affairs, is a near fatal disturbance of their precarious equilibrium. This act of state surveillance tested 'one's soul, one's being' (p. 203). Jane loathes having to let the officer pore over their savings book, which is a 'calendar of their existence' (p. 260) – an image which evokes both economic determinism and the slipping away of their control over time. Jane feels her 'rights as a woman' have been violated (p. 266). Jack is impotent to protect her, but the real wound is existential, 'far, far deeper, in the very springs of life' (p. 162). As Graham Holderness has noted, the novel manages to achieve a state of tension between the naturalistic accretion of surface detail and the spiritual abyss beneath it.[23]

Brierley's detached narration makes it difficult for the reader to decide whether to interpret the Cooks as perfect specimens of working-class servility, whom the state need not fear, or as stoical victims of the code of 'ultra-respectability' (p. 68). Their lack of class-consciousness reflects the historical circumstances of the moderate midlands coalfields, whose miners joined the breakaway Spencer union after 1926 (a forerunner of the UDM in the 1980s), but the Cooks are also representative of the unorganized, lumpen mass of the unemployed and poor, isolated from the community, and any collective historical or political solution. Despite her flailing desire to 'shoot a Cabinet minister' (p. 196), Jane's hatred habitually 'creeps' inwards. The political unconscious of the Cooks' story is the previous century of working-class struggle for emancipation and decent living standards. Having finally obtained a begrudging system of benefits and social safety nets, the unproductive mass are left to a life of subsistence and what Orwell called 'cheap palliatives' (Orwell believed these had averted a revolution – in fact the Cooks consume very few of them). The biblical reference in the novel's time scheme casts an ironic shadow over the narrative: if the world was created in seven days in Judaeo-Christian myth, capitalism has decreated the Cooks' world, leaving them with a mere façade.

While *Means Test Man* begins with unemployment and follows its humiliations and rigours in minute particularity, *Sandwichman* returns to the more conventional *Bildungsroman* format to chart the stages of development leading up to the emasculating moment. The form also allows Brierley to engage directly with the influence of D. H. Lawrence. Arthur Gardner is a self-improving miner whose ambition is to become a teacher. This requires a prodigious feat of intellectual stamina and resilience, as he must take numerous exams, study for many hours at home, and attend college on a day release scheme, as Brierley himself had done. The language of Gardner's aspirations marks him out as a Lawrentian hero. He has a 'spiritual hunger' (p. 7), he wants to 'live wholly' (p. 58) and has a 'deeper sense of living' (p. 86). His efforts to carve out a non-alienated destiny are actively frustrated by a vindictive and envious stepfather (a jealous victim of downward mobility), and a flighty, materialist girlfriend. Nancy's predilection for 'dances and pictures and nice clothes' (p. 32) draws a battle-line between the philistinism of mass culture (Orwell's 'palliatives') and the barely attainable salvation of high culture. Arthur is a precursor of Richard Hoggart's 'scholarship boy', who must cut himself off from his more elemental peers and lead a life of sedentary exclusion and deferred gratification. The gap that opens up between the working-class scholar's new world and his roots is both social and cultural, and most working-class writers have had to negotiate it. Arthur feels his world is 'upside down' (p. 42). His grip on his class identity becomes precarious, particularly when it is mediated through an analysis of education and culture. He refuses the Marxist epistemology of his friend Neil, who sees education as a radical class weapon, not merely a mechanism of exclusion. Arthur also refuses to join the romanticized, fashionable cult of Lawrentianism which has swept through the university, a mixture of bohemian sexual vaunting and phoney worship of the proletarian worker's mystique. Arthur's understanding of the links between intellect and emancipation is still forming. He believes education can liberate his 'real self' (p. 49), as it had aided Lawrence, but without the need for social mobility. He finds social rising distasteful, reminding him of 'climbing deputies and under-managers' (p. 49). Arthur knows that 'however far he reached from the practical atmosphere of his class, he would still be one of them' (p. 49), yet shortly after he admits to his friend, 'I can't grasp the idea of class' (p. 61).

Another precursor of Arthur's predicament is Jude Fawley, Hardy's doomed seeker after knowledge (at one point in the novel, Arthur is dismayed to find his mother reading *Jude the Obscure*'s 'not very pleasant contents' (p. 213)). Just as Jude is stricken by a malevolent fate, so Arthur suffers from tragic errors and bad luck. The clearest resemblance between the two heroes is in the two scenes where Arthur is shown studying at the workplace. In the first scene (pp. 19–21) Arthur is wrestling with a problem of logic 'in spasms' between his duties. He is so absorbed that he is almost cut down by a runaway coal tram, a clear omen. The deftest touch in this scene is the graffiti which Arthur leaves behind him, 'logical symbols on a smooth piece of rock' (p. 20). The indecipherable, mock-primitivist marks are a literal and iconic testimony to the disjuncture between the real, material world and the unattainable, abstracted, dominant, 'logical' culture he aspires to, and which he tries to imprint on the blank page of his own world. Appropriately, it is the logic exam that he later fails, and that ends his academic career. The second work scene, which occupies the first part of chapter 4, is an inverted rewriting of the earlier débâcle. This time Arthur's error is to give way to feelings of masculine aggression. Taunted by a 'ganger' for being a 'bloody college swank' (p. 93) he falls into dialect (a rare occurrence) and has a slanging match. Meantime he makes a serious mistake and causes three trams to run loose, causing a near-fatal accident. His supervisor has the excuse he needs to sack Arthur. Ironically, the absence of a job gives Arthur additional time to study, but the absence of income deprives him of the resources to study. There is an abortive *deus ex machina* near the end of the novel when Nancy, now a fallen woman, reappears in her own car and offers to 'keep' him, which of course his masculine pride refuses, even if the alternative is to go on the tramp. Nancy is another working-class heroine whose only route to independence and social mobility is through sexual favours or prostitution. In working-class texts, cars are nearly always a menacing presence, signifying decadence or the threat of 'luxury'.

If Nancy has become a working girl, her settlement is just one tier of the novel's complex study of the tensions between various modes of work: paid and unpaid; domestic and external; masculine and feminine; manual and mental; productive and artificial; alienated and rewarding. The kinds of work represented, most of which Arthur is involved with, include mining (paid labour), allotment gardening (Arthur is obliged to help his father do this, even though it detracts from his studies), studying, housework drudgery (the last three take place in or around the home), a brief spell as a librarian and trainer at an unemployed skills centre (this is fulfilling but is not part of the 'real' economy so it leads nowhere), parading the streets as a sandwichman (humiliating labour-exchange work), and a period as a WEA evening class instructor teaching drama (ironically, Arthur is quite good at this, but just as he has 'arrived' as a teacher the class closes through poor attendance). The novel is very much a proletarian *Bildungsroman*, as Arthur's life-chances emerge from these different forms of labour, and of course the eventual absence of labour is highly determining. His life is a series of material choices and impositions, a condition which only touches Paul Morel briefly when he obtains his first (and only) job. Arthur's exit from the novel is only superficially like Paul's – though both are leaving their communities after the death of their mothers, Arthur is on the tramp, while Paul's quest is for existential and creative fulfilment. It is difficult to reconcile Arthur's sentiments that 'he was free' (p. 275) with his snowbound disappearance into a workhouse.

Despite this bleak ending, *Sandwichman* is the first working-class novel to look closely at the complex role of adult education in the formation of class and cultural identity. Though Brierley incorporated some of his own experiences into the narrative, it is worth pointing out that by the time the novel was published he had established himself as an author with a respectable publisher (Methuen), and had settled into a secure job as a child welfare officer (a position he kept until his retirement in 1965). In some ways it is a pity Brierley was not more autobiographical and had written a novel exploring that fascinating network of patronage and lucky breaks which aided his own career, and which no working-class author could do without. Brierley belonged briefly to the so-called 'Birmingham group' of writers – Walter Allen, John Hampson and the working-class novelist Leslie Halward were also involved. Brierley owed much of his success to John Hampson, who provided the basic idea for *Means Test Man*.

In Joe Corrie's *The Black Earth* (1939) the destruction of the hero is brought about as much by the repressive, claustrophobic environment of a closed mining community as it is by vindictive mine-owners. It is made clear at the outset that Brandon, a Scottish mining village, is a deadening place:

> the boys of Brandon were doomed the day they were born, doomed to do battle with the coal that was embedded deep in the earth, doomed to be caged in the dirty little town, marry and settle down there to rear still more children to step on the cage. Any other thought was but a dream. (p. 8)

There is no social mobility in Brandon. Even the possibility of a 'heroic' story from within the community is obliterated by a Hardyesque confluence of unpropitious social circumstances, accidents and sheer bad luck. Of course Brandon is a slave to coal production, but Corrie is more interested in the social and psychological scars of proletarian life than with alienated labour, which is an assumed fact of life. During the course of the novel we see the Smith family, whose name signifies their ordinariness, tear themselves apart. The son Jim Smith gives up a promising school career for the pit, not for economic reasons but because of peer pressure, fear of becoming a 'snob', and the sheer difficulty of studying for exams. He eventually finds a possible escape route in amateur football, but the local fame he achieves leads to a swaggering selfishness and a hatred for his parents, whom he blames for holding him back. When his father is paralysed in a mining accident, the family become dependent on Jim's wage, a responsibility he cannot bear. His mother Maggie finally kicks him out for his cavalier attitude, and it is a measure of the bleakness of this novel that there is no reconciliation between parents and son. Maggie's husband Jim finds his only solace in bullying her. While his emasculated male pride is the driving force behind this persecution, the reappearance of one of Maggie's old flames rubs salt in the wound. One of the impressive features of the novel is its sympathy for Maggie, showing her roles of wife and mother strained to breaking point. When she discovers Jack has stolen her savings to place a bet (a desperate and self-destructive attempt to regain his lost economic identity) she storms out of the house. Jack agrees to go to a convalescent home, where he commits suicide: a harrowing end to a story which tracks the collapse of traditional, patriarchal working-class values.

REGION AND NATION

Classifying working-class writers according to their occupational affiliation or background is only one way to map the period. Equally interesting and valid is to look at regional and national identity. This grid reveals a strong anti-metropolitan bias, though the core of London-based authors must not be ignored. The bulk of the remaining part of this chapter will consist of a regionalized commentary on working-class fiction of the 1930s, beginning with Birmingham, the home of Leslie Halward.

Halward, the son of a pork butcher, was a toolmaker and a plasterer. He saw the interwar housing boom from the point of view of a worker, and in a sentiment that Tressell would have appreciated, thought that most of the houses were jerry-built. Strongly influenced by Chekhov, Halward began to get short stories published, and came to fame with a collection entitled *To Tea on Sunday* (1936). His participation in the 'Birmingham group' opened up to him the world of London literati, and the ex-plasterer met the likes of Graham Greene and Edward Garnett. However, his fiction is considerably more downbeat than this success would suggest.[24] The influence of Hemingway can be detected in Halward's clipped, unadorned prose style.

Each short story is a miniature study in bathos and poignant moments. The facts of working-class life are meant to speak for themselves. A labourer weeps when his favourite hod breaks. Another labourer gets drunk and bullies his wife. There is some wry humour at work, but two very bleak stories stand out for their narrative control and power.

In 'The Breadwinner' an unemployed worker and his wife wait for their son to come home with his week's wages. The father wants the money for booze, and flies into a violent rage when he is informed by the son that the wage packet has been mislaid. With the father out of the way, the son gives his wages to the mother. She is distraught at not being able to physically protect him from her husband. In 'A Poor Man's Wife' the bare details of a working-class wife's daily routine show her enslaved position with incredible force. As Engels said, the woman is the proletarian of the family. In a similar vein, a story called 'Sunday Morning' in Halward's next collection *The Money's All Right* (1938) turns a wife's preparation of the Sunday roast into a tense, ritualistic occasion.

Moving northwards, Manchester is the setting for Jack Hilton's novel about a plasterer turned professional boxer, *Champion* (1938).[25] During a spell on the dole, the hero Jimmy Watkins reads Tressell's novel, a 'classic' which 'made him think that conditions hadn't changed much' (p. 119). Though he becomes rich and famous, Jimmy does not abandon his core values, and helps an old friend become an MP. The novel's upbeat ending is in marked contrast to the scepticism of Hilton's autobiography *Caliban Shrieks* (1935): 'Do you forget that governments rule by bread?' (p. 96).

Another Manchester-based novelist, Frank Tilsley, wrote one of the few narratives about white-collar unemployment, *The Plebeian's Progress* (1933).[26] With pitiless scrupulosity, the novel pulverizes the layers of respectability which coat this 'be-collared servitude' (p. 24). After losing his clerical job, Allen Barclay experiences the cut-throat lifestyle of a sales rep. His spirits eventually crack, and he murders his wife to save her any further suffering. As he is hanged, the press announce the beginning of an economic upturn.

One working-class novelist who can match this stark despair is the Liverpool ex-seaman James Hanley. His fiction explores those areas of profound social and psychological dislocation and fragmentation more often associated with modernism. Hanley's divergence from naturalism is not extreme. He writes in a register of understated, haunting, foreshortened immediacy that explores his characters' tortured emotions and outbreaks of violent passion and self-destructive energy. While brutalizing economic factors are always present, Hanley's fiction also creates a strong sense of a debilitating modern condition. Hanley's stories comprise a working-class wasteland in which the anchor-points of secure subjectivity have been cut adrift. The Liverpool location is constantly recycled in his fiction, as the imperial port provides a nexus of contradictory forces: far-flung regions and customary working-class life; absent male breadwinners and feminocentric family rootedness; exotic promise and grinding exploitation. Hanley's characters are often torn apart by these tensions.

Hanley's first published novel *Boy* (1931) achieved notoriety when it was banned for obscenity in 1934.[27] It was not reissued until 1990, thus taking its place alongside those other banished texts of the period, Radclyffe Hall's, *The Well of Loneliness* (1929) and D. H. Lawrence's *Lady Chatterley's Lover* (1930). It is difficult for a modern reader of *Boy* to see any intention to corrupt the reader. In the descriptions of brutal sexual acts, it is clear that the hero is a victim of adverse circumstance. The story concerns the misfortunes of Arthur Fearon, the diminutive son of a brutal Liverpool seaman who stows away on a merchant ship to escape the grinding oppression of his family and dockwork. Given that Hanley ran away to sea aged 13, the novel is loosely autobiographical, but for Fearon there is no salvation either in travel or the pursuit of culture. Hanley is remorselessly anti-sentimental about life at sea. When Fearon has to leave school early to support his family, there is an acute sense of waste. The novel uses the point of view of Fearon's teacher Mr Sweeney to communicate the mood of wasted opportunity. He has seen many bright children like Arthur 'dragged from their benches' (p. 13). Arthur's stunted physique is like a statement of his unreadiness for this move, and his perceptions emphasize the menacing gargantuanism of the adult world. His 'huge', simianized father batters Arthur physically and verbally ('you undersized young pig', p. 17), in the first of a succession of assaults by violent working-class men. The sudden transition from school to work, youth to manhood, is a *rite de passage* that features in numerous working-class novels, and defines very clearly a key moment in the formation of working-class masculinity. But while Harry Hardcastle faked his initiation into a man's world, Fearon suffers two sexual humiliations that almost break his spirit. Firstly, while cleaning out a ship's boiler as one of the 'stinking' duties of his first job, he is set on by his workmates who black his testicles and urinate on him. One way to cope with alienated labour, it seems, is to become hardened and sadistic. This brutal treatment is one of the reasons he stows away on the SS *Hernian*. The womb-like confinement of the coalhold suggests a rebirth, but when he is discovered he is raped by the ship's steward. The reason why this scene outraged the authorities may not only have been its description of a homosexual act. Offence may also have been caused by the implicit critique of an imperial system which relied heavily on the navy. The navy's labour force is just as brutalized as the industrial proletariat on the mainland. The perils of being a 'boy' now include becoming a 'brownie' or sex-object for the crew. Sexual domination is one compensation for stringencies of alienated and exploited labour in a regime where 'an order can squeeze the guts out of labour and extract from it just sufficient to keep the average shareholder from getting really low-spirited' (p. 176). This is a lesson Arthur learns quickly and fatally.

Despite these traumatic experiences Fearon survives and is taken on as a regular seaman. The novel is deliberately vague about Fearon's understanding of the damage inflicted on his psyche. In a letter he writes to his parents (pp. 108–10), he admits briefly that the crew 'interfered' with him, but he also expresses a naïve optimism about his prospects and his hopes to 'become something'. This callow self-awareness is more of a curse than a protection. When the ship docks at Alexandria (still at that time part of the British Empire), Fearon feels for the first time the egotistic thrill of exoticism and colonial prowess. Again, power is expressed in primarily sexual terms. He visits a brothel to prove his newfound masculine potency, but immediately contracts syphilis and becomes gravely ill. To the end, his compromised body is an embarrassment to those around him. In a drunken rage the captain smothers him, falsely claiming in his log that 'Ordinary Seaman Arthur Fearon' was washed overboard in a storm. The brief life of this working-class martyr ends in a series of impersonal communiqués, the discourse of an official cover-up.

Some of the best writing occurs in the brothel scenes, which comprise a heady debunking of imperial mastery and domination. Fearon is both driven and destroyed by an ideology which conflates sexual and colonial conquest. He first goes to a brothel to be 'blooded'. Instead, he has a fit during intercourse, described as a feeling of being overwhelmed: 'Something was sucking him down' (p. 141). Rather than becoming a man, he is merely reaffirmed as a 'Picannin'. So desperate is he to shed this image that he breaks a curfew and returns to the brothel. This time he is determined to enjoy the 'feast of the flesh' (p. 150). Initially, events seem to satisfy his lusts and pent-up frustrations. He gets the prostitute to perform lewd acts, and basks in 'bliss and abandonment' (p. 162). Significantly, the most intense moment in this overheated scene is Fearon's discovery of the power of money: 'The act of handing it over filled him with a sense of power, of ownership, of mastery' (p. 161). But throughout the scene there is a counter-language associated with the prostitute's point of view, which reveals that Fearon's mastery is delusional. To her, he is a 'form of lapdog' (p. 161) and there is a strong suggestion that the real thrill of the sex for both of them is its Oedipal undertow. Once the 'five minutes of excitement' is over, she kicks him out unceremoniously into the 'filth and rubbish' (p. 164). To be 'mastered' by a 'greasy' whore is the ultimate humiliation of his manhood. Driven by his fantasy of 'a certain power', the scene confirms Fearon's powerlessness over his own body. Throughout the novel, Fearon's faltering consciousness is registered in terms of visceral processes – his fragile body is the site of invasions, violent conflicts and unresolved tensions, a trope more frequently associated with feminine experience. His progress can be plotted metaphorically in terms of encounters with menacing waste products and pernicious excretions. He is variously covered in shit, piss, dirt, grease, semen and vomit – after his rape he feels 'covered with slime' (p. 79). Unconsciously, Arthur's quest seems to be for his mother's body. He dies crying out for her, and is thrown into an ocean which the seamen refer to as a feminine monster.

In Hanley's fiction the male hero is essentially emasculated by his class position. The consciousness of this disenfranchisement finds expression in existential yearnings, psychic agonies, and frequent eruptions of violent emotions and actions. There is no solace in either the stability of a close-knit community or the liberating potential of collective action. The social character of the working class is fatally invaded by fragmentation and alienation. The fullest exploration of this bleak picture is in the novels which follow the fortunes of one Liverpool family, the Furys. As the name implies, the Furys embody violent tensions and conflicts.

In *The Furys* (1935), the first novel of the sequence, the pervasive atmosphere of futility and paralysis is given an ironic edge by the fact that the story is set in 1926, the year of the General Strike.[28] Desmond Fury (the oldest son, destined to become a trade union leader) supports the strike, but the rest of the family are hostile or indifferent. A more potent symbol of immobilization than the strike is the figure of the grandfather Mr Mangan, who is catatonic and infant-like. The main narrative focus is on Peter Fury, the returning native who has disgraced himself by being expelled from an Irish ecclesiastical college. His mother is particularly devastated, as she had pinned all her hopes on his taking orders. The reason for Peter's expulsion is kept secret for over 300 pages, during which time Mrs Fury undergoes severe mental agonies as she suspects the truth is immoral. Eventually Peter confesses he visited a brothel (a clear act of rebellion), but to add insult to injury he also begins an affair with Desmond's disreputable wife Sheila. As in *Boy*, there is no healthy expression of sexuality. Peter is attracted to 'fallen' sexuality as a means to throw off his moral training and defy the social constraints of the family and community.

This is not the only example of a fall from grace in the novel. There is a web of incidents and images conveying a powerful sense of doomladen menace, loss, banishment and persecution. Peter's brother Anthony is recovering in an American hospital after having fallen from his ship's mast. Mrs Fury has to make several humiliating trips to the company's headquarters to obtain compensation for the accident. All Mrs Fearon's outings are described as journeys through an alien landscape. When she and her husband Deny Fury go to meet Peter's boat, they carry

Mr Mangan on their backs like a religious burden. The first passenger to emerge from the ship is a celebrated murderer being brought for trial; this is one of the novel's more heavy-handed omens (whose meaning unfolds in the sequel). Mrs Fury undertakes another torturous odyssey when she accompanies her sister to the docks to get a boat to Ireland. After an exhausting journey on foot, there are of course no ships sailing. Mrs Fury, like so many fictional working-class women, is the novel's central symbol of frustrated hopes and limited horizons. Desperate to pay Peter's outstanding fees, she resorts to borrowing from a moneylender Mrs Ragner – a Faustian pact whose terrible consequences are again delayed until the sequel. She also steals her husband's savings, surrendering any vestige of self-respect she possesses. Peter's confession about his affair breaks her spirit. Peter is caught in a social limbo, unable to find a job (even though he is prepared to be a scab worker) or to resolve his affair with Sheila. The only way out of this impasse is to go to sea, the one career his mother was determined he should avoid. It is only at the final leave-taking that a photo of Sheila slips out of his wallet and his mother discovers his terrible secret. She flies into an uncontrollable rage and attacks him physically. Peter represents 'all men, all those who had cheated and insulted her' (p. 549).

In *The Secret Journey* (1936) the pained cycle of reunion, revelation and scattering is repeated.[29] Peter returns home after a year at sea and resumes his liaison with Sheila. Deny Fury's response to the discovery of his wife's theft of his savings is to return to the sea. Mrs Fury falls deeper into debt, and in a desperate attempt to disentangle her, Peter sleeps with Mrs Ragner the moneylender. This classical downward spiral of deceit, betrayal and shifting loyalties has a predictably violent dénouement. When Sheila breaks off the affair, Peter vents his fury by brutally killing Mrs Ragner. The murder scene has strong echoes of nineteenth-century sensationalism, as Peter stuffs her bejewelled hand down her throat. In a demented state, Peter rushes home and proclaims to his mother 'we're free. Free. FREE!' (p. 569). This is one of the most terrifying endings to a working-class novel.

A similar catastrophic atmosphere pervades the short fiction of George Garrett, another Liverpool seaman. In 'Fishmeal' (1936), for example, a ship's stoker throws himself overboard in a fit brought on by illness. John Lehmann believed that Garrett fell victim to the material obstacles in the way of becoming a working-class author, despite being a 'battler against heroic odds'.[30]

The third member of the Liverpudlian cohort of working-class authors is the ex-convict Jim Phelan. His imprisonment was the culmination of a chequered early life that included training as a blacksmith, gun-running for the IRA, and tramping in England and France. His novel *Lifer* (1938) is 'an attempt to lend words to the inarticulate and misunderstood inhabitants of the prisons'.[31] The novel has the moral drive of a muckraking exposé. The hero is not an underprivileged proletarian but a low-grade clerk who is particularly squeamish about his brutalized masculine environment, especially the pervasive threat of being 'bottled' or buggered. In order to assert his masculinity, Arthur beats up a prisoner who makes a pass at him. Once released, Arthur cannot find a job or a secure identity. In a heavily ironic ending, he deliberately commits an offence so that he is re-arrested and returned to the 'security' of prison life. Phelan explains in his autobiography that he wrote the book to keep his sanity and self-respect intact.[32] On his release from prison he was courted by the literary establishment, but refused the offer of a salaried job in favour of tramping: 'they could keep their job, and I would keep Jim Phelan'. This defiance is both Romantic and social, a testimony to the tensions underlying the notion of 'success' for working-class writers.

Moving across the border into Scotland, there is the towering achievement of Lewis Grassic Gibbon's *A Scots Quair* trilogy (1932–4).[33] Grassic Gribbon was the son of an Aberdeenshire crofter. He had a career as a reporter and a spell in the RAF before he turned to full-time authorship. He wrote the work from his home in Welwyn Garden City, a long way indeed from the location of his formative years. Grassic Gibbon took the bold aesthetic decision to focalize the historical sweep of thirty years of lowland Scottish history through a female character, Chris Guthrie. This feminization of the epic form creates an immediate source of tension, in that women are not conventionally regarded as the agency of historical change or the vanguard warriors of class struggle. The decentring of the heroic narrative creates an ironic distance between Chris and the

79

various men in her life who are all players in the public sphere. Her father, for instance, is a dour Scots minister whose fierce class-consciousness is matched only by his patriarchal tyranny over his family. The most corrupting effect of his rule is to be found in his incestuous desire for Chris (justified with an appeal to the Old Testament, pp. 89–90) which creates a ripple effect in her own confused, protective feelings towards her brother Will (pp. 42–44). As in *Cwmardy*, the theme of incest opens up a glaring faultline in patriarchy. But Grassic Gibbon's feminist ethics also extend to a critique of the politics of reproduction. Chris's mother is recognized by the crofter community as little more than a 'breeding sow' (p. 60), and eventually poisons herself and recently born twins as a desperate protest. The Medea-like trauma leaves Chris in little doubt that control of her body is essential to her survival, and in her three marriages she has only one son (on the night she planned to conceive a second, her husband Ewan fails to appear as he has signed up for Flanders; when he comes home on leave from training, he is sexually depraved and already dehumanized – he is later shot for desertion, an attempt to redeem himself in her pacifist eyes). Even when her son Ewan's growth towards class leadership and urban struggle begins to dominate the latter stages of the trilogy (he becomes an icon of all victims of the 'world's masters' while being beaten up in a prison cell, pp. 451–2), the uneven development and eerie resolution of Chris's story is in many ways more formally interesting.

For a start, her class position has been fluid and compromised, more of a zigzag than a linear progression towards militant class-consciousness. Unable to define her social status through productive (paid) work, she is lifted into the despised ranks of the gentry by her marriage to the radical minister Colquohoun, though this does not prevent her supporting the miners in the General Strike. After his death she migrates to the industrial heartland and helps to run the boarding house she and Ewan live in. Technically she is now petty-bourgeois, and her downwardly mobile 'comeuppance' is the butt of many a sneer by locals. After a third abortive marriage, she turns full circle and buys the croft she grew up in. Her return to the land is a hauntingly beautiful personal settlement, but its poetic poignancy is heightened by its historical irrelevance – the local people do not even remember her or her father. At the one point in her life where she is truly independent, she fades into non-signification. On the other hand, Ewan storms out of the narrative into an equally blank future. Having ruthlessly cast off his lover Ellen for her lack of revolutionary resolve, he enters a phase of guerrilla warfare against the state. If Grassic Gibbon could have extended the narrative by another couple of years (he died in 1935), Ewan would no doubt have found his destiny in Spain.

Seen from a modern critical perspective, Grassic Gibbon seems to have had a clear understanding that subjectivity is both socially and linguistically constructed. While showing promise at school, Chris realizes that books and education – and, by implication, English cultural hegemony – threaten to erase her Scottish identity. She is 'two Chrisses', English and Scottish, the former's language 'sharp and clean', the latter's 'coarse and brave' (p. 37). Like all colonial subjects, she is a cultural hybrid, but the split is intensified by her disempowerment as a working-class woman.

Grassic Gibbon's reputation has eclipsed that of James Barke, who questioned his rival's working-class credentials. Barke claimed that the trilogy was fatally weakened by an unfamiliarity with 'the day-to-day actualities of the workers' struggle'.[34] Barke's solution to this problem was *The Land of the Leal* (1939), a sprawling epic covering generations of Scottish history from the 1820s to the present.[35] The novel is not written in dialect, as is *A Scots Quair*, and it has a clear Hegelian forward movement: history achieves class-consciousness in anti-fascism. Like Len Roberts, Andrew Ramsay is killed in Spain, leaving his mother Jean, who was born into the Galloway peasantry, to grieve.

Barke's earlier novel *Major Operation* (1936) is just as formally ambitious as *The Land of the Leal*.[36] It uses montage effects to create a sense of Glasgow as a totality of class forces, the 'Second City of the Empire' in 'dread of the word revolution' (p. 13). These forces resolve into the intertwined stories of two men: 'Big' Jock MacKelvie, a dockers' leader, and George Anderson, a coal agent. When the men meet in a hospital ward, Anderson undergoes a conversion to socialism. He epitomizes the bourgeois 'going over' to the cause of the working class. As his marriage and business collapse, Anderson embraces his new philosophy enthusiastically and soon achieves a martyr's death at the hands of the police. Beneath this propagandist plot, the novel shows that Anderson has reservations about the revolutionary predisposition of the working class. Similarly, Jack's prowess is destabilized by the 'haunting fear of unemployment' (p. 79). The novel is an intriguing blend of 'day-to-day actualities' and quirky, highbrow Marxist chapter titles, such as 'Never Say Never Again (Unity of Opposites)'.

Though most of the texts discussed so far have been non-metropolitan, it would be wrong to assume working-class writing is exclusively regional or provincial. While London often figures as an ambiguous site of mobility and success in novels by northern writers, those writers born and bred in London share many of the same concerns, grievances and aspirations of other working-class authors. The London equivalent of the 'two-nation' journey from north to south is the transition from the East to the West End, from production and poverty (East) to consumption and leisure (West). Most heroes of London working-class fiction must negotiate this frontier at some point. We must not entirely flatten out the differences between London and the regions, of course. London has always had a much richer and more complex ethnic culture than most other cities. It is significant that two of the most important London working-class writers in the 1930s should be Jewish. In the 1930s a new wave of Jewish immigrants fleeing persecution in Europe joined the older Jewish communities established in the nineteenth century. As the Cable Street riots of 1936 showed, the resistance to the Blackshirts combined ethnic and class solidarity. In the work of Simon Blumenfeld and Willy Goldman, the shifting allegiances of class and culture, economic, social and ethnic identity, provide a rich new dimension to working-class fiction.

In Blumenfeld's novel *Jew Boy* (1935), 22-year-old Alec is a victim of traditional sweated labour.[37] He works ten-hour days to produce 'beautiful worsteds' (p. 15). His miserly boss will not even allow the workers to join an anti-fascist march which is supported by virtually the whole of the Jewish East End. Eventually Alec leads a successful strike, knowing full well he will be sacked when the seasonal demand falls off. Alec is a 'double outcast, Jew and Communist' (p. 49). His Communist belief is that 'under the rule of the proletariat Jews would have the same rights as other workers'. As a proto-'Angry' working-class intellectual, Alec lives on the fringes of a bohemian Jewish 'renaissance' that he rejects for its bourgeois romanticism. On the other hand, he is dismayed by the example of Mrs Saunders, an acquaintance of his girlfriend, who has rejected all vestiges of her Jewishness in return for the 'anaemic narrow-minded dreariness of suburbia' (p. 143). If the opposing wings of middle-class culture are both unacceptable to Alec, so is traditional high culture as represented by the 'class' woman he meets at a concert. The basis of the erotic attraction between them is 'a rich woman picking up a page boy' (p. 257) and, try as he might, he cannot dominate her. Instead, he turns to the ex-prostitute Olive, another example of an independent working-class woman. She is happy to live with him and work in a café and has no qualms about having an abortion. Her stoicism is contrasted with his increasingly grandiose schemes, including an abortive plan to emigrate to the Soviet Union: 'it was all one to her...ham and eggs and tea for two, for ever and ever and ever' (pp. 346–7). Olive's bedrock of proletarian consciousness is a foil to Alec's quest for affiliation and identity. Having exhausted all options, Alec is finally revived by meeting the black Communist Jo-Jo, who combines political idealism with an idyllic marriage. He reminds Alec that 'Dis Hitler is a gentleman compared wid some of de white bosses in Africa' (p. 325). Although Alec is far from being a heroicized class warrior, the message reaffirms his mission: the real enemy is capitalism. It is a characteristic feature of socialist fiction of this period that it reverses the narrative closure of classic realism. Where nine-teenth-century novels offered romantic solutions to social conflicts, this fiction provides political solutions to personal crises.

A more detailed recreation of a Jewish East End community is to be found in Willy Goldman's first book, *East End My Cradle* (1940).[38] The novel is so autobiographical as to be barely fictional. It splices together several short sketches and stories that had already been published. This ambiguous structure is emblematic of Goldman's uncertain status within literary tradition: 'I had been trained by miseducation and upbringing to think of [writing] as the prerogative of cranks and idlers'

(p. 203). One way to avoid such a reputation is to identify fully with his own kind, to regard literature as a 'passion' not a profession. In 'In Search of the Muse', he finds inspiration in the social detritus of the East End: 'I saw wretches huddled in doorways and ragged prostitutes slinking by walls and I wept at their misery and my own' (p. 212). But the 'desire to scream the story of our common fate into the face of the world' does not produce a narrative, and we are told of the material and intellectual difficulties of reading and writing. His portrayal of Stepney slums has a Morrisonian unsentimentality, rejecting nostalgia in favour of some scathing, sometimes humorous depictions of the conflicts, tensions and contradictions within a closed, urban community. For example, both his school education and his religious training ('kheder') are repressive and alienating. Real life is found on the streets, where razor gangs and hole-in-the-corner sex are the nearest he can get to the glamorized masculinity of the movies. The wrench from school to work is a 'nightmare of suddenness' (p. 61) and the idea that it will instantly make him a man is a cruel fraud. Jewish working-class girls suffer even more acutely from the disparity between the respectable ideals of femininity that have been drummed into them and the 'hard-boiled, hard-bitten' environment of the sweat-shop (see chapter 14, 'The Sweet Bloom of Womanhood'). Goldman illuminates the bitter ironies that underpin a 'slum' marriage: while it provides women with their only means of escape from the 'hell' of the sweat-shop, it provides men with the cheap consolation of sexist domination.

Even the joys of summer are debunked: 'we saw no poetry in sunshine' (p 111). Though Ken Worpole has characterized Goldman's protagonists as 'Keatsian', the tone of East End My Cradle is too worldly and sceptical to fit that description.[39] Blumenfeld and Goldman revived the 'slum novel' as a response to the social and cultural pressures inflicted on the East End by interwar poverty and the rise of fascism.

The Communist ex-seaman John Sommerfield, on the other hand, turned to a more modernist aesthetic in his novel May Day (1936).[40] Sommerfield disobeyed the Comintern line as he abandoned the traditional plot. The book presents three days in the lives of over ninety 'typical' London workers, their families, and their bosses. This montage is given a distinctly working-class point of view, as all events are overshadowed by an impending May Day demonstration. One of Sommerfield's aims is to show that only collective action can overcome fragmentation and alienation. It is significant that James Seton, the book's Ulyssean wanderer-figure, meets his death at the hands of a police truncheon. While this melodramatic finale creates yet another working-class martyr, it is a reminder that individualism is a dangerous illusion. The order beneath the apparent randomness and meaninglessness of urban life is to be found in a Marxist consciousness and 'the mathematics of class struggle' (p. 171). But the novel is also accessible to the general reader. Beneath the experimental surface there is a relatively conventional plot, in which a 'speed-up' at Langfiers carbon factory (the consequence of a takeover by Amalgamated Engineering Incorporated, who embody the aggressive tactics of interwar monopoly capitalism) becomes the flashpoint for a walkout and a decision to join the May Day rally. The factory is the centre of an interweaving tapestry of segmented lives, including the recently unemployed John Seton and his wife, who regard work as 'the blessed slavery that had come to rescue them' (p. 10). Sommerfield is careful not to glorify any of the working-class characters, though he ridicules the upper-class capitalists. They are either impotent and fossilized (like the paternalist Langfier), decadent and irresponsible (like his son) or ruthless and conspiratorial (like the AEI board). The Communist characters are wiser than other characters, but that does not mean they are happy. Ivy Cutler, for instance, who leads the rebellion of the women machine workers, is shown to be loverless and unfulfilled.

In order to make the action even more responsive to collective agency, Sommerfield draws on two contemporary cultural movements which had the 'people' at the centre of their aesthetic: the cinematic documentary movement and Mass Observation. The former aimed at a style both objective and 'poetic', while the latter 'anthropology of ourselves' modelled itself on photographic realism. Sections of *May Day* read like the voice-over for a documentary: 'When they are twenty-one the factory sees them no more. They would have to be paid an uneconomic wage, so they are replaced by a fresh batch of schoolgirls' (p. 30). Sommerfield's use of the cinematic 'cut' reinforces his political message. As Langfier's limousine sweeps past workers, beggars, war veterans, and mothers committing infanticide, his motion is counterpointed by the windstrewn ubiquity of a Communist leaflet publicising the May Day rally, 'Forward to a Soviet Britain'. As Valentine Cunningham has noted, it is a favourite technique of socialist authors in the thirties to pit the 'voice of the people' against repressive dominant discourses.[41] Sommerfield's 'communist romanticism' embellishes the urban landscape: *The sky oozes soot and aeroplanes, and burns by night with an electric glow*' (p. 3).

May Day continues that minor but vital tradition of the proletarian counter-realist novel pioneered by Tressell. The inherent danger of this approach is that the characters are flat or wooden, and are used as pawns in a totalizing logic.

Finally, it is important to look at the fiction of Ralph Bates, whose career exemplifies the internationalist dimension of the cultural matrix within which 1930s working-class writers moved. Andy Croft illustrates the extensiveness of this network by noting the participants at various left-wing writers' conferences.[42] The Paris Writers' Congress of 1935 included the British delegates E. M. Forster, Aldous Huxley, Ralph Fox, Christina Stead, Walter Greenwood and James Hanley, and writers from 38 other countries, including André Gide, Louis Aragon, Martin Nexo, André Malraux and Henri Barbusse. Forster made a speech against censorship in which he defended Hanley's *Boy* against its detractors. This conference led to the formation of the International Association of Writers for the Defence of Culture, whose second Congress took place in Spain in July 1936, in the early stages of the Civil War. As one of the British delegates, Ralph Bates came to the Congress straight from the front line to put his weight behind the conference's resolution that 'the principal enemy of culture is Fascism'.

Bates, a railway worker by origin, held an important political position in the Communist faction of the Republican government, being the editor of the newspaper of the International Brigade, *Volunteer for Liberty*. He was active in Spanish radicalism from the 1920s, earning a living as an itinerant mechanic. His novels *Lean Men* (1934) and *The Olive Field* (1936) explore the political upheavals in the Spanish Left in the years immediately preceding the outbreak of the Civil War.[43]

Lean Men captures the sense of the swift movement of revolutionary history. The plot revolves around a series of often confusing sectarian conflicts, while the assured hand of the omniscient narrator provides the unifying epic overview:

> There was not a city, town or reasonably large village in which a revolutionary Committee had not existed, ready to seize power. (pp. 306–7)

The strands of action are also linked by dominant metaphors drawn from the Romantic sublime: storms, volcanoes and the 'Promethean' power of the working class. To give the British reader a point of entry into the narrative, the hero is Francis Charing, an English exile who sets up the Centre for Free Studies. This facility is supposedly purely recreational, but Charing wants it to be a base for training Marxist cadres, and for uniting the damaging split between Communists and anarchists. This Utopian hope soon fades as the novel ends with Charing on the run from the government. *The Olive Field* has a more localized approach to the same material, focusing on an Andalusian peasant community to trace the same passions, loyalties and resistances (including an attachment to the Catholic Church which baffles political activists). The quixotic temperament of the Spanish is both a spur and a hindrance to revolutionary progress. In Valentine Cunningham's opinion, Bates had 'written the revolution' in advance of the historical events.[44]

In the 1920s and 1930s the horrors of dehumanization were only too clear in the emergence of mass unemployment and fascism. Working-class fiction played a vital role in reflecting and resisting this modern nightmare.

3

The Influence of Affluence: The Road to 1979

The war in Europe ended on 7 May 1945, when Germany surrendered to the Allied forces. Less than three months later, the Labour Party won the British general election with a huge majority of 146 seats. If ever a day can be chosen as a turning point in British working-class history, 26 July 1945 must be a prime candidate. After the deprivations of the 1930s and the sacrifices of the war, a people's government had at last been elected with the power to implement socialist reforms. The result seemed in one way to be a huge surprise. The Tories, after all, were headed by the great war leader Winston Churchill – surely he would secure the patriotic vote? But the Second World War was really two wars with two aims: a military campaign to defeat fascism; and a political and social campaign to eradicate poverty and the worst forms of social inequality. The Tories were too closely associated in the people's memory with the social horrors of the 1930s for them to be trusted with the job of postwar reconstruction. The war had also familiarized people with the experience of a powerful state, so there was no widespread fear of centralized economic and social planning. Indeed, the election signalled a determination by the British people to challenge decisively the destructive power of *laissez-faire* capitalism. The year 1945 marked a new beginning in the social and political history of Britain, but it was also the culmination of a longer tradition of radical demands for redistribution that had its roots as far back as the second part of Tom Paine's *The Rights of Man* (1792). In the nineteenth century, the Chartist dream was that universal suffrage would create a government that would truly represent the common person against the interests of the élite minority. But despite the gradual introduction of mass democracy into the British political system, a stubborn streak of conservatism in the British working class meant that neither of the first two Labour governments (1924, 1929–31) had secured parliamentary majorities, and a reactionary coalition government ruled Britain from 1931 to the end of the war. Now all that had changed. As the 'Red Flag' was sung in Parliament by jubilant Labour MPs, and Churchill remarked disconsolately that the new government 'would have to fall back on some kind of Gestapo',[1] it was difficult not to agree that a decisive shift in political power had taken place, and that the 'political economy of the working class', as Marx called state regulation of the economy, had finally arrived. It seemed that the protests and struggles of the interwar years, which included the intervention of radical culture, had achieved their purpose of building a new consensus for socialist reforms: full employment based on Keynesian economics; nationalization of the staple industries; the creation of a welfare state and a National Health Service; universal free education; and state patronage of the arts. One indication of the popular demand for such changes can be seen in the unprecedented wartime sales of the Beveridge Report on establishing a social security system. Within a month of its publication in 1942, the Report had sold over 100,000 copies, and a Gallup survey revealed that nineteen out of twenty people knew the essential details: 'full' employment (meaning no more than 8.5 per cent unemployed), a free health service, and child allowances.[2] Whereas the jingoism of the First World War had impeded progress towards socialist goals, the Second World War accelerated such ambitions, as it was from the beginning a war to defend democracy against totalitarianism. With fascism in Europe defeated, the British people demanded their reward.

In their six years of office (1945–1951), the postwar Labour government embarked on a massive programme of reform that transformed Britain into a semi-socialist 'mixed' economy. There was a huge economic, social and ideological investment in what is now called the public sector, as it seemed incontrovertible that unbridled capitalism was wasteful and inefficient (the dole queues of the 1930s were still fresh in the memory). While it was never the intention of the Labour government to own and control all the means of production in the country (nationalization was limited to the most 'needy' of the old staple industries and the public utilities), or to socialize all the institutions of privilege (such as the public schools and the House of Lords), and while such perceived failures to introduce a full-blooded socialist reform of inequality of wealth and opportunity in Britain were soon to be criticized by the British Left, it remains the case that, in Peter Hennessy's words, no period of British history has experienced such a 'progressive phase'.[3] The new institutions of the welfare state, such as the National Health Service, became emblems of the new 'age of consensus' in modern Britain. This consensus lasted over thirty years, until the New Right came to power under Margaret Thatcher, and began to dismantle most of these core postwar reforms.

Yet the postwar Labour government has also been burdened historically with the dour reputation of 'austerity'. While this image was used at the time by Labour's opponents to undermine its achievements, there is no doubt that, compared to the rise of 'affluence' in the late 1950s, the economy could not support a high level of consumption.[4] As a bankrupt nation reliant on loans from America, the government could only pay for its reforms by maintaining the wartime rationing of clothes and food (rationing was not fully abolished until 1956), and exporting most luxury products. A severe winter in 1946–7 weakened the economy further, and caused power cuts and short-time working. The emergence of the Cold War led to an initially secret investment in nuclear weapons research, and defence spending increased further with a rearmament policy provoked by the Korean War. The government's fear of Communist takeovers in ex-colonies (despite its having supported many such forces of resistance during the war) brought about the unprecedented and costly introduction of peacetime conscription: between 1946 and 1960, National Servicemen were sent to all regions of the British Empire, and fought in wars in Malaysia and Kenya. By the end of its rule, the Labour government had introduced charges for eye tests, a symbolic betrayal of its pledges to provide free medical services for everyone regardless of their income. In October 1951,

Winston Churchill returned to power. The Tories reigned until 1964, though it is worth pointing out the fact that in the October 1951 general election, the greatest number of working-class votes ever cast went to the Labour Party – only the peculiarities of the English electoral system meant that the Labour government was defeated.[5]

Though they had a long term in office, the Tories preserved most of the core postwar reforms, while reaping the political benefits of economic expansion and the emergence of 'consumer' capitalism. By the late 1950s, 'austerity' had been supplanted in media and official political discourses by the rhetoric of 'affluence' and 'You've never had it so good': the new emphasis was on consumer goods, social mobility, the pursuit of pleasure, the cult of the teenager, and growing social and sexual freedoms that anticipated the 1960s. Full employment and steady economic growth generated a rise in average living standards, and a spectacular boom in disposable income for the teenager: the young, unmarried worker.[6] Though the experience was by no means universal, the majority of the British working class entered a period of unparalleled prosperity and 'jobs for life' security that was to last until the 1970s.[7]

Some observers saw the socialist reforms of 1945–51 as actually enabling a rebirth of capitalism. This was the argument made in Anthony Crosland's important book *The Future of Socialism* (1956), in which he claimed that most of the demands of prewar socialism had been delivered by a capitalist system 'reformed and modified almost out of existence'.[8] According to Crosland, the old agenda of the Left was effectively redundant: class struggle and public ownership were no longer the means of providing a decent standard of living for the majority. In the same year Crosland's book was published, two major world events seemed to add to the sense that a renaturalization of capitalism and liberal democracy had taken place: the Suez canal fiasco and the Hungarian uprising.

The first of these episodes can be interpreted as a last, futile flexing of Britain's imperial muscle. When President Nasser of the recently independent Egypt nationalized the Suez canal, the major sea-route between Europe and the East, Britain's response was to concoct with Israel and France an excuse for a British invasion. After a period of fighting which lasted several days and left many hundreds of Egyptians dead, the invasion was called off after objections from the Americans; the British prime minister Anthony Eden resigned shortly after. This humiliation gave a boost to the process of decolonization throughout the British Empire, and undoubtedly bolstered the idea that old-fashioned methods of dominating less powerful countries had now been superseded by the all-conquering forces of world trade and international consumer capitalism.

A few months after the Suez débâcle the Soviet Union crushed a democratic uprising in Hungary. The Soviet 'bloc' of Eastern European countries had emerged at the end of the war as a buffer zone between capitalism and Communism. The Hungarian experience (to be repeated in Czechoslovakia in 1968) was an early sign of the forces of internal dissent and nationalism that would eventually contribute to the break-up of the Soviet system in the late 1980s. Many British Communists were disenchanted by the clampdown in Hungary, and looked for a new political realignment. If imperialism had been mortally wounded at Suez, so had Communism at Budapest. In between these ailing metanarratives lay the limitless expanse of a 'refined', benevolent, 'affluent' capitalism. Jimmy Porter captured this sense of disillusionment and the 'end of ideology' in some famous lines in John Osborne's play Look Back in Anger, which appeared on the British stage a few months before the Suez invasion: 'There aren't any good, brave causes left'.[9]

These political and ideological developments had a major impact on the ways in which the social progress of the postwar British working class was perceived, defined and redefined by commentators, sociologists, critics and creative artists, working in old and new media. Working-class fiction can be seen to participate in these debates, and to offer its own insights and illuminations. The central concern of many observers was not political but cultural and even spiritual, and this development was an intensification of sociological trends that began in the interwar years. It was felt that material advance and social mobility were devitalizing working-class culture: if the working class now possessed some of the material security that they struggled to attain for more than a century, wouldn't their class identity, which was forged in such struggles, be eroded? In other words, the anxiety was that affluence would assimilate the working class into an expanding bourgeois lifestyle (the process of 'embourgeoisement') or into a classless mass culture (christened by Richard Hoggart as 'shiny barbarism'[10]). Improved educational opportunities arising from the 1944 Education Act, the expansion of 'white-collar' and adminis-trative occupations, the switch to measuring class position by lifestyle and acquisitions rather than the breadwinner's job, the rehousing of older working-class communities in anonymous high-rise blocks or suburban and out-of-town new estates, the influx of a new black working class – all these factors contributed to a major reassessment of the social and cultural stability of the postwar working class.

Most of the memorable studies were carried out by left-liberal observers who were worried about the fact that while material progress was democratic and desirable, the extinction of the working-class way of life was too high a price to pay for these benefits. The task of recuperating working-class history and traditions before they disappeared for good gave new purpose to some of the socialist fugitives of 1956 who formed the New Left, and led directly to some of the most influential works of postwar social, cultural and literary history: Richard Hoggart's *The Uses of Literacy* (1957), Raymond Williams's *Culture and Society* (1958), *New Left Review* (begun in 1960 under the editorship of Stuart Hall), and E. P. Thompson's *The Making of the English Working Class* (1963).

Paradoxically, this desire to uncover the second 'remaking' and possible dissolution of the working class helped to create a period of unprecedented cultural dominance for working-class writing and representations of working-class life. British cultural production in the late 1950s and early 1960s invested heavily in working-class narratives. In literature, a new generation of working-class novelists rose to prominence: John Braine, Alan Sillitoe, Stan Barstow, David Storey, Keith Water-house. Most of their early fiction was adapted for the cinema by a group of directors and producers with a firmly anti-establish-ment philosophy. Tony Richardson, Lindsay Anderson, Karel Reisz, and John Schlesinger had been active in the 'Free Cinema' movement of the 1950s.[11] In the theatre, subsidies from the Arts Council opened up a creative space partially protected from commercial forces. The Royal Court theatre flourished as a centre for challenging new drama, presenting plays with working-class themes by John Osborne, Arnold Wesker and Bernard Kops. Joan Littlewood's Theatre Workshop in the East End of London also produced pioneering proletarian drama, such as Brendan Behan's *The Quare Fellow* in 1955, and Shelagh Delaney's *A Taste of Honey* in 1958.[12] The new medium of television drama also looked to the working class for vital subject matter, in the plays of David Mercer, the early episodes of *Z Cars* and, of course, *Coronation Street*, which began in 1960.

This period can justly be termed a golden age of working-class literature. The number of first-person narratives is one indicator of a new mood of confidence amongst working-class writers. Although it could still prove difficult for a budding working-class novelist to find a major commercial publisher (both Sillitoe and Braine had their first novels rejected many times in the early 1950s), a successful author could expect to be hugely popular. The virtuous circle of film adaptation and cheap paperback issue could boost sales dramatically. *Room at the Top* (1957) was reprinted eight times in 1959, the year of the film release. As the obscenity trial of the Penguin paperback edition of *Lady Chatterley's Lover* in 1960 showed, the paperback revolution in the publishing industry had made fiction a genuine mass form, bringing both high cultural and popular literature within the purchasing orbit of the working class.

It is probably this period (the three or four years either side of 1960) which most people associate with working-class writing, rather than the 'political' 1930s. The postwar renaissance of proletarian art, 'northern' passion, and 'kitchen sink' realism has also gained cultural status from being merged in literary histories with the mythology of the Angry Young Man. In this mythology, the home-grown version of the rebel-without-a-cause is an anti-hero of the lower classes who voices a protest against the soullessness and conformity of 'affluent' modern life. The Angry Young Man, exemplified by Jimmy Porter in *Look Back in Anger* (though the title is often applied to both author and hero), is liberated through social mobility from the old vocabulary of class struggle, but finds himself in a social limbo, unwelcomed by his new class. Frustrated by the absence of a socialist alternative to sterile conformity, Jimmy finds consolation by converting class-consciousness into sexism – his stoical middle-class wife Alison is the butt of most of his vituperative humour. Jimmy is the pioneer of a new generation of aggressively masculine working-class heroes. Regrettably, in this period even more than others, there is a dearth of working-class women writers.[13] Shelagh Delaney wrote plays, and Nell Dunn can only be described as an honorary proletarian.

The new fiction by Braine, Sillitoe, Barstow and Storey explores the contradictions within the working class's anxious historical movement from 'austerity' to 'affluence'. The novels are particularly valuable for testing the validity of the 'embourgeoisement' thesis.

John Braine's *Room at the Top* (1957) is organized around the hero Joe Lampton's symbolic passage between two Yorkshire towns.[14] Dufton is the place of his birth, and represents the 'zombie' philistinism and old-fashioned working-class values that he leaves behind for the more genteel and prosperous Warley. In Dufton, a place of 'nasty snivelling fears' (p. 34), the snow turns black before it hits the ground (p. 85). Warley embodies 'gracious living' (p. 12) and is for Joe a 'place without memories' (p. 96). Like Paul Morel, Joe's ambition to transcend his class can draw on the combined resources of a primitivist sexual vigour and a heightened aesthetic sense of bourgeois culture. Also like Morel, Joe is not a manual worker but a 'white-collar' pen-pusher: the pragmatic reason for his move to Warley is to take up a promoted post as a local government accountant. Joe's occupational status could be seen to make him typical of the idea that postwar working-class identity was being eroded by an economic shift away from traditional proletarian labour to work of a less determinate class position. But Joe's typicality in this respect can be overestimated, as his success does not come about through the meritocratic route of career opportunity.[15] Though he is a scholarship boy, his rapid social mobility has more in common with the rapidly transformative processes of myth. Moreover, Joe's success is constructed as a mythic story of his own making.

Joe appears to have complete control over his destiny. His pangs of homesickness only last a few seconds (p. 15). He compares himself to a military leader opening hostilities (p. 30) and to a god in control of his destiny: 'What has happened to me is exactly what I willed to happen. I am my own draftsman'

(p. 124). This idea that the novel is an unfolding of Joe's will also comes from the narrative method: the novel is a first-person narration told retrospectively from the point of view of the successful 'Warley' Joe looking back on his ambitious former self. Given that the novel is about conversion to a new life at 'the top', it can be read as an evangelical capitalist fable, a parodic pilgrim's progress, the story of a saint turned sinner: a modern Faust. Most of these mythic dimensions are foregrounded in an early scene where Joe has a 'revelation' about his mission in life. The source of his inspiration is catching sight of a wealthy young man and his girlfriend getting into a sports car. It is as if Joe has glimpsed the Holy Grail:

> I wanted an Aston Martin, I wanted a three-guinea linen shirt, I wanted a girl with a Riviera suntan – these were my rights, I felt, a signed and sealed legacy...I made my choice there and then: I was going to enjoy all the luxuries which that young man enjoyed. I was going to collect that legacy. It was as clear and compelling as the sense of vocation which doctors and missionaries are supposed to experience, though in my instance, of course, the call ordered me to do good to myself not others. (p. 29)

Unlike Paul Morel, Joe's superior intelligence is not manifested in creative art, but in a ruthlessly plotted offensive on the middle-class life he both despises and desires. The contradictions in his transitional situation are glaring: for every claim he makes that he has been revitalized by Warley ('I felt as if I were using all my senses for the first time', (p. 27)) there is a reminder that his emotions have actually been 'devalued' (p. 77).

The mythic dimensions of Joe's progress are incorporated self-consciously into the narrative. They have the effect of enhancing Joe's mystique, while allowing him to keep a self-deprecating distance from gross self-flattery. On several occasions he likens himself to a 'swineherd' pursuing a princess in a fairy story (pp. 58, 203), and at one point to the comic figure of King for a Day (p. 69). Nevertheless, Joe has been 'chosen' (or has chosen himself) and cannot turn back. Despite the apparent self-hatred that the abandonment of his lover Alice Aisgill produces, Joe knows he must possess the capitalist's daughter Susan Brown if his plan is to succeed. The sexual battery he uses to penetrate the fortress of the propertied classes, defloration and impregnation, has more in common with nineteenth-century melodrama than bourgeois sexual sophistication, and is an example of the novel's proletarianization of mainstream elements of literary tradition.

At times, however, Joe's Nietzschean superiority reaches absurd proportions, as in the scene where Alice compares him to Christ: 'I've washed your feet with my tears' (p. 172). Joe's perfect 'fair and Nordic' physique has more than an echo of fascism about it (p. 70). Other heavily contrived plot elements that aid his mission are handled sentimentally. The function of his landlady Mrs Thompson is to be a mother-figure and ease his passage into alien social territory. Joe looks exactly like her dead son who was killed in the war (p. 21). Joe has a reserved place in his adoptive new class.

While the novel is a proletarian fairy-story, it is also rooted in the historical experience of the 1940s. Like much nineteenth-century fiction, the action is displaced into the recent past. The affluent Joe of the present looks back ten years to his formative Warley days. Given that the novel was published by Eyre and Spottiswoode in 1957, this dates the action to 1947, the year in which an unremittingly harsh winter pitched the British economy into crisis. Joe's 'campaign' takes place within a climate of 'austerity', rationing, and the immediate aftermath of the war, not the 'affluence' of the late 1950s when the novel was published. In strict historical terms, Joe cannot be typical of the 1950s, and to make him so is to read 'affluence' back into 'austerity' (had the novel appeared in the early 1950s when Braine first submitted it, this misreading may not have been so available). The 1940s setting makes Joe's ambitions all the more appetizing, and his success all the more remarkable, but a reading of the novel which ignores the retrospective time-scheme underestimates the moral purpose of the narrative structure. Joe the narrator is disenchanted, sated, and pacified by his ten years at 'the top'. He likens himself to a slick commodity: 'I'm like a brand-new Cadillac in a poor industrial area ... plastic and lacquered' (p. 124). He has lost his soul: 'I suppose I had my chance to be a real person'. Even sex, once his most powerful weapon, has become sanitized and contaminated by its likeness to glossy advertisers' images (pp. 183–4). He looks back nostalgically to his vital, vigorous, questing self of the 1940s. At the point at which Britain's new-found prosperity was being celebrated by politicians and the media, Joe's devitalization and conformity can be read as a warning to the working class that the price to be paid for 'embourgeoisement' is cultural emasculation and dehumanization.

Joe's effeminization had already begun all those years earlier. This change is most clearly shown by the recurrent references to his hands. Hands are the traditional signifier of working-class status (metonymically, a 'hand' is a worker). Each of Joe's lovers describes his hands: to Alice they are 'big and red and brutal' (p. 83); to Susan they are 'square and strong' (p. 139); but to the 'tart' whom Joe picks up to appease his guilt over Alice's death, his hands are 'lovely' and 'soft', 'Like a woman's' (p. 231). These are the 'lacquered' hands of a 'Successful Zombie' (p. 123), the capitalist-in-waiting who in Tressell's terms does not work. There is a chilling moment when Joe wanders through the working-class area of Warley and looks with 'derisive pity at the stupid faces around me – the faces of, if they were lucky, my future lorry-drivers and labourers and warehousemen' (p. 226). Joe becomes a company yes-man, a metaphorical 'sandwich-boardman' (p. 13). He has betrayed his working-class origins and become an upper-class commodity, without the will to resist (this theme is pursued in more detail in the sequel *Life at the Top* (1963), where Susan cuckolds him; in the 1970s spin-off TV series *Man at the Top*, however, Joe's ambition and sexual drive have been revived). So although Joe's story can be interpreted as an anticipation of the Thatcherite 'turn' of large sections of the British working class in the 1980s, a more correct reading would place the novel alongside those contemporary Left-cultural jeremiads about the effects 'shiny barbarism' was having on authentic working-class identity.

Another important consequence of the retrospective narrative scheme is that it places the action in the immediate aftermath of the war. The war plays a decisive determining role in Joe's transformation, and is made to conform to his 'elect' progress. Joe served in the RAF, was shot down and imprisoned in Stalag 1000. Instead of attempting to escape, like his upper-class rival for Susan's affections, Jack Wales, Joe rejected this gentlemanly heroism (of the type that graces so many patriotic war films made in the 1950s) and studied for his accountancy exams, as if preparing for the new opportunities of postwar reconstruction.

The more significant intervention of the war, however, is the stray bomb that fell on Dufton and obliterated Joe's house, killing his parents, severing him from his roots, and rewarding him with several hundred pounds of insurance money.

One of the most important scenes in the book occurs in chapter 10, where Joe revisits this bombsite while on a Christmas visit to Dufton. The novel's treatment of the theme of class identity and class-consciousness is at its most intense in this episode. At the same time as he becomes fully aware of his destiny and his invulnerability, Joe's 'unselfish, generous and gentle' relatives (p. 96) remind him of the core values he has abandoned. His aunt is a classic embodiment of traditional working-class decency; she is Hoggart's 'our mam' of the 1920s and 1930s. But her unselfconscious 'language of giving', and some tell-tale moments in the visit, emphasize the fact that her world belongs to the past, while Joe is a creature of the future. No detail is more significant than Joe's distaste for his aunt's tea: 'it was too strong, stuffy and pungent like old sacking' (p. 90). The scene is poised emotionally between Joe's steely determination to conquer the new social landscape and his nostalgia for collective values. In 1947, Joe's relatives would probably have been much more typical of the condition of the working class than he was, but the scene relies again on the teleological aesthetic of his predestination to achieve a resolution of its constitutive tensions:

> A sluggish wind crept down from the Pennines, cold and damp and spiteful, trying to find a gap in my defences. It retired...it had no power over me now, it was a killer only of the poor and the weak. I looked at the small space which had once been my home; I'd come a long way since 1941. (p. 94)

Joe lays his parents' ghosts to rest, and emerges unscathed from the diabolical environment of 'labour in the mills forever' (p. 97).

Room at the Top is a fantasy about social mobility in the years of 'austerity'. It is possible that its publication was delayed until its portrayal of acquisitive lust and working-class 'politics of envy' seemed to reinforce the myths of affluence and the sexualized Angry Young Man.[16] Joe is not a creature of 1950s affluence, or postwar social mobility. He does not take up university education in the wake of the 1944 Education Act; Joe's education was completed during the war. As Alan Sinfield has noted, the intellectual character of 'Angry' and working-class authors belongs essentially to the prewar tradition of the autodidact.[17] The formative years of these authors were the 1930s and 1940s, which may account for the continuing presence in their work of an older working class, and the persistent use of a wary narrative distance from the new shibboleths of success.

This is certainly the case in Alan Sillitoe's first novel *Saturday Night and Sunday Morning* (1958),[18] where the hero Arthur Seaton defines his robust independence against his parents' comfortable, pacified existence:

> in a way he was glad to see the TV standing in a corner of the living room, a glossy panelled box looking, he thought, like something plundered from a space-ship. The old man was happy at last, anyway, and he deserved to be happy, after all the years before the war on the dole, five kids and the big miserying that went with no money and no way of getting any... There are no flies on me, Arthur thought. (p. 20)

> They think they've settled our hashes with their insurance cards and television sets, but I'll be one of them to turn around on 'em and let them see how wrong they are. (p. 114)

Arthur's determination not to conform to standards of respectability manifests itself primarily in a vigorous sexual life. At one stage in the novel he is involved with three women: Brenda, the wife of his workmate Jack; Winnie, Brenda's sister, who is married to a 'swaddie'; and his fiancée Doreen, who lives on one of the interwar out-of-town estates and represents the respectable aspirations of the new, affluent working class. Arthur's virile masculinity is also evident in his productiveness: taking maximum advantage of the piecework system, he earns high enough wages to own a wardrobe full of expensive Italian suits (which he wears over 'soiled underwear', p. 56). He has a level of disposable income that Harry Hardcastle would have found fantastic. Arthur's favourite nephew William ogles Arthur's wage packet, 'a stupefying amount of money' (p. 54). Arthur is certainly affluent in this respect, but he is resistant to the idea that the only way to express a higher standard of living is through either a bourgeois lifestyle (deferred gratification) or consuming the 'shiny barbarism' of mass culture; Arthur is patronizing about television, and has little interest in modern music.

Arthur is neither materialist nor socially ambitious. The novel does not attempt to present him as a clearly defined, emergent force, but gives him instead an abrasive power arising from his wavering social allegiances and values. Arthur is rarely situated outside traditional, industrial working-class locations: he lives a pampered life at home in one of the old terraced streets, a 'solid bloc of anarchistic Labour' (p. 109); he drinks, fights and woos in pubs, and his main recreation is fishing on the canal. Occasionally, the novel embellishes the pre-industrial, rural past, as in Arthur's sentimental memory of his grandfather's forge, which 'had long ago been destroyed to make room for advancing armies of new pink houses' (p. 179). To the extent that Arthur seems destined to marry Doreen and move into one of these properties, his story could be seen as an example of a small degree of social mobility within the working class, though Arthur makes clear that marriage and settling down will be just another 'battle', and there is no possibility that he will be liberated from his job at the lathe in a bicycle factory, a 'monstrous being' (p. 20). Arthur's tirades against the forces of conformity always have a class-conscious edge. He lumps together the state, civil institutions and authority figures (including trade union leaders) as one huge racket:

> Blokes with suits and bowler hats will say: 'These chaps have got their television sets, enough to live on, council houses, beer, and pools – some have even got cars. We've even made them happy. What's wrong? Is that a machine gun I hear starting up or a car backfiring?' (p. 177)

The spectre of a Third World War also undermines shiny barbarism, but Arthur sees little hope in organized resistance. He voted Communist in the last general election more as a prank than a serious political act (p. 28). In the carnivalesque scene at Goose Fair, where Arthur is likened to the Lord of Misrule, he looks out from the top of the Helter Skelter 'wondering how many columns of soldiers could be gathered from these crowds for use in a rebellion'; the next moment 'two hands stabbed into his back and pushed him into oblivion' (p. 143).

Arthur's rebelliousness is essentially a matter of conscious-ness. We are reminded that thought is vital to existence: 'this lathe is my everlasting pal because it gets me thinking' (p. 176). The narrative is told almost entirely from his point of view, and the use of free indirect speech means that the story is dominated by Arthur's vernacular voice (in the film version a voiceover was used to create a similar effect). There is no privileging of standard English, which helps to reduce the damaging gap between the cultural position of the author and that of the characters.[19] As someone who has only vague memories of reading Shakespeare's *Henry V* at school, Arthur has no literary pretensions, but that does not mean his language lacks proletarian lyricism in the frequent use of unliterary similes and vigorous prose:

> For it was Saturday night, the best and bingiest glad-time of the week, one of the fifty-two holidays in the slow-turning Big Wheel of the year, a violent preamble to a prostrate Sabbath. (p. 5)

> His memory acted at first like a beneficial propaganda machine, a retainer and builder of morale, saying that he could not have been so drunk... (p. 10)

Sillitoe's prose goes some way towards meeting George Orwell's dictum that literary English should be the joint product of the poet and the manual worker.

Despite the social and cultural restrictions which loom large in his life, and which he spends much of his time and energy dodging, cheating and outwitting, the mere fact that Arthur's consciousness is continuously operative and questing is an affirmation of a working-class point of view and its right to be part of literary history. An element of primitivist glamour enhances this aesthetic. There is plenty of evidence in the novel for seeing Arthur in Hoggartian terms as an urban savage, living an 'unplanned' life of swift, instinctual responses which are more vital and authentic (if more violent and morally unregulated) than staid working-class conservatism, bourgeois respectability and mass culture's 'standardized' emotional effects. When Arthur vomits over an older working-class woman, her husband makes an ineffective protest (pp. 10–11); Arthur and his cousin Fred turn a drunken driver's car over and become 'ecstatic warriors' (pp. 99–101); the sound of breaking glass revitalizes Arthur's spirits (pp. 93, 176); and at times Arthur's sexuality achieves a Lawrentian depth, 'through to the opened furrows of the earth' (p. 188).

These existential passions are not only a vital response to an alienating mode of production; they are also generated by a largely unmodernized working-class culture in which time is perceived as a relentless cycle of work and play, a 'Big Wheel' of seasonal, communal rituals such as Bonfire Night, Christmas and 'smashin'' Goose Fair (p. 111). Unlike the 1930s, there is more scope for the 'sweet things of life' (p. 177) within this oppressive regime, but there is still little incentive to plan ahead. Yet for all that Arthur's life is episodic and opportunistic (it is worth noting here that the novel began its life as a series of short stories), Sillitoe imposes beneath this working-class picaresque surface a redemptive linear structure. 'Sunday morning' is more than just a time for reflection and repose after the excesses of 'Saturday night'; it also represents renewal and moral growth. Arthur's hedonism runs out of steam when Brenda becomes pregnant and he is beaten up by swaddies (for whom he has a particular hatred, as they remind him of the humiliations of National Service). Yet he knew he had it coming, and sees his recovery as a watershed period, and a prelude to settling down. To emphasize the sense of a symbolic rebirth, Arthur remains in his bedroom 'buried for three days' (p. 155). Doreen is the traditional good woman who can save him from himself. He is also reabsorbed into the older working-class culture in the form of Aunt Ada's huge family, which embraces some 'undeserving' elements (two of her sons were deserters during the war, and she herself resembles a 'promiscuous barmaid' (p. 64)) within an ethos of boundless hospitality and self-help (Arthur takes Brenda to her for an abortion). Aunt Ada's 'tribe' is a stalwart institution of class consciousness, and provides Arthur with the resources to remake his working-class identity. Aunt Ada is the most sentimentally drawn character in the novel, a ripe version of 'our mam'; she is the antithesis of that other nostalgic stereotype, the nagging noseyparker Mrs Bull. It is during Aunt Ada's New Year party, a time of symbolic renewal, that Arthur feels whole again. Though he insists he is 'always a rebel', the novel is uncertain where to direct his antagonisms: at the conformist tendencies in his own class, or the 'impersonal' forces of the modern state, which he barely comprehends.

The other significant character at Aunt Ada's party is the black serviceman Sam. Though he is the butt of racist humour, the festive camaraderie of the occasion extends to him also, and seems to offer him a tentative place within this older working-class culture. Sillitoe introduces the theme of emergent black British culture at a late stage in the novel, to parallel the narrative uncertainty about Arthur's class trajectory. The novel signals that the growing presence of blacks in working-class communities may require an extension of the defining features of traditional working-class identity (productive labour, poverty, propertylessness) even though the historical experience of the two cultures may not be shared. If Sam represents the Caribbean community, Doreen's mother's lover Mr 'Chumley' represents the Asian dimension to postwar immigration. Arthur responds to him with condescension and pity, but the significance of the novel's introduction of two black characters counteracts Arthur's dismissiveness. It may be no coincidence that in the year the novel was published there were race riots in Nottingham and London's Notting Hill. In the opening factory sequence of the 1960 film version, directed by the European émigré Karel Reisz and scripted by Sillitoe, the camera dwells on a black worker – 'He's alright' says Arthur's voiceover, though the characters of Sam and Chumley are both omitted from the story.

Also omitted from the film adaptation, for which Sillitoe wrote the screenplay, was the character of Winnie. Her sexual promiscuity, which is more than a match for Arthur's, was presumably regarded as too shocking to be publicly screened and consumed, and her removal also created a conventional romantic triangle (Arthur, Brenda, Doreen). Even if Winnie's lubricity is ignored, Brenda's lack of guilt about her adultery and her evident pleasure in her affair with Arthur constituted a major departure in post-Kinseyan British culture, even though she is 'punished' with an unwanted pregnancy. It would be misleading to claim that Sillitoe is consciously progressive in his portrayal of gender. Arthur's views on women are at the best patronizing: 'women were more than ornaments and skivvies; they were warm, wonderful creatures that needed and deserved to be looked after' (p. 36). At his worst he is sadistic: his first response to Brenda's announcement of her pregnancy is to feel 'brutal and exultant' (p. 58). Yet there is no doubt that the emphasis in working-class texts of this period (and the 'kitchen sink' film versions) on men and women enjoying sex, helped to break down some of the remaining barriers of Victorian prejudice against sexual frankness in cultural representations of contemporary British life.

Sillitoe's early fiction is reminiscent of nineteenth-century naturalism in its gritty portrayal of closed working-class communities. Unlike most other working-class fiction of the period, he is refreshingly uninterested in the themes of social mobility, education and breaking away. The social trajectory of many of his characters is in the other direction – a descent into criminality and disaffection. It is often in the submerged social regions of the lumpenproletariat or underclasses (Gissing's 'nether world') that Sillitoe searches for the most authentic proletarian experiences and language. This approach may have been a way of avoiding the artistic influence of that other Nottingham-born novelist D. H. Lawrence, under whose shadow Sillitoe (like Walter Brierley) had to find an original voice. It may also be a comment on the dislocations of working-class identity taking place in a time of transition. Several of Sillitoe's early stories are narrated by or are about juvenile delinquents and petty criminals, including 'The Loneliness of the Long Distance Runner' and 'The Decline of Frankie Buller', both of which appeared in the 1959 collection of short stories *The Loneliness of the Long Distance Runner*.[20]

The narrator of the title story is Smith, a teenager who has been sent to an Essex borstal for burglary. Though his name implies his ordinariness, he has a talent for cross-country running, and if he pleases the governor and wins enough races, he can look forward to an early release. His dilemma is similar to Arthur Seaton's reluctance to conform to society's rules: will Smith deliberately lose the Blue Ribbon Cup race and sabotage the governor's plans to turn him into a 'race horse' (p. 18)? Given Smith's hatred of authority, his decision to throw the race comes as no surprise, though he is aided in his decision by the discovery that he has pleurisy. His private war is expressed in class-conscious language. On his arrival at the borstal, he notices the governor's 'lily-white, workless hands' (p. 9). His mission is to get 'a bit of my own back' (p. 45). Contradictions emerge from the meditations he has on his long, solitary

105

training sessions. He sees a purpose in 'scribbling down' (p. 13), yet he includes 'pen-pushers' in his catalogue of 'pot-bellied' candidates for assassination (p. 15). He is fiercely unintellectual, but he declares his intention to have his experiences published if he should get caught again. A flashback to his upbringing provides a conventional sociological perspective on his deviancy: he is the son of a hedonistic single mother, a classic case of postwar 'maternal deprivation'. Smith's mother spends the £500 insurance money she has received from Smith's father's death in an industrial accident in one prolonged 'binge' of treats and watching endless television. Her type had already appeared in the role of Helen in *A Taste of Honey* and resurfaces as Billy Casper's mother in Barry Hines's *Kes* (1968) and Kelly Brown's mother in Pat Barker's *Union Street* (1982). These texts suggest that affluence and 'candy-floss' values contaminate the older generation more easily than the younger generation, who are in a position to reject their parents' materialism. Smith fools around with the television, including watching with the sound turned down – 'it was so funny the whole family nearly went into fits on the brand new carpet that hadn't yet found its way to the bedroom' (p. 22). But the power of advertising has so whetted his appetite for consumer goods – 'the telly made all these things seem twenty times better' (p. 21) – that Smith is driven to steal. This ironic treatment of the theme of affluence recurs in 'The Ragman's Daughter' (1963),[21] where the petty-thief narrator and his female partner relish 'stealing stuff for kicks' (p. 13), and redistribute stolen cash around their community. Smith's ambivalent attitude to sport as a route to the new 'talent class' also anticipates the theme's sceptical treatment in David Storey's *This Sporting Life* (1960) and Barry Hines's *The Blinder* (1966).

In 'The Decline of Frankie Buller' there is a rare example of Sillitoe using a story to reflect on the problems of being a working-class writer. The story revolves around the embarrassing gap between his bohemian life in Majorca (where he lived in the 1950s, and where he knew Robert Graves) and his roots. Sillitoe proposes two solutions to this problem. First, he is self-deprecating and apologetic about success and the profession of writing. He refers to 'what has come to be called my study' in a 'ramshackle Majorcan house'; he mimics the surprise of 'visitors' that he can possess a library that includes classics (p. 154); he admits to feigning an accent when he meets childhood friends (p. 172). The second way to bring the two worlds closer together is, paradoxically, through writing. While he admits that books are now a 'foliage' that partly conceals his 'real personality', it is only through narrative that he can revisit his 'natural state' as a childhood member of Frankie Buller's gang. The involvement of a cuckoo's song in provoking childhood memories betrays Sillitoe's reliance on Romanticism. In Wordsworth's 'To the Cuckoo' (1802), the bird's song is credited with the power of returning the listener to the 'visionary hours' of childhood. The embedded account of gang warfare in 1930s Nottingham constructs Buller as a tragic emblem of the raw humanity Sillitoe feels he has lost. To the young Sillitoe, Buller 'seemed like a giant' (p. 156), but when he meets him years later he realizes Buller has been given electrical shock treatment to make him 'responsible' and 'conforming' (p. 172). Sillitoe wonders whether the 'coalblack bag inside' has survived (p. 173). The destruction of Buller's 'dark inspired mind' (p. 174) coincides with 'the city's advance' (p. 167). The story is self-consciously nostalgic for the lost world of the unregulated prewar working class, but the tone of sentimentalization is redeemed by Sillitoe's acknowledgement that 'you can't wind back the clock' (p. 154).

Sillitoe admitted in a preface to *Saturday Night and Sunday Morning* that he had not worked in a factory since the early 1940s, and that his fiction was not aiming at documentary realism but a radical, humanist exploration of the interiority of working-class characters who may or may not themselves be consciously radical.[22] As Smith says in 'The Loneliness of the Long Distance Runner', 'I'm a human being and I've got thoughts and bloody secrets' (p. 13). Sillitoe can be placed within a prewar tradition of Marxist aesthetics which stressed the importance of creating a fully rounded working-class consciousness in fiction: this view was held by such critics as Rex Warner, Ralph Fox and Alick West in Britain, and George Lukács in Europe; all such views were influenced strongly by Engels's notion of the 'triumph of realism'.[23]

The hero-narrator of Stan Barstow's first novel *A Kind of Loving* (1960) is neither macho nor a rebel.[24] Indeed, he seems to be constructed by Barstow as a counter to the Angry Young Man. Vic Brown is a draftsman in a large, modern engineering works. Though he is not university educated, his job is markedly middle-class and 'respectable' in character when compared to Arthur Seaton's semi-skilled factory labour. Vic has no particular grudge against the establishment, and no conscious aspirations to reject his community. He is a decent bloke who can expect to meet a nice woman, settle down and look forward to possible promotion (a thousand a year) and even buying his own home. He admires his sister Chris, a schoolteacher who has married an upper-middle-class schoolmaster. Vic seems to typify the idea that affluence was bringing about a gradual convergence of lifestyles between the classes, and in the process narrowing the options for unorthodoxy. Unlike Joe Lampton and Arthur Seaton, Vic is defined by his lack of virility and drive. Underneath his sexist banter, he is actually squeamish about sex, though he blames his environment for this awkwardness: 'I think it's shabby and dirty as well, because it's something nobody talks about' (p. 111). He is afraid to admit to his mates that he is more interested in love than sex (p. 16). He vacillates continually about his precise feelings for his lover Ingrid. After they have had premarital sex, he loses interest in her, but when she becomes pregnant he does the expected thing and marries her: 'life is no fairy tale' (p. 215).

Like Doreen in *Saturday Night and Sunday Morning*, Ingrid lives with her mother in newer suburban housing, a 'little modern semi' (p. 54). Marriage to her should represent for Vic a step up from his more traditional working-class roots (his father is a miner). However, Vic and Ingrid cannot afford their own place and living with her mother turns out to be disastrous as she is possessive and envious. As so often in working-class fiction, it is the mother-figure who represents a stifling conformity to standards of respectability. Ingrid's mother is bigoted, Tory and racist (p. 222). When the drunken Vic vomits over her, it is difficult not to read the act as an infantile revenge fantasy (Arthur Seaton also vomits over an older woman). When Ingrid loses the baby, Ingrid's mother tries to reclaim her daughter, while Vic accuses Ingrid of being frigid. It transpires that Ingrid feels inhibited living under the eye of her mother, so the couple move out into shabby lodgings and try to start again. An uneasy, stoical calm is restored, as it is clear that Vic does not love Ingrid. In the sequel to the novel, *The Watchers on the Shore* (1965), Vic leaves Ingrid and escapes to London, where he has an affair with an actress.

But the earlier novel is poised on the cusp of 1960s freedoms. Vic's bohemian, metropolitan destiny is anticipated in his growing interest in high culture, which also sits awkwardly with his family's expectation that he take an interest in traditional working-class cultural activities such as his father's brass band (p. 119). Vic works part-time in a gramophone and music shop, develops a taste for classical music, and eventually accepts the owner's offer of a full-time position. Vic makes the transition between C. P. Snow's 'two cultures' of science and art. Though the novel is a reworking of *Love on the Dole* in an affluent setting, it is also poised to become a *Künstler-Bildungsroman*. High culture is the antidote to both traditional working-class culture and mass commercial culture. 'Liking something that's worth liking' is a conventional liberal-humanist ideal, though Vic has much to learn. He beams about his most recent acquisition, 'Tchaikovsky's Pathetic Symphony' (p. 174). What Raymond Williams has called the 'orthography of the uneducated' rears its clownish head again at this moment.[25]

In the same year as *A Kind of Loving*, a first novel appeared by another Yorkshire miner's son. David Storey's *This Sporting Life* (1960) explores the inner life of a professional rugby league player.[26] Storey drew on his experience as a professional footballer in the 1950s, and reworked the themes of working-class ambition and ambivalent provincial success first seen in *Room at the Top*. Storey's main contribution to the renaissance of northern working-class fiction in this period was to introduce a new tone of existential bleakness.

Though Arthur Machin's £500 signing-on fee catapults him into the ranks of the talent class, he is a destructive and repressed character, unable to disentangle himself from his gladiatorial image. He purchases a large car and a television, two icons of affluence, but he cannot escape the fact that he is a commodity. To reinforce this point, we discover that the owner of the rugby club, Weaver, also owns the factory Arthur works at. Arthur is sexually desired by Weaver (p. 30), Weaver's wife (pp. 98–107), and the talent scout 'dad' (p. 30). He tries to find solace in a bitter and corrosive relationship with his landlady Mrs Hammond. But she is more repressed than he is, 'keeping her stinking feelings back' (p. 162). The only time he uses the word 'love' to describe their suffocating relationship, she spits in his face (p. 175). She is haunted by the memory of her husband, who died in an accident at Weaver's factory. This death also stalks the narrative as a reminder of the destructiveness of industrialism, though Arthur accuses Mrs Hammond of driving her husband to suicide (p. 180). Their affair deteriorates into violence, but Arthur's obsessiveness still leads him to refuse the opportunity of an affair with Mrs Weaver. Once Mrs Hammond dies prematurely, Arthur continues his soulless routine: 'I had no feelings. It was no good acting any longer as if I had' (p. 229). Paradoxically, the achievement of the confessional narrative form is to give a voice to this emptiness.

Storey's second novel *Flight Into Camden* (1961) was also a conspicuous new departure in that the story is told by a miner's daughter, Margaret.[27] She embarks on a doomed affair with Howarth, a college lecturer, and agrees to elope with him to London. Though a sense of futility and despair is never far away, Margaret is prepared to be unconventional and undertake the classically male voyage away from her northern roots to the ambiguous satisfactions of southern, metropolitan culture. There are feminist dimensions to the novel's exploration of female desire. Margaret rejects the idea that her destiny lies in motherhood (p. 59). Despite her father's abusive remarks about her immorality (she is a fallen woman in his eyes), she feels uniquely alive (p. 148), and is prepared if necessary to break with her parents for good. It is also made clear that a conspiracy of men defeats her. Howarth grows tired of her, claiming (in an echo of Paul Morel's hectoring of Miriam) that she will not give herself to him completely (p. 150). He pretends that her parents are ill as a ruse to get her to go home, and then writes a cowardly letter calling off the affair. Her brother Michael, a university lecturer, is vindictive and possessive. On the other hand, Margaret has no aspirations beyond her romantic obsession with Howarth. She is left in limbo, awaiting the new feminism of the 1960s.

In the absence of any female working-class novelists in this period, Storey's feminocentric narrative is particularly valuable.

The next important fictional portrayal of working-class women's experience to appear on the literary scene, as we shall see, was also produced by an honorary working-class woman writer, Nell Dunn. Storey's manoeuvre conformed to his theory that the 'move south' by male working-class writers represented a process of feminization.[28] Storey himself went to the Slade School of Fine Art in London, and for several years in the 1950s oscillated between a 'northern' life as a footballer and a 'southern' life as an artist and budding writer. These inner tensions and conflicts could be seen as aesthetically productive, as they informed much of his later fiction.

Raymond Williams also took up the theme of social mobility and cultural displacement in his first, autobiographical novel, *Border Country* (1960).[29] Williams was the classic scholarship boy: the son of a signalman, educational success propelled him from a village in the Welsh Borders to the high culture and metropolitan life of Cambridge. By 1960, Williams had established himself as one of the leading figures in the New Left revival, and had become an influential literary and cultural critic. In *Culture and Society* (1958), Williams traces the evolution of a central dissenting tradition in post-Romantic British culture, giving a prominent place to D. H. Lawrence. In the collection of essays given the title *The Long Revolution* (1960), Williams looks ahead to the future development of this tradition. 'Realism and the Contemporary Novel' puts forward the Lukacsian view that realism should inscribe individual experience within the social totality. Fiction should strive for 'The balance ... in which both the general way of life and the individual persons are seen as there and absolute'.[30]

In *Border Country*, Williams put some of these ideas and themes into practice. The novel revolves around the hero's anxious revisiting of his roots. Matthew Price, a London University history lecturer, is summoned back to his parents' Welsh home as his father is dying (a similar 'returning native' motif is used in David Mercer's 1960 television play *Where the Difference Begins*, in which two socially mobile brothers meet up at their mother's funeral). In order to include in the narrative an exploration of the 'long revolution' of working-class history and politics, and to put the individual characters in a dialectical relation to the 'general way of life', Williams abandons a linear time scheme in favour of an oscillation between the present day

111

and a series of flashbacks to his father's role in the General Strike of 1926. Williams believed that 1926 was a decisive moment in Welsh proletarian history, representing both a devastating defeat and a consolidation of a defensive class consciousness.[31] Matthew's father is not particularly militant in the strike, but he suffers from the victimization that follows its collapse. Matthew has to struggle with the meanings of his father's history and the light in which it casts his own achievements as an academic historian specializing in Welsh labour history: 'he was trained to detachment...and the detachment was real in another way. He felt, in this house, both a child and a stranger' (p. 83). He comes to the realization that 'by measuring the distance, we come home' (p. 351), but the bridging of the two worlds of knowable communities and the intelligentsia remains an ambiguous possibility rather than a reality:

> The landscape of childhood never disappears, but the waking environment is adult: the street, the committee, the long, quiet library, the file of revised manuscript, the books shifting under the arm as you run for the crowded bus. The personal meaning is evident in every shape in this country, every sound of the loved voices, but the public meaning is elsewhere, in a different negotiation and in another voice. (p. 307)

In *Border Country*'s sequel, *Second Generation* (1964), Williams continues the search for a narrative 'negotiation' between Wales and England, working-class culture and intellectuals, history and modernity.[32] The novel focuses on the Owen family, who migrated from South Wales to Oxford in the 1930s in order to find work in the car industry. By the start of the 1960s, Harold Owen is a senior shop steward at the factory, and a bastion of 'trade union consciousness'. His son and daughter are more troubled, and feel divided between the city's two halves, industry and the academy. Peter Owen is a Matthew Price figure. He chooses to abandon his postgraduate research into sociological theory to work independently on working-class migration patterns, even though this decision jeopardizes a promising academic future. While Peter sees his decision as negotiating a rapprochement with his family history, his father berates him for being sentimental and rash: 'you want to go back where I started' (p. 345). Peter's sister Kate gives up her academic prospects for the more gender-bound reason of supporting the family in a needy moment, though she also becomes active in the Labour Party. After a brief affair with a middle-class bohemian, she rejects the 'old bourgeois fantasy' of a 'personal breakout through sex' (p. 272) just as such ideas were becoming newly fashionable.

The centrality of the trope of the 'border' in Williams's fiction is reminiscent of the 'political' interwar years, where the metaphor referred to intellectuals 'going over' to the proletariat, and to volunteers crossing the mountains into Spain. The ghosts of older class and political struggles haunt postwar working-class fiction, and Williams makes a robust attempt to lay these ghosts to rest and to move on.

But realism was not the only way to respond to the theme of breaking away. Keith Waterhouse's comic novel *Billy Liar* (1959) deals with one Saturday in the life of a working-class rogue who tries to make life conform to his fantasies of glamorous power and success.[33] Waterhouse's own career as a witty Fleet Street columnist is reflected in the fact that Billy is a would-be comedian and comic scriptwriter. He works in a funeral parlour, mistreats his girlfriends, and lampoons many aspects of working-class and provincial life. His ambition is to move to London to work in radio (a move anticipated by several 'Angry' predecessors: the middle-class Oxbridge fugitive Lumley, the hero of John Wain's *Hurry on Down* (1953), ends his picaresque adventures writing radio comedy; Jim Dixon in Kingsley Amis's *Lucky Jim* (1954) leaves his university lectureship to take up a job (and a girlfriend) in London's publishing industry). Billy's response to the cultural sterility of his environment is to reduce affluent working-class life to a series of comic stereotypes, such as the bluff Yorkshireman (p. 138) and the 'dark satanic teashops' (p. 24). While this debunking has a value, his shallowness and self-centredness is a problem for the reader. He is unmoved by his grandmother's death, for example (p. 169). After a series of backlashes in his personal, working and romantic life, he decides not to take the train to London, though just how chastened he is remains unclear.

Waterhouse's satire is refreshing if superficial. There is no reason why working-class culture should be immune from comic deflation from within its own ranks. The stage, musical, and film versions of *Billy Liar* were all very successful. As

113

Richard Hoggart points out in *The Uses of Literacy* (1957), a rich vein of debunking, irreverent and often ribald humour has long been a hallmark of working-class culture.[34] While this quality has been under-represented in working-class fiction, the postwar period offered new creative opportunities for working-class writers in radio comedy, television 'sit-coms' and 'soaps', and led to some contemporary masterpieces of proletarian humour and comedy-drama, particularly in the 1960s: *Coronation Street* (still running) and *Steptoe and Son* are two obvious examples, while *Till Death Us Do Part* produced that memorable patriarchal know-all Alf Garnett.

Unfortunately, Alf Garnett's tirades against authority are seriously disfigured by sexism and racism. He blames most problems on two sources: the government and black people. In his tabloid view of society, black people are uncivilized and a threat to the British way of life. In fact the postwar Labour government granted British passports to all commonwealth citizens in 1948 and actively recruited Caribbean workers to fill labour shortages, a policy that continued throughout the 1950s. Black people became the new working class of postwar Britain. By the end of the 1950s there were black communities in most major British cities: London, Bristol, Birmingham, Liverpool, Cardiff, and Glasgow. The race riots of 1958, the operation of a colour bar by landlords and employers, and the passing of the 1962 Immigration Act (which introduced the first restrictions to primary male immigration on overtly racial lines, as black immigrants now needed work permits to enter the country), show the depressing lack of intervention by the state to raise general awareness about the social and cultural position of blacks in postwar Britain. Despite this inaction, in the 1950s there were burgeoning numbers of Caribbean novelists based in London. It is an ironic fact that in the era of decolonization, London became the literary capital of the West Indies. This flowering of Caribbean literature included V. S. Naipaul, George Lamming, Roger Mais, John Hearne and Sam Selvon. Selvon will be looked at briefly here, as he exposes the common ground between black settlers and the white working class.

Selvon came to England from Trinidad in 1950 and stayed until 1978, when he re-emigrated to Canada. His fiction is particularly illuminating about life in London for the first waves of mostly single black men looking for work and lodgings, and adjusting to a new society. His two early books *The Lonely Londoners* (1956) and *Ways of Sunlight* (1957) are also memorable for Selvon's comic approach to the themes of cultural displacement and racism.[35] Much of the comic effect comes from the use of a modified form of Creole dialect by the characters and the narrator. This street vernacular defamiliarizes the London setting and infuses the landscape with cultural difference. The areas around Bayswater Road and Ladbroke Grove become 'the water' and 'the grove', men are 'tests', and one short story is about 'obeah in the grove'. The fiction is littered with lively rogues on the make, and with characters trying to come to terms with proletarianization and loss of status (see particularly 'Calypso in London' and 'Working the Transport' in *Ways of Sunlight*). Selvon's heroes face racism in and out of the workplace, but they are also gently mocked by the narratives for their fecklessness and scapegoating of women.

Selvon's Marxist orientation becomes clear in a didactic passage in *The Lonely Londoners*:

> Wherever in London that it have Working Class, there you will find a lot of spades. This is the real world, where men know what it is to hustle a pound to pay the rent when Friday come ... It have a kind of communal feeling with the Working Class and the spades, because when you poor things does level out, it don't have much up and down. (pp. 73–7)

The white British working class could well have learned these lessons of solidarity and respect for difference, rather than succumbing to the time-honoured ruling-class device of divide-and-rule. As George Lamming recounted in *The Pleasures of Exile* (1960), many immigrants found white working-class poverty hard to accept. But Selvon's novels were effectively excluded from the British literary tradition for several decades. The only white British writer to take up the opportunity to embrace black culture was the middle-class Colin MacInnes in his 'London' trilogy, *City of Spades* (1957), *Mr Love and Justice* (1960) and *Absolute Beginners* (1958), which features the 1958 Notting Hill riots. MacInnes's vision of a London transformed by black and youth culture is as much mythic as it is realistic, however. For example, one of the leading characters in *Absolute Beginners* is called 'the Hoplite', a term used for a footsoldier in ancient Greece, and hardly a word to emerge from within working-class vernacular discourse.

The picture drawn so far of working-class fiction in the postwar years has featured mostly familiar names: Braine, Sillitoe, Barstow, Storey, Williams, Waterhouse. This clutch of mainly northern writers comprises a literary canon for the late 1950s and early 1960s. For a brief period, working-class creativity was at the forefront of British culture – film adaptations boosted paperback sales of the novels, 'kitchen sink' drama on stage and television thrived, working-class rock-and-roll bands began to rise to stardom, and Britain was soon to elect its first grammar-school-boy prime minister in the form of Harold Wilson. There has never been a time of such cultural pre-eminence in the history of the British working class. But it is important to note that this achievement was based to a large extent on the depoliticization of the explicit content of the literature. As Stuart Laing notes of the period, the celebration of working-class writing took place in a 'peculiarly "non-political" political context'.[36] Unlike the 1930s, there was little interaction or collaboration between working-class writers and the radical intelligentsia, even with the emergence of the New Left from the embers of the discredited post-1956 Communist Party. However, that does not mean there were no active working-class novelists with a more direct political purpose. Another reading of the postwar period is possible which foregrounds a number of neglected Communist writers, notably Jack Lindsay, Len Doherty and Herbert Smith, who examined in a more explicit fashion than their canonical counterparts the failures of the new Britain.[37] The novels of the non-Communist Sid Chaplin are also important in this context, as they deal with the mining communities of the north-east, a missing dimension in the more famous texts. These largely forgotten texts also pose a challenge to the idea that working-class fiction only began to flourish in the late 1950s as a response to 'affluence', when the focus of most debate was on social mobility and the erosion of working-class identity. Sid Chaplin's early novels, for example, appeared at the end of the 1940s.

The period immediately after the Second World War was a lost opportunity for the working class to attain a real and lasting degree of cultural power in Britain. Although the Arts Council was founded in 1945 out of the wartime Council for the Encouragement of Music and the Arts, its function was to redistribute high culture, not to give greater autonomy and importance to working-class cultural traditions and educational institutions such as the prewar Labour colleges and WEAs. No direct subsidies were provided by the Arts Council for writers, and the patronage of left-liberal publishing outlets such as *Penguin New Writing* went into decline, itself closing in 1950. Instead of rising to prominence as the organic intellectuals of a new, socialist Britain, working-class writers had to resort to commercial publishers. John Lehmann, a major patron of working-class writing in the 1930s, believed that this lack of economic support for working-class writers after the war was justified because Britain was becoming more classless: 'the conception of "working-class literature" is itself out of date in the age and country of the welfare state.'[38] Stuart Laing summarizes this position as a 'widespread view' that 'both working-class writing and political literature were obsolete forms'. Any attempt to maintain these traditions would be seen as 'an anachronistic attempt to revive 1930s' forms and perspectives'. In such a hostile climate, 'anachronistic' working-class authors who were uneasy about aspects of the postwar settlement were 'facing increasing difficulty in being accepted as worthwhile contributions to the business of contemporary fiction'.[39]

Given this lack of encouragement, the publication of Sid Chaplin's first two works, *The Leaping Lad* (1947) and *The Thin Seam* (1950), seems all the more valuable.[40] Chaplin was a self-educated north-eastern miner whose long career lasted from the 1930s to the 1980s.[41] He published his first stories in *Penguin New Writing*, and gathered them together in *The Leaping Lad*. The stories are an evocation of aspects of Chaplin's childhood years in the 1920s, including memories of the General Strike. In 'Grace Before Meat', a miner steals turnips to feed his starving family. The story takes issue with Christian morality, and supplants 'Thou shalt not steal' with 'the earth is the Lord's' (p. 93), a distant echo of agrarian radicalism. In 'Easter 1927' the child's naïve point of view allows for the weaving together of the themes of defeat, loss and regeneration. The effect is both lyrical and ironic, as the child does not perceive the symbolic relevance of the Easter setting in relation to his community's despair. In one of the strongest stories, 'Hands', a family conflict between a miner and his father turns into a chilling reminder of the destructive forces of alienated labour. The son's anger at his father's disapproval of his sexual laxity leads to carelessness at the coalface which in turn causes a roof-fall. This buries his father; only his hands are visible protruding from the rubble. The image captures the material oppression of language; a 'hand' is a mere 'appendage of the machine', in Marx's terms, and in this image of exploited labour the Oedipal drama finds a terrible resolution.

In an essay called 'A Story-teller's Story', Chaplin claims that his fiction has its roots in oral tradition, and that his work can therefore be seen as a form of 'folk' art: 'the essential inner core is the talk of men going to and from the coal'.[42] But while *The Leaping Lad* evokes some of the rhythms of community life, *The Thin Seam* displays a self-consciousness about literary narrative and language. The novel is lyrical and formally ambitious, though Chaplin's aesthetic aims are not in the last instance separable from his exploration of the impact on working-class communities of the postwar settlement.

The Thin Seam has a quasi-modernist structure. In Russian Formalist terms, the *fabula* (the raw sequence of events) concerns the return of an idealistic miner Christopher Jack to his local village. He has just emerged from a Working Men's College and is determined to become a local Labour leader, but this ambition is thwarted by his inability to reintegrate into the community. He begins to write in the hope this will help him to resolve his inner turmoil. The *sjuzet* (plot) reorders these events in order to intensify Jack's dilemma. The main action of the narrative occupies just one night-shift down a mine. Jack and his mates work in a 'little hell' (p. 12): 'A man takes off his clean clothes and puts on his pit gear...but between the acts lies a lost world' (p. 16). Details about Jack's life enter as flashbacks, emphasizing the conflict between his two selves, the autodidact writer and the labouring man of the people. He has to decide which 'world' he truly belongs in. A roof-fall and the rescue of a trapped workmate bring out powerful emotions of camaraderie in him.

He also realizes that writing can evoke the beauty as well as the horror of underground work. The journey out of the pit is a 'caravan to the sun' away from the 'pulsating enfolding waves' of nature's primeval embraces (p. 64). The temptation to glorify or over-romanticize the miner's labour is tempered by mock-epic allusions: the odyssey to the coalface is 'a voyage as tempestuous in its own way as any fishing boat putting out from Shields or Whitby' (p. 19) and Jack feels 'agony recollected in partial tranquillity' (p. 21) about his unresolved role. It is not made clear whether or not writing can ultimately heal the divisions within himself. While Jack's predicament is possibly the first example in postwar literature of the 'anxious returner', he analyses his dilemma in socio-economic not psychological terms:

> all scholarship battens on the backs of the workers, and with a sense of horror I saw that although the primrose path was open to me and that not a soul would ever condemn me for taking it, just the same I knew that all the time I would be supported on the bowed, sweated shoulders of my father and others like him. I might later become a left-wing leader and 'fight' for them, but it would be from a comfortable and assured position that I would 'fight'. To take their part would in no way redeem my position. I would still be a deserter. My people in one world, myself in another, completely and utterly alien. (p. 32)

Whether or not this kind of language could be called 'anachronistic' in 1950, Chaplin kept the vital issues of labour movement politics and class betrayal on the literary agenda. The tendency of late-1950s cultural sociology was to marginalize the 'self-improving minorities' of working-class communities; Richard Hoggart omitted trade union leaders and labour radicals from *The Uses of Literacy* on the rather unconvincing grounds that they were not the target of mass publicists and cultural debasement (p. 11). A knock-on effect of this deprivileging of the political consciousness of the working class was that the precise social and political character of the new Britain was often overlooked in favour of convenient generalizations such as 'affluence' and democracy. One important exception to this trend was a study of a Yorkshire mining community, *Coal is Our Life* (1956).[43] The aim of this investigation was to study the impact of the nationalization of the coal industry on 'Ashton' (the invented name recalls Mass Observation's 'Worktown'),

119

and to see whether an improved standard of living had altered the traditional pattern of social relations. The authors' conclusions contradict 'facile assumptions' that the postwar settlement has created more opportunities for 'embourgeoisement' and 'escape' (p. 9). Many miners 'see themselves opposed to the same forces as before nationalization' (p. 77). The old problems of job insecurity and low social mobility still apply: 'the promise of security, prosperity and a new life flowing from nationalization and the welfare state was a lie' (p. 9). The idea that there has been a Hegelian 'break' at the end of the war is also illusory: the progression from the bad old prewar days of private ownership, the dole, and the Spencer Union, to the brave new world of state ownership, full employment, and the NUM has brought about only cosmetic changes. Most of the coal industry's profits from 1946 to 1953 (when the study was undertaken) have been given to the mine-owners in compensation. The ability of NUM representatives to act is impeded by their loyalties being divided between the workers and the state. Hence 'the actual changes have been absorbed into the miners' traditional ideology rather than transformed it' (p. 76). While this 'traditional ideology' remains in place, women in the coalfields will remain subjugated (p. 181). The study is particularly illuminating about miners' reluctance to change the 'traditional' sexual division of labour. Even the Women's Section of the local Labour Party has a 'social rather than political character' (p. 166). Many marriages become 'empty and uninspiring relationships' (p. 183). The destructive effects of alienated labour pierce the most intimate areas of life.

The Marxist bias of *Coal is Our Life* identifies economic and industrial power, not social and cultural change, as the agency of cultural decline in mining communities (when the book was reissued in 1969 during a wave of pit closures, the 'lie' of nationalization seemed an incontrovertible fact). It implies that the way forward for the working class is to demand true control over its economic destiny, so that (as Marx had said) both men and women could achieve their full potential. These themes were taken up by the Communist miner Len Doherty in his two novels *A Miner's Sons* (1955) and *The Man Beneath* (1957).[44] Both novels deal with questions of leadership and cohesion within mining communities (and, by analogy, the working class as a whole).

In the former novel there is another 'revisitor' in the shape of Robert Mellers, who has been released from gaol after serving a three-year sentence for assaulting a rival trade union leader. It takes Mellers the course of the novel to win back the respect of his old colleagues and friends, and to revive the local Communist branch. His triumphal moment is getting back his job at the pit, 'a world where sunshine and life and beauty do not exist except in men's minds, but are carried by them everywhere and always' (p. 264). The trajectory of the hero is towards a reabsorption into the collective agency of the community, not a 'flight' or 'escape' from it.

Another area in which the novel is politically more progressive than its canonical counterparts is the exploration of women's experience. Two subplots develop the theme of women's entrapment. The first subplot follows the marriage of a new party member Jud Rodgers and his wife Jean. When he begins to neglect her for party work, she complains 'I think I'm only headcook and bottle-washer around here' (p. 58). Jud goes to Mellers for advice, and is given a swift lesson in sexual politics: 'The women are just as important as the men' (p. 167). The old idea of 'work and politics for the one and the kitchen for the other' needs radicalizing:

> 'Your wife meets more economic problems right in her own kitchen than half the blokes who're supposed to be experts... show her how her own housework and shopping fit in with the things that you're fighting for... it's going to be you that'll have to make the sacrifices... the way to show you're sincere is to stop at home with her.' (p. 175)

Mellers's marriage-guidance is more than effective, as Jean feels wanted and is motivated to become politically active. She does not gain economic independence, but she has a new life outside the home.

A second subplot shows that Jean is not an isolated example. A local campaign for improved recreational facilities for children produces an 'avalanche' of women volunteers: 'From all over the village the women had come – young ones and old ones, quiet sympathizers and virulent crusaders' (p. 166). As importantly, 'alliances were being forged between those from the old village and those from the new estate now that they had this common interest'. The women's action is vital in preventing fractures within the community.

The Man Beneath is formally more ambitious than its predecessor. The novel may have been influenced by *The Thin Seam*, as it uses the device of a truncated time-scheme. Jim Harris, a miners' representative, lies buried beneath a roof-fall at the coalface. Believing he is certain to die, he experiences his life flashing before him in 'spasmodic, disconnected scenes he would never ordinarily have recalled' (p. 26). This near stream-of-consciousness technique mingles together various aspects of his career and personal life. He personifies many features of the historical course of the labour movement: he remembers the defeat of 1926, having to abandon college in the 1930s to support his family, being radicalized by the war, and disillusioned by nationalization:

> The miners first hailed this as a new era in their working lives, but doubts and criticisms gradually began to appear. There was still conflict between the men and the management, and union men found themselves in the ambiguous position of being expected to show loyalty to both sides. (p. 65)

He remembers that the man most likely to replace him is the Communist Johnny Morgan. Morgan is not presented as a character with all the answers. On the contrary, he is Harris's protégé. This undoctrinaire approach to Communism could be a response to the chastening events of 1956. Harris also recalls a poignant episode when he took Morgan to see an old, dying, and still fiercely radical miner, who had in his possession an eighteenth-century manuscript of a speech by a miners' leader. The encounter is a powerful lesson in the importance of preserving and mobilizing labour traditions and history; it also makes a self-referential point about the value of working-class writing.

Harris's successes as a union leader are not matched in his personal life: his marriage is a failure. His wife is a strong woman who resents being made to feel 'ordinary' through his neglect (p. 166). She punishes him by having an affair: 'Somebody's been around your property and you don't like it' (p. 164). His burial in the mine seems metaphorically like retribution for not being able to 'imagine a woman's side of it' (p. 176), though as he is rescued he knows he will have plenty of time to do precisely that. His wife's lover leaves the village, and the community, like the hero, survives another threat to its existence.

After a period of dormancy in the 1950s, Sid Chaplin returned to the literary scene with *The Day of the Sardine* (1961) and *The Watchers and the Watched* (1962).[45] The former novel is a useful foil to *Saturday Night and Sunday Morning*. The hero Arthur Haggerston is an underachiever, drifter, and a bit of a rogue in a north-eastern working-class community. His one aim in life is to avoid becoming a 'sardine', meaning literally a worker in the local sardine factory, and metaphorically a conformist (the word recalls Joe Lampton's 'zombies'). He has a series of picaresque adventures, including affairs with older women and involvement in a local street gang. The most compelling theme in the novel concerns Arthur's Oedipal conflict with his bigamist father. After they fight, his father agrees to divorce Arthur's mother. Having rescued the remnants of his family, Arthur is a reformed character and finally succumbs to a job in the sardine factory. In his new fifteen-guinea suit he is 'all dressed up and nowhere to go' (p. 263). He lacks direction, but has no ambition to escape.

A new cause emerges for the hero of *The Watchers and the Watched* in the form of racism. Tiger Mason is an ordinary 'independent working man' (p. 94) until he becomes swept up in a race riot. Having just ducked out of an offer by the local community to lead a rent-eviction campaign, Tiger impulsively sides with the besieged black and Asian residents, to the horror of many of his neighbours. His attempts to enlighten his community about the capitalist causes of racial division fall on deaf ears. The novel is a vital reminder that beneath the new affluence lay a new black working class.

The Communist novelist Herbert Smith also used his fiction to emphasize the importance of racial awareness. In his London novel *A Morning to Remember* (1962), the familiar convention of the industrial accident is used to glorify the heroism of a black worker.[46] When a group of power-station workers are trapped in a gas-laden pit, they are rescued by the valiant and reckless daring of Ron, an unskilled black labourer. His courage shocks his white colleagues into an awareness of their racism: 'the sacred rite of restoring a man to life had been a lesson' (p. 91). In

Smith's earlier novel about a strike in a west London engineering factory, *A Field of Folk* (1957), the management justify the introduction of a speed-up by claiming they must supply military parts quickly for the war in Malaya.[47] In Alan Sillitoe's 1961 novel *Key to the Door*, Arthur Seaton's brother Brian is sent as a National Serviceman to fight in Malaya but refuses to shoot a Communist insurgent when he has him in his gunsights.[48] The setting of British working-class life in a global capitalist and colonialist context can also be found in Jack Lindsay's 'Novels of the British Way' series, in particular *Rising Tide* (1953), which deals with the London docks strike of 1949.

THE PRICE OF COAL – THE PERMISSIVE YEARS

If the impact of 'affluence' on working-class life in the 1950s was often exaggerated, there is no doubt that the 1960s and 1970s were years of unprecedented prosperity for many working-class people. Between 1955 and 1969, for example, average earnings rose by 130 per cent.[49] The election of two Labour governments in this period (1964–70 and 1974–9) seems to show, at least superficially, that Britain needed another injection of state socialism in order to meet people's aspirations for a freer and fuller life. In the wake of economic justice came a whole new sensibility of personal freedom. In particular, pressure had built up in the 1950s for the liberalization of laws governing sexual behaviour: there was a strong demand for emancipatory state action in the areas of homosexuality, abortion, contraception and divorce. By the end of the 1960s, permissive legislation had been introduced on all these fronts: in 1967 abortion was legalized, private homosexual acts for consenting males over 21 were decriminalized (lesbians remained legally invisible), and the National Health Service was allowed to provide free contraception (under the title 'family planning' rather than 'birth control'); in 1969 the grounds for divorce were liberalized to include incompatibility. Harold Wilson's Labour government also expanded the higher education system, building several new 'campus' universities, and setting up the correspondence-based Open University for adult returners. There was also a change in education policy away from grammar schools towards non-selective comprehensive secondary education. To under-write this process of modernization, the government promised a Wellsian investment in the 'white heat' of new technology. These well-intentioned developments were undoubtedly de-signed to unblock some of the rigidities of the class system by making refinements to the postwar 'consensus'. As Anthony Crosland emphasized in the 1950s, well-managed capitalism could deliver socialist goals. In his formulation, working-class politics would become increasingly concerned with social rather than economic issues.

This Whiggish view of postwar history was not shared by the New Left in the 1960s and 1970s. While recognizing that living standards had risen for many people, Left analysis shifted away from conventional economistic Marxism towards a much more pluralistic analysis of the destructive effects of consumer capitalism and the means of liberation from what Marcuse called 'liberty within a system of servitude'.[50] While the struggle of the proletariat for control of the means of production was still regarded as vital, the western working class was no longer credited with the sole historic responsibility for the overthrow of *laissez-faire*. Revolutionary agency shifted to a host of new causes, ranging from decolonization (according to Stokely Carmichael, 'the proletariat has become the Third World, and the bourgeoisie is white western society'[51]) to a 'revolution in perception' within the individual psyche.[52] The range of new struggles included the emancipation of blacks, women and sexual minorities; the transformation of personal life and the psyche; the expansion of consciousness (with the aid of drugs if necessary); the establishment of communes and alternative lifestyles; the revival of pacifism and the 'flower-power' of the hippies; forms of violent and non-violent direct action including 'days of rage' and sit-ins on university campuses; rock festivals, 'protest songs' and the folk music revival; and the Situationist theories of society as a disruptable 'spectacle'. The American war in Vietnam was a major catalyst for many of these new and revived forms of protest. As the first 'TV war', images of American casualties and atrocities shocked the general public. This outrage fed into a widespread condemnation of America's anti-Communist policies and the support given to the war by other western governments, including Britain and France. In

May 1968, students in Paris rioted, workers downed tools, and a revolutionary alliance of the new and old radical forces seemed to be occurring. The alliance crumbled quickly, but 1968 has become a legendary year in the postwar radical calendar, symbolizing a Utopian potential for a new kind of society based on the infinite transformation of the self and the end of 'one-dimensional' capitalism.

The extent to which this 'spirit of renewal', in Christopher Booker's words,[53] actually transformed traditional working-class culture and consciousness in Britain is debatable. While the British New Left saw the urgent need to unite the aims of intellectuals and the labour movement, achieving this synthesis proved more difficult. For example, Arnold Wesker's Centre 42 project, an attempt to turn the Roundhouse theatre in north London into a cultural base for workers and artists, floundered quickly. It may have been the year of the Paris riots, but 1968 was also the year in which women workers at the Ford car plant in Dagenham won a groundbreaking case for equal pay. Unreconstructed trade union consciousness was alive and kicking. John Goldthorpe's important sociological study *The Affluent Worker in the Class Structure* (1969) debunked the idea that the 'embourgeoisement' of the working class was taking place. When car workers at the Vauxhall plant in Luton were asked to which class they belonged, 14 per cent claimed to be middle class, while 67 per cent assigned themselves to the working or lower classes.[54]

As much as it was inspired by 'new needs and satisfactions',[55] the British public in the 1960s was outraged by the rediscovery of poverty and deprivation in welfare state Britain. As the *May Day Manifesto 1968* put it, 'post-war capitalism, even at its most successful, creates and ratifies new kinds of poverty'.[56] Jeremy Sandford's *Cathy Come Home* (1967) followed the misfortunes of a young married working-class couple who get trapped in a downward spiral to homelessness.[57] The story caused a public controversy when it appeared initially as a television drama-documentary directed by Ken Loach, who was establishing himself as a major figure in British radical culture. Sandford's novelization shows the precariousness of working-class affluence and the close proximity of the poverty trap. Cathy feels she is 'living on the edge of an abyss' (p. 51). The slide into poverty begins with remarkable ease. When Cathy becomes pregnant and her husband Reg is injured at work, the loss of earning power means they can no longer afford to live in their 'posh' flat. The waiting list for council housing is formidable, and private landlords are reluctant to take children. The couple begin a series of fugitive steps down the accommodation and social ladder. Their residences comprise: living with Reg's mum; a slum tenement; a 'one-up, one-down' in a New Town; a caravan; a car; a derelict house; a makeshift tent; and a women's hostel. The 'burden' of children is finally lifted when they are taken into care.

By the late 1960s, the disenchantment of the labour movement with the Labour government reached a peak when new legislation to curb trade union rights was proposed. But the election of a Tory administration in 1970 committed to a tough new industrial relations policy led to a revival of conventional labour militancy. Two major strikes by the miners in 1972 and 1974 led to the government's eventual downfall and the election of another Labour term of office. Any plans this government had for socialist policies were scuppered by a massive hike in oil prices and a run on the pound. In 1976 the International Monetary Fund agreed to bail out the British economy on the condition that cuts in public spending were made. By the late 1970s, a party that only thirty years previously had created the welfare state was busy making cuts in education and public services. The public sector unions went on strike in protest, and the so-called 'winter of discontent' of 1978–9 whetted many voters' appetites for a new right-wing political ideology that promised to sweep away 'old-fashioned' socialism. In May 1979 Margaret Thatcher became Prime Minister, and the second 'remaking' of the British working class began in earnest.

The response of working-class novelists to the permissive agenda of the 1960s and 1970s suggests that the new causes and freedoms did not permeate very far into working-class culture and consciousness. While some writers explore the themes of social and sexual emancipation, the majority of texts also articulate the persistence of class boundaries and traditional forms of oppression and deprivation.

According to Philip Larkin, the sexual revolution 'began in 1963, between the end of the Chatterley ban/ And the Beatles' first LP'.[58] In the same year, the publication of Nell Dunn's series of vignettes *Up the Junction* seemed to confirm Larkin's wry pronouncement.[59] Dunn's sketches of the Battersea working class focused on the sexually promiscuous escapades of a group of young women. The frankness of their unselfconscious language is as shocking as their deeds: 'I like it rough. You get more feelin' out of it that way' (p. 16); 'Let's face it, you get a bit irritated seeing the same man all the time, it's boring' (p. 38). Though Rube, Sylvie and the others still live within their knowable urban community, their lifestyle is associated with the pleasures of 'shiny barbarism' and the glamour of Americanized mass culture. The stories are lathered with the romantic imagery of pop songs, living for today, speed, and American cars – one of the Battersea lads drives a 'beat-up Buick' (p. 32). The book appears superficially to be emblematic of the onset of the 'swinging sixties', but such an interpretation would be misleading. The sexual freedom of these Battersea women is not based upon the use of new forms of contraception such as the pill, and an appalling backstreet abortion signals the end of this 'butterfly' period:

> Finally the ambulance arrived. They took Rube away, but they left behind the baby, which had now grown cold. Later Sylvie took him, wrapped in the *Daily Mirror*, and threw him down the toilet. (p. 67)

The welfare state is also a conspicuous absence. In the book's ugliest scene, a single black mother has a miscarriage on the floor of a woman's hostel. The matron 'left the baby on the floor' (p. 46). Beneath the superficial glamour is the persistent grime of slum life: 'She is pretty in the dirty café' (p. 24); 'He combs his hair and I look at the early morning sun dappling the filth' (p. 36); 'The hard little balls of her ankles are black with dirt' (p. 37); 'Flecks of soot, large as pennies float down in the hot afternoon' (p. 40). The narrative is more rooted in the 1950s than the 1960s. The sketches even revive that prewar folk devil the 'talleyman', who relishes ripping off black customers: 'the further they get in debt the dirtier they become' (p. 104). The final sketch, 'The Children', is extremely bleak: 'Johnny throws a stick at a swan. "Me mum don't care what time I come in of a night. She's always watching telly"' (p. 110). Sex, booze, camaraderie and racism are consolations for alienated labour: 'We laugh, twenty-five women hunched over three long tables, packing cheap sweets for Christmas. Thick red fingers, swollen with the cold, flash from tray to box' (p. 25). Though the women have little control over their destiny, they do have a strong sense of community. Dunn's narrative technique of foregrounding untagged conversation creates the impression of an oral, unlettered culture; just the type of nostalgic, non-bourgeois collectivity celebrated by Richard Hoggart in *The Uses of Literacy*. Dunn also immerses her incongruous 'heiress from Chelsea' persona in this milieu and becomes an honorary working-class woman.

Dunn's second novel *Poor Cow* (1967) abandoned the ensemble approach for a more conventional focus on a single character, provocatively named Joy.[60] Joy is hardly a typical working-class woman; she is more like a *demi-mondaine*, living up to the stereotypical implications of her 'slum-white legs' (p. 9). She is married to a petty crook, wishes to be a 'mum and a glamour girl' (p. 130) and takes full advantage of the new sexual freedoms. She works as a bar-maid, model and good-time girl. Her conversion to promiscuity is completely guilt-free:

> Proper lusty I was getting – it used to be love but it's all lust now – it's so terrific with different blokes. Sometimes you fancy it all soft and other times you want them to fuck the life out of you. Well you can't get that from the same bloke can you. (p. 64)

Though this vernacular frankness has feminist potential, the confessional mode and the 'orthography of the uneducated' can also be cruel to Joy. Writing to her imprisoned husband, she waxes lyrical: 'I'm so raped up in Your love I never want to be unraped' (p. 50).

The theme of male sexual adventurism is pursued in Bill Naughton's *Alfie* (1966).[61] Alfie is a sex-obsessed, 1960s version of Arthur Seaton. He is single-mindedly dedicated to a libertine lifestyle in 'swinging' London. He keeps diary notes of his lovers' menstrual cycles, and he sees husbands as a joke. Unlike Arthur Seaton, Alfie is not defined by alienated labour (he occasionally does a driving job but is happy to sponge off his women) and the social range of his peccadilloes is considerable. One of his lovers is a physiotherapist, another is a successful businesswoman. To the modern reader, Alfie's appalling sexism is almost unreadable. He is not averse to beating up one of his

129

lovers (p. 108) and is generally a bully and a slob. His first-hand experience of an abortion chastens him but only temporarily: 'life is definitely loaded against the woman' (p. 148). He also suffers a serious illness, an attack of impotence, and a rejection by his most prestigious lover Ruby. But just as his amorous lifestyle begins to look threadbare, a sentimental ending to the novel reunites him with his 'Thursday night bint'. The most redeeming moments of Alfie's laddish Cockney narrative occur when class-consciousness surfaces, as in the description of Ruby's 'poncey' penthouse flat: 'handsome thick red carpet and mirrors you can see yourself in all over the place. In fact she's almost too good for me – with a set up like that' (p. 97). But only 'almost'.

The more challenging theme of working-class homosexuality is explored in David Storey's *Radcliffe* (1963).[62] This is a very rare theme in working-class writing. Clancy Sigal joked about the autoeroticism of miners in *Weekend in Dinlock* (1960).[63] On a trip down the mine (a conscious reworking of Orwell), the journalist Sigal points out to his favourite miner that 'the subterraneanism of homosexuality must be around somewhere' and gets the reply, 'Ah, lad, that is a funny thing indeed you're saying' (p. 29). Pat Barker's novel about the First World War *The Eye in the Door* (1993) features an affair between an officer and a gay infantry-man, and Jeanette Winterson's *Oranges are not the only fruit* (1985) explores the even rarer literary phenomenon of working-class lesbianism. But in general the theme has been very submerged in working-class fiction. In *Radcliffe*, gay sexuality is repressed and destructive.

Radcliffe follows the intense, tortured and ultimately fatal relationship between Leonard Radcliffe, son of a declining gentry family, and Vic Tolson, a manual worker. Their attraction finds its purest expression in violence, intimidation and debasement. Tolson's viciousness includes putting shit in one of Radcliffe's sandwiches, striking him with a hammer, and subjecting him to oral rape. Radcliffe finally retaliates by killing Tolson with his own claw hammer – this object figures as a malevolent phallic symbol throughout the novel. Radcliffe goes mad and dies in an asylum. Storey's characteristic tone of despair and existential emptiness is intensified by the Gothic setting and mood. Radcliffe lives in 'The Place', an ancestral mansion surrounded by new council housing. The imminent demise of his line is anticipated in his grotesque nightmares, in which titanic armies sweep over his body. His doomed affair with Tolson is therefore an act of monstrous class betrayal. The relationship can be read as a metaphor for the postwar decline of the traditional legitimacy of the aristocracy and their most potent symbol, the country house. Radcliffe and Tolson are Gothic *doppelgängers*: 'Vic was my body, and I was his soul' (p. 342). On the other hand, the novel could powerfully reinforce a stereotypical view of homosexuality as unstable and deviant.

Returning to more conventional territory, Storey's novel *Pasmore* (1972) traces the development of the postwar scholarship boy into the post-Robbins era of university expansion.[64] Colin Pasmore, a London University history lecturer from a working-class background, embarks on a dispirited affair as an escape from his stalled marriage. Objectively, Colin seems a shining example of postwar social mobility: he has a secure profession, a middle-class wife (the daughter of a doctor), a house and a family. But despite writing a book on nineteenth-century evangelicalism, his own life feels purposeless. He makes a futile and damaging attempt to re-establish contact with his father, a miner. All the familiar landmarks in his life recede until his life revolves around a small rented room. The narrative is also stripped bare of any embellishments, being limited mostly to laconic dialogue and prosaic actions. The novel is a powerful evocation of a post-1960s cultural malaise. Colin is worse off than his 'Angry' predecessors, as he lacks their vitality. When he returns to his family after his 'journey', he still 'dreamed of the pit and the blackness' (p. 171). It is a measure of how far working-class fiction has come from the prewar era that this fear has little to do with the material facts of poverty or losing one's job, though it may have much to do with losing contact with one's roots. In *Saville* (1976), Storey turned away from the contemporary scene altogether in order to recreate the world of his childhood.

Storey's fiction draws on social contradictions that were only too apparent in the Britain of the late 1960s. Though the Labour government had set itself against the élitism of grammar schools and put its weight behind the more egalitarian comprehensive system of secondary education, private education was left untouched and continued to supply most graduates to prestige universities. There was still a high demand in the economy for traditional unskilled labour (the coal industry, for example, employed over 300,000 miners in the 1970s), and the majority of children from working-class families remained excluded from higher education.[65]

The stories of Barry Hines, who began his literary career in the late 1960s, explore the lack of real opportunity for working-class youth in modern Britain. Though Hines, like Storey, is a beneficiary of postwar reforms (he was born in a Yorkshire mining village, went to grammar school, became a teacher and finally a full-time writer of novels, TV scripts and screenplays), his fiction deals with the experience of the majority who were not so fortunate or gifted as himself. His most famous novel is *A Kestrel for a Knave* (1968), usually known by its film version title *Kes*.[66] The story is set on a postwar housing estate on the outskirts of a south Yorkshire mining town (Barnsley), and focuses on the relationship between an underachieving school-leaver, Billy Casper, and a kestrel he has captured and trained. Billy is attracted to the bird as compensation for the deprivations in his family life. He has a feckless single mother (an echo of Helen in *A Taste of Honey*) and a brutal older half-brother Jud who regularly batters him (at one level the novel is about child abuse and the absence of social services). The only impact made by affluence on Billy's life has been completely negative. His mother and Jud neglect him for their own pleasures, which could be read as confirmation of Richard Hoggart's fear that the working class was being dehumanized by consumerism and mass society. Billy is forced to take on a paper-round to try to earn some spare money. He also resorts to stealing, though the novel makes clear that petty criminality is a response to his environment. The story begins with a 'proletarian dawn' scene that emphasizes deprivation: Billy shares a bed in a curtainless bedroom with Jud, who wakes Billy up deliberately when he goes off to the early shift at the pit; there is no food for breakfast, and Billy is sent to the grocer's to ask for more credit; his mother means well but cannot show affection and clearly uses Billy as an errand-boy to make up for her deficiencies (the scene revisits the old problem of 'maternal deprivation'). Billy has no Aunt Ada to turn to; there is no trace of the nostalgic, older working-class community in the novel. It is as if a Hegelian break in

132

history has taken place, leaving Billy stranded on the bleak fringes of affluence. Though Jud is a miner, the culture of traditional labour and class solidarity is absent from the story. In a careers interview he is summoned to on his last day at school, Billy is horrified at the prospect of going down the mine (indeed, the brutal Jud has more in common with Ned Narkey than the heroic miner of left-wing mythology). Billy is a waif and a fugitive, endlessly ducking, dodging and raiding.

The only sanctuary for Billy is his relationship with the kestrel, in which he can find both an opportunity for creativity, and an emotional release. He discovers the bird while walking in nearby woods, and senses unconsciously that he and the kestrel have something in common. The novel draws on the pastoral tradition by structurally opposing urban corruption and alienation to a redemptive nature. But this polarization of nature and culture is only superficial: Billy steals the bird and keeps it locked up at the bottom of his garden (this is a grave error, as it puts the bird within the orbit of Jud, who kills it as punishment for Billy spending a betting tab that would have netted Jud enough winnings to 'have had a week off work', p. 149); and his only friend emerges from the heart of the ideological state apparatus in the form of his English teacher Mr Farthing, who moves benignly between his and Billy's worlds. Mr Farthing manages skilfully to coax Billy into telling his classmates about training the kestrel, and later the same day hears a more intimate account from Billy in the garden shed. This is the novel's most poignant scene, as Billy is beginning to find a voice, express himself and show his sensitive side. While these qualities almost transform Billy into a noble savage (Jud lampoons him as a 'wild man' (p. 36)), the social gulf between Billy and Mr Farthing is too great to be suspended for very long. Tension soon resurfaces when Mr Farthing unwittingly reclaims linguistic authority in the conversation, showing his greater mastery of metaphor and allusion. Discussing the bird's silent method of flight, Billy says 'you feel like poking your ears to make 'em pop because it goes that quiet'. Mr Farthing comes up with the image of a 'pocket of silence' and then quotes a poem by Lawrence, at which point Billy clams shut (pp. 118–19).

For all his liberal-humanist compassion, Mr Farthing's function as an English teacher is to induct Billy into the linguistic and ideological conventions of standard English. While on his paper round, Billy steals a moment to read comics and is shown as a primitive, infantile reader (p. 15). Billy's illiteracy and his exclusion from the normative culture of standard English is shown further in his attempt to acquire a book on hawks. He is refused access to the public library as he is not a member. The exchange with this particular gatekeeper of culture is both amusing and anguished (pp. 32–3). Billy cannot comprehend bureaucracy and resorts to stealing from a book-shop. Billy's poor literacy is shown most movingly in the 'Tall Story' he writes during his English lesson. The brief sketch of a happy family life is like a miniaturized negative image of the whole novel: Billy wakes up 'in a big hous up moor edge' to 'backen and egg and bred and butter', and to find Jud 'goind the army' and his father coming home to take him to the cinema (p. 73). The fantasy is both social and Freudian. The 'family romance' of Billy's 'tall story' reaches its conclusion at the end of the novel, when he breaks into a disused cinema in a state of shocked grief at the death of the bird. Billy's thoughts return to a primal scene: the moment when his father left the family after finding Billy's mother and 'Uncle Mick' 'staring and flushed' on the sofa. The discovery happened after he and Billy had been at this cinema, an experience Billy remembers as womb-like: 'the warmth there...Billy between his dad and another man, tiny between them...a bag of sweets between his thighs' (pp. 118–19). The real emptiness in Billy's life is the absent father, and Jud is a travesty of a substitute. Billy's final fantasy is of himself and Kes hunting Jud down like a wild animal. This scene is also the culmination of the narrative treatment of the primeval relation-ship Billy has with food. Any treat is usually followed by a terrible punishment, as if a fundamental insecurity about pleasurable consumption underlies working-class life. Billy spends Jud's bet on fish and chips, a 'portable feast' (p. 125), while a free 'strip of beef' goes to the hawk.

If the revelation about the absent father seems sentimental, *Kes* shows in stark terms the re-emergence in the 1960s of an affluent 'underclass' of the socially disadvantaged and dysfunc-tional. The narrative structure emphasizes Billy's precarious position on the edge of a Fall into manhood. The action is restricted to Billy's last significant day at school (represented by the careers interview) and the story of the discovery and training of the hawk is told in flashback. However, the novel is not unremittingly bleak, as Billy's peregrinations are littered with comic jinks and antics as he constantly brushes up against authority. His headmaster Mr Gryce sees Billy's generation as the cocky, disrespectful ingrates of postwar reforms and social permissiveness, 'when every boy quotes his rights' (p. 56). Gryce makes a direct reference to the 'affluence' thesis: 'But what do I get from you lot? A honk from a greasy youth behind the wheel of some big, second-hand car... You're just fodder for the mass media!' But his denunciation of democratic progress is undermined by the school's arbitrarily brutal regime. The novel's use of sudden shifts from high comedy to arbitrary violence is shown most effectively in the PE scene. Mr Sugden's absurd pretensions on the football field turn into a sadistic vendetta against Billy off the field. He punishes Billy's poor football skills by forcing him to take a prolonged cold shower: 'he resembled an old print of a child hurrying towards the final solution' (p. 105).

Kes was published in the legendary year of 1968. While continental revolution seems a million miles away from Billy's tragedy, the novel has the radical aim of exposing the failure of egalitarian ideology in general, and the educational system in particular. By the mid-1970s, the working class had asserted their traditional industrial muscle, and Hines responded to this resurgence with the television drama *The Price of Coal* (broadcast in 1977).[67] Like the film version of *Kes* (1970), this was another collaboration with Ken Loach. The novelization followed in 1979, which shows that for some working-class writers the McLuhanite revolution was a reality, and electronic media were taking priority over the printed book.

In *The Price of Coal*, Hines formally divides his penchant for tragicomic effects into two ensemble stories about the same Yorkshire pit. The first, comic piece 'Meet the People' shows the pit preparing for a royal visit; the second, tragic story 'Back to Reality' revisits the familiar convention of the mining disaster. In 'Meet the People' most of the humour comes from the absurdities of 'tarting the pit up' (p. 8) for the royal gaze, including such moments as the laying of turf over a slagheap, the painting of a brick holding up a sash window, the barring of miners in overalls (their normal work-clothes) from the main office block (after the disaster, a distraught miner leaves a symbolic smudge on the wall of the manager's room, p. 115), searching a lunchbox for explosives, and observing the sycophantic paranoia of the local management. Some of the miners' quips are reminiscent of Tressell's workers: 'One of the men asked if He was looking for a job. Another replied that He could have his' (p. 8). The ironic use of 'He' throughout the story is an effect that only the literary version can create.

Hines uses 'Back to Reality' to attack the vulturous insensitivity of the television and newspaper press. One of the wives of a trapped miner berates a reporter: 'You weren't willing to write sob stories about us in the '72 and '74 strikes were you?' (p. 150). To prevent the disaster scenes becoming sentimental, Hines counterpoints the scenes at the pit with the home life of Syd, one of the most sceptical of the miners. Syd's family is also full of underlying tensions. When Syd is badly injured in the explosion, his son Tony, also a miner, still feels his mother's emotional reserve (p. 119).

In addition to the revival of industrial militancy, the 1970s saw other major tensions emerge and resurface. The 'Troubles' returned to Northern Ireland, leading to the deployment of British troops and the reconstruction of the IRA. A revival of Scottish nationalism led to an unsuccessful attempt by the Labour government to introduce devolution for Scotland. There was also a significant resurgence of organized racism in the form of the National Front, who blamed rising unemployment on black immigration, and who met with fierce resistance from anti-racist campaigners. These fractures in the postwar settlement both obstructed and aided the development of class-consciousness. The decolonization of British culture became a potent new force for literature, producing a new generation of Scottish and black British writers. While Scottish writers are looked at in the next chapter, mention can be made here of the innovative fiction of Buchi Emecheta, a Nigerian-born writer whose early novels lay bare the welfare state in ways no 'indigenous' working-class writer had done.

The *May Day Manifesto 1968* is adamant that immigrant blacks are the new working class of Britain:

> In Britain, the immigrant poor are living out, more sharply than any other identifiable group, the whole range of general social

136

deprivation: in the decaying centres of cities, in overcrowded schools, in bad housing, in the low wages of unskilled work. Yet this experience, which is in fact a concentration of a general problem of the society, and which is imposed, in similar ways, on other groups of the unsettled poor, is displaced, internally and externally, by the false consciousness of skin colour. (p. 167)

This summary describes the essential milieu of Emecheta's fiction, with the notable exception of the further oppressive and distorting influence of patriarchy. Emecheta's heroine Adah has to cope with the humiliations of proletarianization and sexual inequality.

Second-Class Citizen (1974) is based on Emecheta's own experiences.[68] The novel follows the progress of Adah, a Nigerian Ibo librarian, who emigrates to London in the early 1960s to join her husband, an accountancy student for whose training she is paying. In Lagos, Adah led a bourgeois lifestyle and had a servant. When she arrives in London, her status suffers two immediate blows: her husband Francis treats her like a maid, and their accommodation is very poor. Adah has two lifelines: her career and her feminism. Although she feels that all blacks are treated like second-class citizens, her job in a public library is a source of self-esteem and real material rewards, such as holiday pay. One of the glaring contradictions in Adah's situation is that she wants to embrace a westernized lifestyle but is 'treated like a native girl' (p. 75) by many aspects of the social system. The novel illuminates the differing roles allotted to women by the African and western cultures she inhabits. Francis expects her to work to support his studies, and is uncomfortable with being in the role of the sole breadwinner while Adah has her children. These values are an ironic reversal of the feminist argument for women's work, which is based on the idea of emancipating women from a dependency on men's income. As her marriage disintegrates, Adah realizes that her only escape route is to give up her job and rely on 'Assistance' (social security) which gives her the bare independence she needs to be able to leave Francis. Yet this is the same welfare state which cannot provide decent housing for immigrants. Adah also begins to write. She is conscious of being a pioneer. Though not the first African woman writer, she is the first immigrant woman novelist in Britain. Though Francis burns her first manuscript, and though the material obstacles in the way of becoming a writer are formidable, Adah discovers her literary voice.

The brief clues we are given about the content of Adah's first novel make it sound suspiciously like *In the Ditch* (1972), Emecheta's first novel but a chronological sequel to *Second-Class Citizen*.[69] *In the Ditch* is about Adah's life as a single mother with five children on a 'sink' housing estate which is due for demolition. Despite its dilapidated state, the estate provides a sense of community for Adah. She is inexorably forced into more and more reliance on the welfare system, until it is impossible for her to carry on with her job at a museum:

> Her socialization was complete. She, a coloured woman with five kids and no husband, no job, and no future, just like most of her neighbours – shiftless, rootless, with no rightful claim to anything. Just cut off...That closed her middle-class chapter. From then on she belonged to no class at all. She couldn't claim to be working-class, because the working class had a code for daily living. (p. 42)

The novel ends with Adah in a state of social transition, seeking new definitions of the working class which will encompass her experience. As a dweller in a near-slum environment, and a member of the new 'lumpen' underclass, she is a harbinger of significant social and literary developments in the 1980s and 1990s.

4

Post-industrial Fictions

The election of the Tory government in 1979 marked a sea-change in postwar British history, and resulted in a drastic reshaping of the British working class. The new Tory administration under the premier Margaret Thatcher was committed to policies of monetarism, deregulation, privatization of nationalized industries and services, the crushing of trade union power, and virulent anti-Communism. This was a 'New Right' philosophy which saw the 'market' and 'market forces' as sacrosanct, and which believed that the role of the state was to unfetter *laissez-faire* capitalism from the socialist restrictions of workers' rights and state planning. Adam Smith's 'invisible hand' (under its new soubriquet 'trickle down') would redistribute wealth from the haves to the have-nots. The Tories set about undoing not just the reforms of the postwar years but the whole socialist heritage of the last 150 years. The British working class was to be returned to a condition in which there was no right to job security, no right to organized self-protection, and in which the discourse of social relations was ruthlessly commodified: the 'cash nexus' became the primary signifier of the value and quality of the social fabric. 'Thatcherism', as this ideology has come to be known, based its appeal on the mentality of the entrepreneur, the owner of a small business, and the self-employed artisan and skilled working-class sector (ironically, the latter were often the backbone of radical movements in the last century). Thatcherism managed skilfully to divide the working class: it rewarded its supporters with lower direct taxation and the right to buy their council home at huge discounts, and gave access to quick profits from the purchase of shares in privatized industries; at the same time, Thatcherism demonized any organized resistance to its policies as the 'enemy within', and used the power of the state to punish its traditional class enemies.

The Thatcher government also had historical accident on its side. For the first few years of its office, there was something of a popular backlash against its cuts in public spending and bullish Cold War rhetoric. In 1981 a series of youth riots swept through Britain's inner cities, and in the same year the miners forced a government U-turn on a programme of pit closures. Public opinion polls showed the Prime Minister was deeply unpopular. But in early 1982 Argentina invaded the Falkland Islands. Parliament, the church and the press responded with jingoistic enthusiasm to the ensuing war, and the Tories' political fortunes were dramatically revived – they went on to win general elections in 1983, 1987 and 1992. With a renewed mandate and a huge majority in Parliament, the government embarked on a revanchist strategy of teaching lessons to its opponents and settling old scores. The 'old' staple industries of shipbuilding, steel and coal were the first in line for attack. The crucial confrontation was, predictably, with the miners. The great strike of 1984–5 marked the last real chance for organized British labour to successfully oppose the philosophy and destructive social consequences of *laissez-faire* market forces. Once the miners' strike was lost, the coal industry was massively run down and the rump of remaining pits were eventually privatized. The dockers, steelworkers, teachers, nurses, car-workers, anti-nuclear campaigners, New Age travellers attempting to get to Stonehenge – all met the same intransigent response from a government who brandished the weapons of high levels of unemployment, anti-trade union legislation, Tory control of the press, Cold War hysteria, and the 'political' mobilization of the police. Over the same period the Labour Party inexorably moved to the right, and abandoned any pretence of reversing the majority of core Tory reforms should it come to power. The collapse of the Soviet Union and the Communist regimes in Eastern Europe in the late 1980s bolstered the notion that capitalism was here to stay for the foreseeable future, and enhanced the fashionable intellectual premise that *fin de siècle* western society was witnessing the 'end of history'.

By the late 1990s, a colossal transfer of economic power from the public to the private sector has taken place in Britain. Traditional working-class communities organized around large-scale manufacturing industry have all but disappeared from British social life; the social imagery of such communities has become nostalgic, while the 'affluent' working class has been heralded by conservative politicians as evidence of a new 'classlessness'. The replacement of productive labour by 'service' and leisure industries, the trend towards low-paid, insecure and non-unionized labour, massive long-term unemployment, reliance on welfare benefits – this erosion of working-class autonomy, the 'feminization' of the economy, are processes that have accelerated the fragmentation of class-consciousness. While it is fallacious to claim that the working class has disappeared, it is true that its traditional economic base, and the class-conscious protective power that was built upon it, have been largely obliterated. As Jeremy Seabrook has noted, the most authentic working-class communities are now to be found in the Third World or in the ranks of 'techno-peasants'.[1] The use of class as a primary signifier in official discourses has waned in favour of a return to an older vocabulary of rich and poor. This emphasis on poverty rather than capitalist exploitation has had the ideological effect of submerging working-class identity (or significant fractions of it) into a heterogeneous, proletarianized underclass of alienated social groups, defined by their economic unproductiveness and an inability to participate fully in society: families living on social security, single parents, the disabled, the homeless, delinquents, drug addicts. Significantly, the deepest literary exploration of this new slum life has been conducted by women working-class writers.

While many of the Utopian hopes of the 1960s have floundered, and there has been a reproletarianization of large sections of society, the pluralization of radical movements has continued to produce new and revitalized forms of political and cultural protest, and new voices of disaffection. Some examples that can be cited include: Rock Against Racism and 'rap' music; the gay 'outing' campaign; Women Against Violence Against Women; the amendment of CND's constitution to allow it to challenge non-nuclear warfare (effective in the Gulf War of 1990–91); the anti-poll tax campaign; Live Aid; and various forms of environmental and 'green' direct action to oppose new roads, pollution, and the importing of nuclear waste into Britain for reprocessing. Micro- and lifestyle politics have developed from the 1960s and 1970s dictum that 'the personal is political', though the emergence of Aids has dealt a blow to the association of personal emancipation with promiscuity. In the universities, poststructuralist theories entered the academic mainstream, and challenged the validity of western liberalism's 'essentialist' myths of the free individual. In this new paradigm, the human subject is a product of language, and language is indelibly marked by social conflict and contradiction. While this position allows for the continuation of the discourse of class as a factor in the interpretation of cultural texts, it does not give any particular role or value to working-class cultural production, as all texts have class conflict inscribed in them. Postmodernist theories have also marginalized the importance of class. Working-class traditions have been reduced to redundant metanarratives or textual constructions. There is a danger that postmodernism gives intellectual legitimacy to 'late' capitalist exploitation, instead of critiquing its destructive qualities.[2] At the opposite pole to these high-intellectual theories is the continuing work of the Federation of Worker Writers and Community Presses, though its small-scale publishing base cannot sustain long works of fiction.[3]

The social development of the working class in the 1980s and 1990s has resembled a return to the insecure 1930s, but without a Popular Front to rally around. It is perhaps no surprise to find renewed tones of bleakness, futility, nostalgia and defensiveness in working-class fiction of this period. David Storey, for example, looked back to the working-class community of his childhood for inspiration, though this did not include an engagement with the broader dimensions or key moments of working-class history.[4] Barry Hines's *Looks and Smiles* (1981) took the temperature of the early years of Thatcherism by revisiting the social territory of *Love on the Dole*.[5] The novel can also be read as a transplanting of *Kes* into the 1980s, where the problem for the school-leaving generation is no longer 'affluent' dehumanization but the precise opposite: economic blight. Though the hero Mick Walsh has a supportive family and wants a respectable trade, his future comprises a life on the dole or a succession of dead-end, underpaid jobs. He dabbles in petty crime while under the influence of his friend Alan, who has joined the army. Alan's tales of a swaggering military life are music to Mick's ears, though Hines makes clear that such a move will brutalize him.

Mick is also humiliated by the fact that his girlfriend Karen has a job in a shoeshop. While Mick suffers from the traditional emasculation of the male worker, Karen personifies the emergence of a 'feminized' workforce. She represents the national shift away from manufacturing and primary production to retail and service industries, which has brought with it a corresponding erosion in security, status and high wages (deemed 'flexibility' in the jargon of the 'free' market). The difference between the significance of Karen and her fictional predecessor Sally Hardcastle, who also stays in work while the men in her life are thrown onto the dole, is that the new ideology of global capitalism preaches that there will never be a return to traditional forms of job security premised on a patriarchal division of labour: the era of the self-improving respectable artisan is finally over. Whether or not this process has been exaggerated, its impact can be seen in the burgeoning of women's working-class fiction in the 1980s and 1990s.

This intervention reflects both the new economic and social realities and the analysis of these changes by feminist writers and scholars. A major revaluation of the class position of working-class women took place in the mid-1980s in two books: Beatrix Campbell's *Wigan Pier Revisited* (1984) and Carolyn Steedman's *Landscape for a Good Woman* (1986).[6] As the title of Campbell's book indicates, she undertook to rewrite the Orwellian quest for 'northern' working-class respectability in feminist and feminocentric terms. For Campbell, working-class women have always been the true repositories of the proletarian condition, and the regressive feminization of the postmodern economy only makes this fact more apparent:

> Most men grieve for the loss of their skills, but don't notice the deskilling of women in their communities through marriage to themselves and then motherhood. When a secretary, lathe operator or cook turns to part-time cleaning in the prime of her life, isn't that as tragic as an engineer reduced to lavatory cleaning in his mid-forties? (p. 117)

143

Where Orwell attacked socialists for their dogma and highbrow self-righteousness, Campbell wants the socialist tradition to face up to its responsibilities and break away from the 'epic nostalgia' of masculine labour:

> many of those good old values rested on the weary labours of women...are not the clerks and cleaners and caterers of the health service the contemporary heroines of the workers' movement?...The changing profile of work and workers demands a leap of the political imagination, the making of alliances between producers and consumers which no amount of epic nostalgia can conceive. (p. 225)

Carolyn Steedman specifically attacks the postwar Left's blindness to issues of gender. She notes that the 'scholarship boy' myth may have performed a useful role as a critique of social mobility, but it denied her a subjectivity as a 'scholarship girl'. Her generation of university-educated women from working-class backgrounds 'could not be heroines of the conventional narratives of escape' (p. 15). Both Campbell and Steedman target Jeremy Seabrook's work as the prime example of 'epic nostalgia'. Seabrook's argument that the latest remaking of the working class has completed its dehumanizing bondage to materialism and individualism is berated by Campbell for a 'gushing pessimism' which ignores 'new forces within popular politics and new forms of political struggle' (p. 225). Seabrook's answer to this charge is worth quoting at some length as it suggests that such feminist critiques of the 'good old values' can provide intellectual respectability for the latest phase of capitalist exploitation:

> The differential suffering which capitalism inflicts on men and women needs to be acknowledged and resisted in all its forms; but it is doubtful whether a competitive comparison of levels and kinds of torment does much more than profit capitalism, like all divisions between victims. It would be debilitating if the rich offering of feminism were to be used to write off a past that saw desperate struggle and valuable achievement, whilst at the same time it remained content to analyse and attack patterns of exploitation as though these were immutable and unchanging, so that we become blind to newer forms and patterns of exploitation and forms which an evolving capitalism inflicts upon women.[7]

There is a consensus in this debate that new social configurations and relations of gender have appeared in response to a revitalized *laissez-faire*. The main disagreement revolves around the type, degree and inclusiveness of the emancipatory potential of these changes. This tension informs most recent working-class fiction, particularly that by women writers.

Pat Barker's first novel *Union Street* (1984) broke new ground by re-inventing old social territory.[8] Though the title invokes community life, the portrayal of a contemporary north-eastern working-class street focuses on the disintegration of women's lives in a social milieu that is deeply regressive. In order to explore the interiority of women's experience, the novel is divided into seven sections. Each segment (with one important exception) is devoted to the story of a female resident of the street. Paradoxically, this structure, which enables a pioneering psychological and emotional representation of different generations of working-class women, also stresses their isolation from each other and the fast-disappearing community. There is no common core to this ensemble experience other than the shared stoicism and often violent sufferings of gender itself. Unlike *Up the Junction*, which *Union Street* superficially resembles, there is no thread of contemporary cultural reference linking the stories. What Raymond Williams calls the 'general way of life' is almost entirely absent, as each story rarely strays beyond the consciousness of its benighted and domesticated heroine. Hence it is difficult to date the action precisely, or to locate the influence of regionalism on the lives of these women. Of course, these absences could be the whole point of Barker's understated approach. Not only have working-class women in this region suffered exceptionally from lack of opportunities to work outside the home (unlike the mill towns of Lancashire and Yorkshire, for instance). There is also a singular lack of an indigenous literary tradition for the modern working-class woman writer to invoke and work within. It is not really so surprising, therefore, to find a strong reliance on D. H. Lawrence both for some of the plot situations ('Muriel Scaife', for example, echoes Lawrence's 'Odour of Chrysanthemums'; the sex scene in the underpass in 'Joanne Wilson' resembles a scene between Gerald Crich and Gudrun in *Women in Love*) and in interior monologue passages. But Barker adapts Lawrence to her own feminist agenda. Barker's main aim is to show that working-class femininity, as constructed by those largely absent contexts of capitalist and patriarchal power, is a process of almost unremitting gloom and entrapment. It is this separate sphere of essentially feminine ordeal and trial which mediates elements of class-consciousness.

The most horrific illustration of this aesthetic comes in the opening story of the youngest character, Kelly Brown. This story is an antitype of a *Bildungsroman*, in that the painful *rites de passage* of breaking away from the family and becoming independent are grossly perverted into a fable of male sexual violence. The story's indebtedness to 1970s feminist analyses of the oppressiveness of conventional notions of femininity is apparent. After being raped by a man who is symbolically a substitute for her absent father, Kelly embarks on a series of self-punishing renunciations of her feminine identity: she indulges in uglification, foul language, destruction of public and private property, and excremental pleasure. By debasing herself in this way, she repudiates her constructed identity and reclaims her body in its 'wild' and 'savage' state (p. 54). Moreover, she attains an unprecedented degree of class-consciousness: a key scene involves her breaking into a 'smug' middle-class home and vandalizing the bedroom, a 'temple to femininity' (p. 53). The story also represents Kelly's transformation as mythic, as her animalistic talents take on the trappings of an urban She-Devil. Locked into a repetition compulsion of haunting the scene of her violation, Kelly awaits new male predators, only to humiliate them with her castrating gaze: 'She knew she had the power' (p. 49). But the story has an optimistic ending, with the possibility that Kelly will return to social life. The mechanism for this resolution is both sentimentally feminist and quasi-mystical. In a local park, Kelly meets the ageing Alice Bell, whose story concludes *Union Street*. They meet under a tree which represents symbolically the tree of life, 'withered and unwithering' (p. 265), and the meeting effects a mythical circle of female bonding: Kelly is the virgin to Alice's crone.

The preponderance of female bodily 'essences' in the stories also creates the strong impression that these working-class women inhabit an elemental world of feminine experience, though there is always a danger that such an approach reinforces biological reductionism. The inability of these women to control their own bodies (except in Kelly's demonic form), coupled with the social backwardness of the setting (it is still difficult to get an abortion in Union Street), positions the narrative uncomfortably on the edge of a form of cultural voyeurism.

In line with most of the other women's fiction studied below, male characters and masculinity are, in Seabrook's words, 'written off'. The only sympathetic men in the novel are sexually unthreatening or inert (Muriel Scaife's dying husband, Lisa Goddard's stunted would-be lover), or are ready to undergo a feminist conversion, as in the elderly George Harrison's specular confrontation with a vagina (to mark his special status, he is given a story of his own). A miners' strike is mentioned but it has no relevance for the women. So, if the overall point is that history as conventionally defined has passed these women by, the essential critical question is the extent to which the novel colludes with that disempowerment.

In her next two novels *Blow Your House Down* (1984) and *The Century's Daughter* (1986) Barker took different fictional routes to the illumination of the contemporary plight of working-class women in the north of England.[9] The former novel is a thinly fictionalized account of the 'Yorkshire Ripper' murders of the 1970s, seen through the eyes of a number of women, some of whom become victims. While Barker tries to deglamorize the folk-devil mystique that has accrued to the psychopathic serial killer figure in popular culture, the presence of this lurking menace inevitably gives a sensationalist charge to the narrative. The latter novel feminizes the proletarian 'epic' by revisiting twentieth-century working-class history through the life of Liza Jarrett, who is born at the very beginning of the century. The result of this shift of gender is that private rather than public history is foregrounded. Liza outlives most of her peers only to see the community she has lived in for decades bulldozed, and to suffer the final humiliation of being mugged. Her present-day predicament interconnects with that of another significant 'feminized' experience, the tribulations of a gay community worker Stephen. His rapprochement with Liza is an affirmation of the male sexual alternative to the destructive forces of heterosexual masculinity. A growing interest in male bonding has informed Barker's highly acclaimed trilogy of novels about the First World War, *Regeneration* (1991), *The Eye in the Door* (1993) and *The Ghost Road* (1995).

An eccentric matriarchal culture is the subject of Jeanette Winterson's first novel *Oranges are not the only fruit* (1985).[10] The book is a comic, postmodern, feminist reworking of the autobiographical *Bildungsroman*. It is also a bittersweet revenge on the Lancashire evangelical family who adopted and raised Winterson. The heroine 'Jeanette' is an incredibly rare literary phenomenon: a lesbian, working-class scholarship girl. She is an ironic travesty of her intended destiny: instead of becoming a mature member of the religious elect and élite, she becomes (in her mother's terms) an ungodly paragon of sin. This development is not a conscious act of sexual politics on the heroine's part. It is only subsequently, with a university education, that the logical connection between her upbringing's marginalization of men, the imposed disgust of sexuality (which produces many a comic scene, such as the singing of hymns on a Sunday to drown out the sound of next door's 'fornication'), and the erotics of female intimacy becomes clear to 'Jeanette'. She seems, in fact, to have adversity on her side, as she inherits a sense of mission and matrilineal determination:

> I had no quarrel with men. At that time there was no reason that I should. The women in our church were strong and organized. If you want to talk in terms of power I had enough to keep Mussolini happy. (p. 124)

As the playful reference to fascism indicates, the novel explores the relations between power, freedom, sexuality and narrative. The self-consciousness of this interplay shows Winterson's awareness of postmodernist ideas about the discursiveness of reality, history as a set of competing narratives, and the constructedness of subjectivity. The novel places the naturalistic *Bildungsroman* inside the anachronistic structure of the books of the Old Testament, interleaves the story of 'Jeanette' with parodies of romances and fairy-tales, and halts the narrative altogether for a digression on storytelling (see 'Deuteronomy'). Any story, Winterson implies, is inevitably a record of barbarity, whether in the guise of biblical law or aestheticized romances. But storytelling is also a sphere of fantasy, alternative realities, and the transformation of the self. Winterson's juxtaposition of the naturalistic and the fantastic is a modest venture into 'magical realism' (the excellent 1989 BBC adaptation of the novel was deficient in this respect, as it omitted the fantasy passages).

Oranges are not the only fruit is one of the most original and sophisticated contributions to the tradition of working-class fiction. Its distance from the pieties, earnestness and unremitting gloom of many a naturalistic working-class *Bildungsroman* is both admirable and healthy. On the other hand, the exclusion from the narrative of patriarchal influence leads to the diminution of any discourse of class in the novel. Jeanette's father appears fleetingly, usually in a groggy condition after having slept off his shift-work. His insignificance, and the novel's focus on (frequently eccentric) religious culture and repressed sexuality, means that the socio-economic factors in the life of this Pennine community are a vague backdrop, and 'Jeanette' remains conspicuously 'untypical'. Her later novels *The Passion* (1987) and *Sexing the Cherry* (1989) move further away from both class-consciousness and naturalism into the fertile regions of historiographical metafiction and 'magical realism'.

Livi Michael's fiction, on the other hand, remains firmly rooted in the tradition of proletarian naturalism. Indeed, her trilogy of novels about the lives of women in the contemporary 'nether' regions can be seen as a revival of 'slum' fiction. But *Under a Thin Moon* (1992), *Their Angel Reach* (1994) and *All the Dark Air* (1997) also show the influence of Pat Barker's evocation of a claustrophobic and elemental women's culture.[11] There are few traces of the naïve optimism of *Up the Junction* or the early stages of *Cathy Come Home*; nor is there a sense that women's social problems can have political solutions. The profound pessimism of the novels is a testament to the bleakness of the social landscape in a Britain of post-industrial decline.

The first two novels of the trilogy develop Barker's technique of segmenting the narrative into brief lives of several women from the same community. In *Under a Thin Moon* the bulk of the narrative is a juxtaposition of two 'typical' female characters from a northern council estate: Wanda, a single parent, and Laurie, a student. The constraints of Wanda's life are summed up in the novel's opening image: her futile attempt to remove the residue of scum from around her bath. Although George Orwell cautioned against founding proletarian literature solely on the fact that the kitchen sink smells, Michael's fiction aims at resensitizing the reader to the squalid texture of everyday life in Britain's underclass. To unsettle the complacency of the public's attitude to poverty, she shows the ease with which standards of respectability can crumble in such an environment. Wanda works in the sub-economy as a barmaid, succumbs to casual prostitution, batters her child, and finally commits suicide. Laurie also finds solace in 'feminine' forms of crime, in her case frequent bouts of shoplifting. She seems to gain little from studying in higher education, and some barbed humour is directed at literary theory (p. 142), though this experience is only very sketchily realized. The only note of hope seems to come in the novel's closing scene, where Wanda's daughter Coral, some years later, turns to writing as a means to understand and hopefully transcend her mother's death.

Their Angel Reach is more concerned with the perpetual threat of male violence against women, and the ways in which this threat has become an appalling yet ambiguous factor in the female psyche. The most disturbing story is 'Living with Vampires', in which Lizzie, an unemployed artist and victim of a sadistic prolonged rape, finds she is excited by hard-core pornography. She is attracted by the fantasy element in pornography, that it 'made sex easy' and free of responsibility (pp. 323–4). But she is also aware that pornography glorifies classic images of female subordination. She eventually exorcises her anxieties by painting a surreal portrait of a vampire, the potent Gothic symbol of the male exploitation of women.

In 'Lower than Angels', the overweight heroine Janice is also turned on by sado-masochistic sex, which is far preferable to 'jerky, unsynchronized humping' (p. 231). An alternative rejection of patriarchal norms takes place in 'Not Even the Rain'. Karen, a housewife, feels her 'seventeen years keeping house and bringing up kids didn't count' (p. 43). She embarks impulsively on an affair with her friend Vi, but has no consciousness of sexual politics to guide her next step: 'For the first time in her married life she didn't care' (p. 47). But self-abandonment may constitute in itself a new form of freedom.

All the Dark Air deals more overtly than the other two novels with the tension between 'masculine' and 'feminine' discourses. The conflict between the two spheres is personified through the relationship of the heroine Julie and her boyfriend Mick. She looks after their ramshackle home, falls pregnant, and attends New Age classes in 'Mind Power'. He takes hard drugs, sells copies of *Socialist Worker*, and thinks her mystical solutions to social problems are mere bourgeois diversionary tactics to dilute the class struggle. While his reductionist Marxism is not presented sympathetically, Julie lacks class-consciousness. Looking at a couple of young hooligans, she ponders, 'These were the people Mick was trying to save' (p. 226). But buoyed up by some successful meditations, Julie's concluding thoughts suggest a possible compromise:

> if you wanted to change the world like Mick you had... to change, not just the world you could see, but all the unending labours of the dead. Everything the dead left behind changed the living world in unseen ways. And if you wanted to change the world like Julie you had this to understand, not just karma, or what was left from your own past lives, but what the dead had left, and the presence of what the dead had left, on the streets... (p. 321)

Alongside the feminization of working-class fiction in the 1980s and 1990s, there has been a major revitalization of the fiction of the Celtic fringe, notably Scotland.[12] The twin forces of de-industrialization and nationalism have combined to produce a renaissance of Scottish proletarian and vernacular novelists: William McIlvanney, James Kelman, Agnes Owens, Jeff Torrington, Irvine Welsh, and Alan Warner. That does not mean there is a 'school' or movement at work, as these writers have their own approaches to their material. Though Kelman and McIlvanney both write about alienated working-class men, Kelman uses stream-of-consciousness modernist techniques, while McIlvanney prefers to remain within a more traditionally realist mode. Owens frequently portrays working-class women in a dehistoricized context. Torrington takes a comic, maggoty approach to the decline of traditional working-class culture. Welsh and Warner explore the new youth underclass of 'rave' and 'chemical' culture. Yet despite these aesthetic differences, these writers share with their English counterparts an interest in exposing the decline of traditional industrial society, and the particular impact this process has on gender roles, the formation of subjectivity, and class-consciousness. As the old familiar landmarks disappear, a new landscape of insidious oppressions and ambiguous potentialities emerges.

Kelman's fiction has progressed from tiny vignettes of working-class experience to lengthy stream-of-consciousness narratives. All his fiction is concerned to render the existential interior life of a fractured, often wandering and centreless post-industrial working-class consciousness. His favourite technique is to abandon punctuation in order to give the impression of fully opening up his characters' consciousness. Although this method is reminiscent of high modernism, Kelman has claimed that his influences are not English or Anglo-American but European, particularly Dostoevsky and Kafka.[13] His nationalist rejection of English cultural hegemony also extends to his frequent use of an uncensored, earthy vernacular; Kelman regards standard English as a form of cultural oppression. This anti-literary discourse is usually generated by aggressively masculine characters. A number of his early short sketches are about men who are alienated from their wives. In 'Where but What', for instance, a man who is rooted to his armchair complains: 'That back of mine's fucking killing me so it – murder! All she did but, nodded her head, nodded her fucking head.' The story ends on a sexist crescendo:

> It annoys you. I used to, get annoyed; I used to get fucking annoyed, with her, the wife, she made me fucking angry. I used to get really fucking browned off – worse, worse, I mean worse than that, really fucking angry, it fucking[14]

The effect of the interrupted ending is to imply a level of deflationary irony is at work, so that this Alf Garnett-style bluster is actually meant to be ineffectual. But it is not always so easy to decide if Kelman endorses the language of his unreconstructed Glasgow personae. For some of these characters, class-consciousness is a stubborn refusal to accept that the world has changed.

The Busconductor Hines (1984) is a portrait of Robert Hines, a fundamentally respectable family man trying to hold on to his job and his sanity.[15] His job grinds him down, and his prospects look bleak: first, the role of conductor is being threatened by single-operator buses; second, his rebellious instincts lead him to almost daily confrontations with management, though he is denied the dignity of being sacked for malingering. He finds consolation in smoking, drinking, and the tender satisfactions of his family. Significantly, he has to decide whether or not to agree that his wife should turn her part-time secretarial job into full-time work. While he contemplates the 'broo' or dole, Sandra becomes more secure – a classic expression of the feminization of the economy. Robert does not displace his resentments onto Sandra, however. His idiosyncratic response to his alienated condition is to mentally and physically wander. Long sections of the narrative are taken up with his 'speculative musings' (p. 93). The most lyrical passages in the novel comprise Robert's awkward philosophizing:

> The lines split and the curves tailed off. A pile of lines left lying about. Each being there for the taking. What you do is choose one – like Hines. Hines has chosen 1 and this 1 leads maybe as far as the sky and that point up there, the point is somewhere up there you see and there is no lurch backwards because the line is always curved, the choice is being made; either you fucking go or you do not fucking go. (p. 102)

The play on the use of '1' (one, the first, I) reveals a lurking self-consciousness in the narrative about issues of identity and agency. A more straightforward decolonization of literary language occurs in the novel's numerous parodies of the discourse of authority. For example, Hines attends a disciplinary meeting,

> in order that he might explain certain conductorial deeds of a nefarious nature and be brought to account for the same, that a rightful retribution might be passed upon him. (p. 207)

None of these discursive strategies can save his job. This point is made clear by the decisive intervention of the transport workers' union in support of his case. The novel ends on a note of anticlimax, with the start of another working day.

In Kelman's latest and longest novel about a working-class Glaswegian, *How late it was, how late* (1994), the hero does not have the familial compensations available to Robert Hines.[16] Sammy McGarrigle, an unemployed petty thief, wakes up one Sunday morning in a bedraggled, down-and-out state, unable to remember what has happened to him the previous day. After a skirmish with the 'sodjers' (the 'polis' or police), he goes blind and discovers that his girlfriend Helen has left him. The novel follows the first week of his readjusted life. He has a series of prolonged, bruising, and at times Kafkaesque encounters with the authorities, including a battery of interrogations by the benefits agency, the police, a doctor and a lawyer. In Foucauldian terms, Sammy's existence is 'disciplined' by these discourses of state power. His amnesia and blindness is construed as a psychological disorder, the ruse of a criminal, or a side-effect of a poor diet. The factitiousness of these constructions of his condition is exposed by the novel's own hermeneutic code, which does not resolve the enigma of the missing patch of time, the location of Helen, or the exact cause of the blindness. The bulk of the novel comprises the inconsequential ramblings of Sammy's fragmented consciousness. The suddenness with which Sammy is socially marooned in the midst of civilization gives the novel the quality of a morality tale. He is in a state of extreme alienation and insecurity: 'It wasnay his body. His fucking body man it wasnay his fucking body. It wasnay his body' (p. 75). Although Glaswegians he meets are generally kind to him, and despite receiving help from his son near the end of the novel, Sammy flees the city and heads for London. The novel is a bleakly comic narrativization of the situation's two central tropes of insecurity and dislocation: blindness and absence.

Generationally, Kelman lies between McIlvanney, Torrington and Owens, who were born in the 1930s, and Welsh and Warner, who were born in the 1970s. This grasp of a longer perspective on modern Scottish history may be one reason why Jeff Torrington takes a comic, bathetic approach to the postwar clearances of the traditional Glaswegian working-class communities. In his debut novel *Swing Hammer Swing!* (1992), Torrington looks at the demolition of the Gorbals in the 1960s through the eyes of an aspiring writer and bohemian *manqué* Tom Clay.[17] He is an autodidact, atheist and ex-railwayman who has chosen a life on the 'broo' to give him time to write. So far he has accumulated twenty volumes of diaries, but at the opening of the novel he is forced to sell his typewriter to buy his wife a gift to celebrate the imminent birth of their first child. This act of self-sacrifice contains a witty, self-referential joke about loss of identity: his typewriter has a faulty letter 'i', and is therefore 'I-less'.

As a resident of one of the condemned slum dwellings, it

seems that Clay's whole lifestyle is about to be dramatically shifted towards conformity in the form of a new estate, and family responsibility. On the brink of this social catastrophe, he finds consolation in some picaresque adventures and observing the surreal antics of the local cinema which is desperately trying to attract new customers. One publicity stunt for the Beatles cartoon film *Yellow Submarine* involves kitting out the projectionist in a mock-up deep-sea diver's suit; he is duly pelted with snowballs by local youths. With Clay's wife conveniently absent in hospital, he embarks on his own variety of Bloomian wanderings and sexual peccadilloes. His sexual morality is a case of a contest between his 'Macdougall' (cock) and 'Jeremiah' (conscience). He has a skirmish with local hoods, and attacks his sister-in-law's materialism, calling her modern furnishings 'visual muggery' (p. 30).

The novel is a comic period piece, a celebration of the eccentricities and kitsch highlights of this transitional moment in Scottish, urban working-class culture. There is a slight danger that the historical setting allows for a displaced indulgence in sexist stereotyping (Clay's wife spends her time reading magazines and manicuring her nails), but the narrative does not pretend that Clay is a paragon of either virtue or reliability. The comic approach can also be read as a defensive response to the momentous historical significance of the relocation of the urban Scottish working class. Clay's sardonic hauteur towards his community and his sentimental attachment to slum life do not comprise a serious grasp of the transformative social forces at work.

William McIlvanney's fiction takes a more conventional, naturalistic approach to the exploration of working-class masculinity under stress. In his early novel *Docherty* (1975) he looks back to the Edwardian period to illuminate the historical process of the formation of working-class respectability in an environment of economic hardship and emotional volatility.[18] The hero Tam Docherty, a socialist miner's leader, believes that decency and moral standards are powerful class weapons that must be zealously defended. This code extends from castigating one son for taking a job in a non-unionized mine, to demanding that another son marry his pregnant girlfriend:

We walk a nerra line. Ah ken hoo nerra it is. Ah've walked it a' ma days. Us an' folk like us hiv goat the nearest thing tae nothin' in this world. A' that filters doon tae us is shite. We leeve in the sewers o' ither bastards' comfort. The only thing we've goat is wan anither. That's why ye never sell yer mates. Because there's nothin' left tae buy wi' whit ye get. That's why ye respect yer weemenkind. Because whit we make oorselves is whit we are. Because if ye don't, ye're provin' their case. Because the bastards don't believe we're folk! (p. 277)

Tam dies a hero's death trying to save the life of a fellow miner.

At the other end of the historical continuum, *The Big Man* (1985) shows the collapse of this patriarchal platform for class-consciousness.[19] With all the mines closed, and traditional sources of skilled and unskilled male labour all but extinct, the social basis for Tam Docherty's brand of authority and agency has vanished. Instead we see Dan Scoular, an Ayrshire ex-miner, displace his fierce prowess onto bare-knuckle fighting. The novel is organized around a Faustian pact. Dan signs up with a Glasgow gangster for an illegal contest against 'Cutty', an ex-boxer. Though he wins the fight, Dan immediately renounces his involvement with the underworld. He gives some of his winnings to Cutty, beats up his boss, and returns home to await his fate. Paradoxically, the fight revives his class-consciousness: 'only the promoters had won...he was enlisted in a war' (pp. 216, 249). The poignancy of this reawakened hostility to the 'dark and uncontrollable forces' of capitalism (p. 18) is sentimentally intensified by Dan's reconciliation with his wife Betty. Their marriage had been in steep decline as years of the dole took their toll of Dan's spirit, his ambition, and his ability to live up to his local fame as the community's 'heritage' (p. 52). Given that Betty left her 'lumpen middle-class' family (p. 35) and a university course to marry Dan, she has had much to grieve about. The disintegration of Dan and Betty's relationship reflects the wider fragmentation of the working class; after he has agreed to fight, Dan confesses that he cannot trust himself to be faithful to the customs and values that have bred his character (pp. 124–5). By the end of Dan's voyage of self-discovery, there is some evidence that traditional, 'epic' masculine working-class culture can survive into the post-industrial era.

Not all Scottish working-class writers are so obsessed by masculinity. In a recently published autobiographical fragment called 'Marching to the Highlands and Into the Unknown' Agnes Owens concludes:

> I suppose you could say my life was a struggle, as it is with most men and women of the working class even in years of good employment. I always worked when possible at anything I could find, ie., in shop, office and factory. That was in the good old days when work brought satisfaction even if it was a hassle.[20]

Ironically, once the 'years of unemployment' arrived in the 1980s, writing became her main source of income: 'This was great, but didn't pay the rent, so I continued to clean houses' (p. 175). She is grateful to be a published author, but with no access to capital she is not much more secure than when in the 1940s she migrated to the Highlands looking for work. This confession is a salutary reminder that the social basis of the literary establishment still disadvantages those from less privileged backgrounds. For the working-class woman, who is expected to 'clean houses', the obstacles in the way of literary success are particularly formidable.

Given the frankness and clarity of this brief review of her life and career, Owens's novel about a working woman striving for some kind of independence is rather disappointing. The narrator of *A Working Mother* (1994) is so laconic as to be almost disembodied.[21] There is so little social or historical reference that it comes as something of a surprise to find that the story is set in the 1950s. The foregrounding of absence could be an attempt to universalize Betty's experience, or to emphasize the sense of a historical vacuum within which working-class women's experience has languished for so long. The fragility of the narrative becomes apparent at the end of the novel, when we discover Betty in a present-day mental hospital regaling a fellow patient with her story. It transpires that the closure of Betty's desire to become independent in postwar Britain is an act of malign Nemesis: her lover Brendan murders her boss Mr Robson, who used to masturbate behind a screen while Betty typed for him; and her husband Adam, for whom she has 'funereal' feelings (p. 112), takes the children and decamps to one of Betty's workmates. Given the cruelty of history, there is perhaps some justification for Betty's failure to engage with the historical context of her rebellion.

157

History has also been singularly unkind to Scotland's urban youth. With the emergence of the Aids epidemic in the 1980s, it became increasingly apparent that Edinburgh constituted one of Britain's major centres for drug-taking. The sharing of needles was spreading the Aids virus more rapidly than sexual transmission. The discovery of such cultural squalor beneath the beauty and antiquity of the capital city revived the old class imagery of 'two nations'. It seemed that the response of youth to the prospect of a future on the 'broo' was self-abandonment and an immersion in a hedonistic, self-destructive underclass existence, cut off from all conventional moral discourses. Drug addiction has become the demonic and demonized reflection of a commodified, fetishized and irresponsible capitalist system. Addiction ritualizes the alienation of the body by inducing a relentless cycle of narcissistic pleasure and loss of self-control. While the drugs problem extends way beyond Scotland, of course, it is the young Scottish writer Irvine Welsh who has quickly established a 'cult' reputation as the spokesperson for the new junkie culture. His picaresque novel *Trainspotting* (1993) is a witty, lively and frequently repugnant account of the insalubrious adventures of an Edinburgh addict.[22]

The vitality of the writing comes from the rawness of the vernacular language and the debunking of the western Enlightenment tradition. The narrator 'Rent Boy', an ex-apprentice, and his assortment of junkie cronies have absolutely no interest in the ideals of liberty, equality or fraternity (indeed, at the end of the novel, Rent Boy betrays his friends and absconds with the proceeds of a drugs deal), or in self-improvement, rationality and citizenship – all those codes are dead narratives. Bodies are merely receptacles for stimulants: drugs, booze, semen. Generally, a needle brings more pleasure than a penis, and at one point in the novel a penis provides the vein for an injection. Any sex that does take place almost by definition has to be morally perverse. Hence the hero has sex with an under-age girl (at first unknowingly, then knowingly) and with the pregnant girlfriend of his dead brother (to add further spice to this scene, he tries to bugger her in the toilet during the funeral wake).

Irvine writes with a knowing degree of iconoclastic and understatedly intellectual humour that redeems many of the stomach-churning moments of bodily incontinence. In one scene, the hero has to fish around in his own shit to retrieve some opium suppositories – a comic imagining of the Freudian idea of shit as infantile 'gold'. In another scene, Rent Boy's friend Kelly rebels against the poor working conditions of her waitressing job by contaminating customers' food with a vile assortment of bodily emissions. Though the literary debt is not acknowledged, this class-conscious scatology reworks a moment from Orwell's *Down and Out in Paris and London* (1933), in which an anarchist *plongeur* spits into the soup before it is served. Rent Boy is actually the most enlightened of his gang, and at times erupts into politically aware tirades, such as his attack on Scottish nationalism, another phoney ideology:

> Ah hate cunts like that... Cunts that are intae baseball-batting every fucker that's different; pakis, poofs, n what huv ye. Fuckin failures in a country ay failures. It's nae good blamin it oan the English fir colonising us. Ah don't hate the English. They're just wankers. We are colonised by wankers. We can't even pick a decent, vibrant, healthy culture to be colonised by. No. We're ruled by effete arseholes ... Ah hate the Scots. (p. 78)

Voluntary exile is the only feasible solution to such cynicism, so it is fitting that Rent Boy escapes to Amsterdam, another drugs capital.

Alan Warner's response to 'rave' culture in his first novel *Morvern Callar* (1995) is to abandon altogether the tradition of virile male narrative.[23] His novel is a female Gothic, in which a young supermarket worker on a Scottish island wakes up one morning to find her boyfriend has committed suicide. Far from being upset, she disposes of the body, claims his inheritance and his first novel, and abandons herself to 'Youth-Med' holidays and 'rave' orgies. The story reads like a macabre Celtic version of a 1970s feminist emancipation narrative. By the end of the novel, Morvern seems to be on the brink of a further metamorphosis into a fertility symbol. She is pregnant with a 'child of the raves' (p. 229) and spends most of her time haunting a dark wood. Clearly, this association with nature creates the possibility of some form of mystical transformation, but the reader is left guessing.

Turning from Scotland to Ireland, a brief mention can be made of the popular novels of Roddy Doyle. Though Doyle is from a lower-middle-class background, and has admitted to being a sympathetic 'spectator' of working-class Dublin life, his comic fiction celebrates the vibrancy, stoicism and resourcefulness of that community.[24] *The Commitments* (1987), *The Snapper* (1990), and *The Van* (1991) form the so-called 'Barrytown' trilogy, focusing on the Catholic Rabbitte family. *The Commitments* follows the rise and fall of a local soul band, *The Snapper* shows the rugged determination of the pregnant heroine to face up to the prejudice and hypocrisy in her family and community, and *The Van* is about an abortive attempt by the unemployed hero to start a mobile burger business. *Paddy Clarke Ha Ha Ha* (1993) is a *Bildungsroman* about a boy growing up in the 1960s and coming to terms with the break-up of his parents' marriage, and *The Woman Who Walked Into Doors* (1996) explores domestic violence through the eyes of its victim, a working-class housewife. The hallmark of Doyle's style is the granting of autonomy to his characters through the use of unmediated dialogue, a technique reminiscent of Nell Dunn's *Up the Junction*. Doyle's foregrounding of domestic and family experience is further evidence of the 'feminization' of working-class culture, though his fiction contains no explicit engagement with the 'general way of life' in contemporary Ireland.

So long as capitalism requires the existence of a working class, there will be a working-class literature. By mapping the long and varied tradition of working-class fiction from the middle of the last century to the present day, it is hoped this book may give some encouragement to any working-class authors who still feel that they are denied a 'literature of their own'.

Notes

CHAPTER 1. FROM CHARTISM TO SOCIALISM

1. See my introduction to Ian Haywood (ed.), *The Literature of Struggle: An Anthology of Chartist Fiction* (Aldershot: Scolar Press, 1995).
2. Thomas Cooper, *The Life of Thomas Cooper: Written by Himself* (Hodder and Stoughton, 1892); quoted in Haywood (ed.), *The Literature of Struggle*, 8.
3. Haywood (ed.), *The Literature of Struggle*, 59.
4. See: Martha Vicinus, *The Industrial Muse: A Study of Nineteenth Century British Working Class Literature* (Croom Helm, 1974), ch. 3, and 'Chartist Fiction and the Development of Class-based Literature', in Gustav Klaus (ed.), *The Socialist Novel in Britain: Towards the Recovery of a Tradition* (Brighton: Harvester, 1982); Jack B. Mitchell, 'Aesthetic Problems of the Development of the Proletarian-Revolutionary Novel in Nineteenth-Century Britain', in David Craig (ed.), *Marxists on Literature* (Penguin, 1975); Mary Ashraf, *Introduction to Working-Class Literature in Britain*, Part 2, *Prose* (Berlin, 1979), pp. 64–71 (this is a very rare book, though it is available at the Marx Memorial Library in London); Gustav Klaus, *The Literature of Labour; Two Hundred Years of Working-Class Writing* (Brighton: Harvester, 1985), ch. 3.
5. I quote from the original text of *Sunshine and Shadow*, hence the reference to chapters rather than page numbers. I hope to bring out a modern edition of the story in 1998.
6. Thomas Miller's *Godfrey Malvern, or The Life of An Author* (1843), while written by a lower-class author who received many subsidies from the Royal Literary Fund, is not about the working class, though it does offer the first realistic portrait of Victorian Grub Street.
7. Louis James, *Fiction for the Working Man 1830–1850* (1963; Penguin University Books, 1974), 25.

8. See Peter Keating, *Working Class Stories of the 1890s* (Routledge and Kegan Paul, 1971).

9. Arthur Morrison, *Tales of Mean Streets* (1894; Boydell and Brewer, 1983).

10. Peter Keating, *Working Class Stories of the 1890s*, p. xv.

11. Peter Keating, *The Haunted Study: A Social History of the English Novel 1875–1914* (1989; Fontana, 1991), 316.

12. Gareth Stedman-Jones, *Languages of Class* (Cambridge: Cambridge University Press, 1983), ch. 4. See also Eric Hobsbawm, 'The Formation of British Working-Class Culture', in *Worlds of Labour: Further Studies in the History of Labour* (Weidenfeld and Nicolson, 1984).

13. See Paul Salveson, 'Allen Clarke and the Lancashire School of Novelists 1890–1914', in Gustav Klaus (ed.), *The Rise of Socialist Fiction 1880–1914* (Brighton: Harvester, 1987).

14. Robert Blatchford, *Merrie England* (1892–3; Journeyman Press, 1976).

15. Peter Keating, *The Haunted Study*, 313.

16. I use the original text, hence the references to chapters rather than pages.

17. See Brunkild de la Motte, 'Radicalism, feminism, socialism: women novelists', in Gustav Klaus (ed.), *The Rise of Socialist Fiction*.

18. D. H. Lawrence, *Sons and Lovers* (1913: Penguin, 1974); Allen Clarke, *The Men who Fought for us* (Manchester: Labour Co-Operative Newspapers Society, 1914); Robert Tressell, *The Ragged Trousered Philanthropists* (1914, restored text first published in 1955; Grafton, 1988); Patrick MacGill, *Children of the Dead End* (Herbert Jenkins, 1914). I am indebted to Jack Mitchell for this comparative approach: see his essay 'Early Harvest: Three Anti-Capitalist Novels Published in 1914', in Gustav Klaus (ed.), *The Socialist Novel in Britain*.

19. There is a small but significant body of critical work on Tressell. See: Jack B. Mitchell, *Robert Tressell and the Ragged Trousered Philanthropists* (Lawrence and Wishart, 1969); F. C. Ball, *One of the Damned: The Life and Times of Robert Tressell* (Weidenfeld and Nicolson, 1973); David Pierce and Mary Eagleton, *Attitudes to Class in the English Novel* (Thames and Hudson, 1979), pp. 79–82; Raymond Williams, 'The Ragged Arsed Philanthropists', in *Writing in Society* (Verso, 1982); Wim Neetens, *Writing and Democracy: Literature, Politics and Culture* (Brighton: Harvester, 1991), ch. 6; Pamela Fox, *Class Fictions: Shame and Resistance in the Working-Class Novel, 1890–1945* (North Carolina: Duke University Press, 1994), ch. 2. It is heartening to see that in 1997 Flamingo Books have reprinted Tressell's novel with an Introduction by Gary Day, under the imprint 'Modern Classics'.

20. Pamela Fox, *Class Fictions*, 63.

21. Peter Keating, *The Haunted Study*, 314.
22. Martha Vicinus is possibly too cautious in her belief that the main legacy of Wheeler's novel was its subject matter and its class-consciousness. See Martha Vicinus, 'Chartist Fiction and the Development of Class-based Literature', 23.
23. Jack B. Mitchell, *Robert Tressell and the Ragged Trousered Philanthropists*, 16.
24. Pamela Fox, *Class Fictions*, 70.
25. Raymond Williams, Foreword to Jack B. Mitchell, *Robert Tressell and the Ragged Trousered Philanthropists*, p. xiii.
26. Jack B. Mitchell, *Robert Tressell and the Ragged Trousered Philanthropists*, 9.
27. George Lukács, *History and Class Consciousness* (1920; Merlin, 1971), 51, 80.
28. Quoted in Jack B. Mitchell, *Robert Tressell and the Ragged Trousered Philanthropists*, 7.
29. John Carey, *The Intellectuals and the Masses* (Faber, 1991); Wim Neetens, *Writing and Democracy*, 154.

CHAPTER 2. BLACK EARTH: THE INTERWAR YEARS

1. See Allen Hutt, *The Postwar History of the British Working Class* (Left Book Club, 1937), ch. 1.
2. See Eric Hopkins, *The Rise and Decline of the English Working Classes 1918–1990: A Social History* (Weidenfeld and Nicolson, 1991), ch. 1.
3. See Raphael Samuel, Ewan MacColl and Stuart Cosgrave, *Theatres of the Left 1880–1935: Workers' Theatre Movements in Britain and America* (Routledge and Kegan Paul, 1985).
4. James Welsh, *The Underworld* (Herbert Jenkins, 1920).
5. The ad appears at the end of Welsh's novel *The Morlocks* (Herbert Jenkins, 1924).
6. Harold Heslop, *The Gate of a Strange Field* (Brentano's Ltd., 1929). For an overview of Heslop's career, see Gustav Klaus, *The Literature of Labour*, ch. 5.
7. Quoted in Andy Croft, *Red Letter Days: British Fiction of the 1930s* (Lawrence and Wishart, 1990), 31.
8. Ethel Carnie Holdsworth, *This Slavery* (Labour Publishing Company, 1925). For further information on Carnie Holdsworth, see Ruth and Edmund Frow, 'Ethel Carnie, feminist and socialist', in Gustav Klaus (ed.), *The Rise of Socialist Fiction*. Pamela Fox looks at the romance elements in both Carnie and Wilkinson in *Class Fictions*.
9. Ethel Carnie, *The Lamp Girl* (Headley Brothers, 1913), 193.

10. Mary Ashraf, *Introduction to Working-Class Literature in Britain*, Part 2, 195.

11. For a discussion of the Plebs League, see Janet Batsleer, Tony Davies, Rebecca O'Rourke, Chris Weedon, *Rewriting English: The Cultural Politics of Gender and Class* (Methuen, 1985), ch. 3. A useful introduction to the historical events of the General Strike is Margaret Morris, *The General Strike* (Journeyman, 1976).

12. The best summative discussions of working-class fiction in this period can be found in Andy Croft, *Red Letter Days*, and Valentine Cunningham, *British Writers of the Thirties* (Oxford: Oxford University Press, 1988), ch. 10.

13. Walter Greenwood, *Love on the Dole* (1933; Penguin, 1976).

14. The novel is attacked by: Carole Snee, 'Working Class Literature of Proletarian Writing', in John Clarke (ed.), *Culture and Crisis in Britain in the Thirties* (Lawrence and Wishart, 1978); Roy Johnson, 'The Proletarian Novel', *Literature and History*, Autumn 1975; Stephen Constantine, '*Love on the Dole* and its reception in the 1930s', *Literature and History*, Autumn 1982. For a defence of Greenwood's methods, see Roger Webster, '*Love on the Dole* and the aesthetics of contradiction', in Jeremy Hawthorn (ed.), *The British Working Class Novel in the Twentieth Century* (Edward Arnold, 1984).

15. Roger Webster, '*Love on the Dole* and the aesthetics of contradiction', 53.

16. Raymond Williams, 'The Welsh Industrial Novel', in *Problems in Materialism and Culture* (Verso, 1980), 220.

17. Rex Warner, 'Education', in C. Day Lewis (ed.), *The Mind in Chains: Socialism and the Cultural Revolution* (Frederick Muller, 1937), 46; Ralph Fox, *The Novel and the People* (1937; Lawrence and Wishart, 1979), 34.

18. Harold Heslop, *Last Cage Down* (1935; Lawrence and Wishart, 1984); *Goaf* (The Fortune Press, 1934).

19. Lewis Jones, *Cwmardy* (1937; Lawrence and Wishart, 1986); *We Live* (1939; Lawrence and Wishart, 1988).

20. Frederick Boden, *Miner* (Dent, 1932); *A Derbyshire Tragedy* (Dent, 1935).

21. Walter Brierley, *Means Test Man* (1935; Nottingham: Spokesman Books, 1983); *Sandwichman* (1937; Merlin, 1990); Joe Corrie, *The Black Earth* (George Routledge, 1939).

22. Quoted in Andy Croft's Introduction to *Means Test Man*, p. xi.

23. Graham Holderness, 'Miners and the Novel: From Bourgeoisie to Proletarian', in Jeremy Hawthorn (ed.), *The British Working Class Novel in the Twentieth Century*.

24. Biographical details are drawn from Halward's autobiography *Let Me Tell You* (Michael Joseph, 1938). See also *To Tea on Sunday*

(Methuen, 1936) and *The Money's All Right and Other Stories* (Michael Joseph, 1938).

25. Jack Hilton, *Champion* (Jonathan Cape, 1938). Hilton's autobiography is entitled *Caliban Shrieks* (Cobden-Sanderson, 1935).
26. Frank Tilsley, *The Plebeian's Progress* (Gollancz, 1933).
27. James Hanley, *Boy* (1931; André Deutsch, 1990).
28. James Hanley, *The Furys* (Chatto and Windus, 1935).
29. James Hanley, *The Secret Journey* (Chatto and Windus, 1936).
30. George Garrett, 'Fishmeal', in John Lehmann (ed.), *New Writing*, II (The Bodley Head, 1936). See also John Lehmann, *The Whispering Gallery* (Longman, Green and Co., 1955), 259.
31. Jim Phelan, *Lifer* (Peter Davies, 1938), Preface.
32. Jim Phelan, *Tramp at Anchor* (George C. Harrap, 1954).
33. Lewis Grassic Gibbon, *A Scots Quair* (1932–4; Penguin, 1986).
34. Quoted in Valentine Cunningham, *British Writers of the Thirties*, 309.
35. James Barke, *Land of the Leal* (Collins, 1939).
36. James Barke, *Major Operation* (Collins, 1936).
37. Simon Blumenfeld, *Jew Boy* (1935; Lawrence and Wishart, 1986).
38. Willy Goldman, *East End My Cradle* (1940; Robson Books, 1988).
39. Ken Worpole, *Dockers and Detectives: Popular Reading, Popular Writing* (Verso, 1983), 105.
40. John Sommerfield, *May Day* (1936; Lawrence and Wishart, 1984).
41. Valentine Cunningham, *British Writers of the Thirties*, 317.
42. Andy Croft, *Red Letter Days*, 51–4.
43. Ralph Bates, *Lean Men: An Episode in Life* (Peter Davies, 1934); *The Olive Field* (1936; Hogarth, 1986).
44. See Cunningham's Introduction to Ralph Bates, *The Olive Field*.

CHAPTER 3. THE INFLUENCE OF AFFLUENCE

1. Quoted in Peter Hennessy, *Never Again: Britain 1945–1951* (1992; Vintage, 1993), 82.
2. Hennessy, *Never Again*, 73.
3. Hennessy, *Never Again*, 454.
4. See Michael Sissons and Peter French (eds), *Age of Austerity 1945–1951* (1963; Penguin, 1964).
5. Hennessy, *Never Again*, 452. See also Jeremy Seabrook and Trevor Blackwell, *A World Still to Win: The Reconstruction of the Postwar Working Class* (Faber and Faber, 1985), ch. 4.
6. Mark Abrams, *The Teenage Consumer* (London Press Exchange, 1959).
7. Arthur Marwick, *British Society Since 1945* (Penguin, 1982), Parts 1 and 2.

165

8. C. A. R. Crosland, *The Future of Socialism* (1956; Jonathan Cape, 1957), 61.

9. John Osborne, *Look Back in Anger* (1957; Faber and Faber, 1976); 84. See also Daniel Bell, *The End of Ideology* (Illinois: The Free Press of Glencoe, 1960).

10. Richard Hoggart, *The Uses of Literacy* (1957; Penguin, 1958), 157. See also Stuart Laing, *Representations of Working-Class Life 1957–1964* (Macmillan, 1986).

11. See: Tom Maschler (ed.), *Declaration* (MacGibbon and Kee, 1957); Robert Hewison, *In Anger: Culture in the Cold War 1945–1960* (1981; Methuen, 1988), ch. 5.

12. See John Russell Taylor, *Anger and After: A Guide to the New British Drama* (1962; Penguin, 1968).

13. For a feminist critique of the Angry Young Man, see Micheline Wandor, *Look Back in Gender* (Methuen, 1987).

14. John Braine, *Room at the Top* (1957; Penguin, 1969).

15. See Stuart Laing, 'The Morality of Affluence: John Braine's *Room at the Top*', in Chris Pawling (ed.), *Popular Fiction and Social Change* (Macmillan, 1984).

16. Stuart Laing, *Representations of Working-Class Life 1957–1964*, 59–60. See also Harry Ritchie, *Success Stories: Literature and the Media in England, 1950–1959* (Faber and Faber, 1988).

17. Alan Sinfield, *Literature, Politics and Culture in Postwar Britain* (Oxford: Basil Blackwell, 1989), 234–5.

18. Alan Sillitoe, *Saturday Night and Sunday Morning* (1958; Pan, 1960).

19. See also Alan Sillitoe, Introduction to *A Sillitoe Selection* (Longman Imprint Books, 1968).

20. Alan Sillitoe, *The Loneliness of the Long Distance Runner* (1959; Grafton, 1986).

21. Alan Sillitoe, *The Ragman's Daughter* (1963; Pan, 1972). 'The Ragman's Daughter' comes first in this collection of short stories.

22. Alan Sillitoe, Preface to *Saturday Night and Sunday Morning* (Grafton, 1985).

23. For an overview of this tradition, see Raymond Williams, *Culture and Society 1790–1950* (1958; Penguin, 1979), Part 3, ch. 5, 'Marxism and Culture'.

24. Stan Barstow, *A Kind of Loving* (1960; Penguin, 1972).

25. Raymond Williams, 'The Ragged Arsed Philanthropists', 265.

26. David Storey, *This Sporting Life* (1960; Penguin, 1965).

27. David Storey, *Flight Into Camden* (1961; Penguin, 1972).

28. See David Craig, 'David Storey's Vision of the Working Class', in Douglas Jefferson and Graham Martin (eds), *The Uses of Fiction: Essays on the Modern Novel in Honour of Arnold Kettle* (Milton Keynes: Open University Press, 1982).

29. Raymond Williams, *Border Country* (1960; Hogarth, 1988).
30. Raymond Williams, *The Long Revolution* (1960; Penguin, 1965), 308.
31. Raymond Williams, 'The Welsh Industrial Novel', in *Problems in Materialism and Culture* (Verso, 1980).
32. Raymond Williams, *Second Generation* (1964; Hogarth, 1988).
33. Keith Waterhouse, *Billy Liar* (1959; Penguin, 1988).
34. Richard Hoggart, *The Uses of Literacy*, 57.
35. Sam Selvon, *The Lonely Londoners* (1956; Longman, 1987); *Ways of Sunlight* (1957; Longman, 1987).
36. Stuart Laing, *Representations of Working-Class Life 1957–1964*, 221.
37. See Ingrid von Rosenberg, 'Militancy, Anger and Resignation: Alternative Moods in the Working-Class Novel of the 1950s and 1960s', in Gustav Klaus (ed.), *The Socialist Novel in Britain: Towards the Recovery of a Tradition* (Brighton: Harvester, 1982). Jack Common's autobiographical novel *Kiddar's Luck* (1951), which is scathing about social mobility, could also be added to the list of 'alternative' postwar novels.
38. Lehman is cited in Stuart Laing, *Representations of Working-Class Life 1957–1964*, 59.
39. Stuart Laing, *Representations of Working-Class Life 1957–1964*, 60, 61.
40. Sid Chaplin, *The Leaping Lad* (1947; Longman, 1971); *The Thin Seam* (Pheonix House, 1950).
41. There is an interview with Chaplin in Jeremy Hawthorn (ed.), *British Working Class Fiction in the Twentieth Century* (Edward Arnold, 1984).
42. Sid Chaplin, *The Leaping Lad*, 2, 4.
43. Norman Dennis, Fernando Henriques and Clifford Slaughter, *Coal is Our Life: An Analysis of a Yorkshire Mining Community* (1956; Tavistock Publications, 1976).
44. Len Doherty, *A Miner's Sons* (Lawrence and Wishart, 1955); *The Man Beneath* (Lawrence and Wishart, 1957).
45. Sid Chaplin, *The Day of the Sardine* (Eyre and Spottiswoode, 1961); *The Watches and the Watched* (Eyre and Spottiswoode, 1962).
46. Herbert Smith, *A Morning to Remember* (Lawrence and Wishart, 1962).
47. Herbert Smith, *A Field of Folk* (Lawrence and Wishart, 1957).
48. Alan Sillitoe, *Key to the Door* (1961; Pan, 1963).
49. Arthur Marwick, *British Society Since 1945*, 118.
50. Herbert Marcuse, 'Liberation from Affluent Society', in David Cooper (ed.), *The Dialectics of Liberation* (Penguin, 1968), 180.
51. Stokely Carmichael, 'Black Power', in David Cooper (ed.), *The Dialectics of Liberation*, 169.
52. Herbert Marcuse, *An Essay on Liberation* (1969; Penguin, 1972), 44.
53. Christopher Booker, *The Neophiliacs: A Study of the revolution in*

English life in the fifties and sixties (1969; Fontana, 1970), 9.

54. John H. Goldthorpe, David Lockwood, Frank Bechhofer and Jennifer Platt, *The Affluent Worker in the Class Structure* (Cambridge: Cambridge University Press, 1969), 174–6.

55. Herbert Marcuse, 'Liberation from Affluent Society', 178.

56. Raymond Williams (ed.), *May Day Manifesto 1968* (Penguin, 1968), 20. See also Margaret Lassell, *Wellington Road* (1962; Penguin, 1966); Ken Coates and Richard Silburn, *Poverty: the Forgotten Englishmen* (Penguin, 1970).

57. Jeremy Sandford, *Cathy Come Home* (Pan, 1967).

58. Philip Larkin, 'Annus Mirabilis', in *High Windows* (1974; Faber and Faber, 1986), 34.

59. Nell Dunn, *Up the Junction* (1963; Virago, 1988).

60. Nell Dunn, *Poor Cow* (1967; Virago, 1988).

61. Bill Naughton, *Alfie* (Panther Books, 1966).

62. David Storey, *Radcliffe* (1963; Penguin, 1965).

63. Clancy Sigal, *Weekend in Dinlock* (1960; Penguin, 1962).

64. David Storey, *Pasmore* (1972; Penguin, 1980).

65. Raymond Williams (ed.), *May Day Manifesto 1968*, 26–7.

66. Barry Hines, *A Kestrel for a Knave* (1968; Penguin, 1983).

67. Barry Hines, *The Price of Coal* (1979; Penguin, 1982).

68. Buchi Emecheta, *Second-Class Citizen* (1974; Fontana/Collins, 1982).

69. Buchi Emecheta, *In the Ditch* (1972; Flamingo, 1985).

CHAPTER 4. POST-INDUSTRIAL FICTIONS

1. Jeremy Seabrook and Trevor Blackwell, *A World Still to Win*, Part 3.

2. See Fredric Jameson, *Postmodernism, or The Cultural Logic of Late Capitalism* (Verso, 1991).

3. Dave Morley and Ken Worpole, *The Republic of Letters: Working Class Writing and Local Publishing* (Comedia, 1982).

4. David Storey, *Saville* (1976; Penguin, 1978); *A Prodigal Child* (1982; Penguin, 1984).

5. Barry Hines, *Looks and Smiles* (1981; Penguin, 1983).

6. Beatrix Campbell, *Wigan Pier Revisited: Poverty and Politics in the 80s* (Virago, 1984); Carolyn Steedman, *Landscape for a Good Woman: A Story of Two Lives* (1986; Virago, 1989).

7. Jeremy Seabrook and Trevor Blackwell, *A World Still to Win*, 173–4. See also: Jeremy Seabrook, *Working Class Childhood* (Gollancz, 1982); *Landscapes of Poverty* (Oxford: Basil Blackwell, 1985).

8. Pat Barker, *Union Street* (1982; Virago, 1984).

9. Pat Barker, *Blow Your House Down* (1984; Virago, 1986); *The Century's Daughter* (Virago, 1986).

10. Jeanette Winterson, *Oranges are not the only fruit* (1985; Pandora, 1989).
11. Livi Michael, *Under a Thin Moon* (Secker and Warburg, 1992); *Their Angel Reach* (Secker and Warburg, 1994); *All the Dark Air* (Secker and Warburg, 1997).
12. See Gavin Wallace and Randall Stevenson (eds), *The Scottish Novel Since the Seventies* (Edinburgh: Edinburgh University Press, 1993).
13. See the interview with Kelman in the *Independent on Sunday*, 28 April 1991.
14. James Kelman, *Greyhound for Breakfast* (1987; Picador, 1988), 134–5.
15. James Kelman, *The Busconductor Hines* (1984; Dent, 1987).
16. James Kelman, *How late it was, how late* (1994; Minerva, 1995).
17. Jeff Torrington, *Swing Hammer Swing!* (1992; Minerva, 1993).
18. William McIlvanney, *Docherty* (1975; Sceptre, 1993).
19. William McIlvanney, *The Big Man* (1985; Sceptre, 1992).
20. See Owens's collection of short stories *People Like That* (1996; Bloomsbury, 1997), 169–76, 175.
21. Agnes Owens, *A Working Mother* (Bloomsbury, 1994).
22. Irvine Welsh, *Trainspotting* (1993; Minerva, 1997).
23. Alan Warner, *Morvern Callar* (Jonathan Cape, 1995).
24. Roddy Doyle, interview in the *Independent on Sunday*, 6 June 1993, 3.

Select Bibliography

The place of publication is London unless otherwise stated. Each author's works are listed in chronological order of first publication.

WORKS OF FICTION

Barke, James, *Major Operation* (Collins, 1936).
—— *Land of the Leal* (Collins, 1939).
Barker, Pat, *Union Street* (1982; Virago, 1984).
—— *Blow Your House Down* (1984; Virago, 1986).
—— *The Century's Daughter* (Virago, 1986).
Barstow, Stan, *A Kind of Loving* (1960; Penguin, 1972).
Bates, Ralph, *Lean Men: An Episode in Life* (Peter Davies, 1934).
—— *The Olive Field* (1936; Hogarth, 1986).
Blumenfeld, Simon, *Jew Boy* (1935; Lawrence and Wishart, 1986).
Boden, Frederick, *Miner* (Dent, 1932).
—— *A Derbyshire Tragedy* (Dent, 1935).
Braine, John, *Room at the Top* (1957; Penguin, 1969).
Brierley, Walter, *Means Test Man* (1935; Nottingham: Spokesman Books, 1983).
—— *Sandwichman* (1937; Merlin, 1990).
Carnie Holdsworth, Ethel, *The Lamp Girl* (Headley Brothers, 1913).
—— *This Slavery* (Labour Publishing Company, 1925).
Chaplin, Sid, *The Leaping Lad* (1947; Longman, 1971).
—— *The Thin Seam* (Phoenix House, 1950).
—— *The Day of the Sardine* (Eyre and Spottiswoode, 1961).
—— *The Watchers and the Watched* (Eyre and Spottiswoode, 1962).
Clarke, Allen, *The Knobstick* (1893).
—— *The Daughter of the Factory* (1898).
—— *The Red Flag: A Tale of the People's Woe* (Twentieth Century Press, 1908).

170

—— *The Men who Fought for us in the 'Hungry Forties': A Tale of Pioneers and Beginnings* (Manchester: Labour Co-Operative Newspapers Society, 1914).

Corrie, Joe, *The Black Earth* (George Routledge, 1939).

Doherty, Len, *A Miner's Sons* (Lawrence and Wishart, 1955).

—— *The Man Beneath* (Lawrence and Wishart, 1957).

Dunn, Nell, *Up the Junction* (1963; Virago, 1988).

—— *Poor Cow* (1967; Virago, 1988).

Emecheta, Buchi, *In the Ditch* (1972; Flamingo, 1985).

—— *Second-Class Citizen* (1974; Fontana/Collins, 1982).

Garrett, George, 'Fishmeal', in John Lehmann (ed.), *New Writing*, II (The Bodley Head, 1936).

Goldman, Willy, *East End My Cradle* (1940; Robson Books, 1988).

Grassic Gibbon, Lewis, *A Scots Quair* (1932–4; Penguin, 1986).

Greenwood, Walter, *Love on the Dole* (1933; Penguin, 1976).

Halward, Leslie, *To Tea on Sunday* (Methuen, 1936).

—— *The Money's All Right and Other Stories* (Michael Joseph, 1938).

—— *Let Me Tell You* (Michael Joseph, 1938).

Hanley, James, *Boy* (1931; André Deutsch, 1990).

—— *The Furys* (Chatto and Windus, 1935).

——*The Secret Journey* (Chatto and Windus, 1936).

Haywood, Ian (ed.), *The Literature of Struggle: An Anthology of Chartist Fiction* (Aldershot: Scolar Press, 1995).

Heslop, Harold, *The Gate of a Strange Field* (Brentano's Ltd., 1929).

—— *Goaf* (The Fortune Press, 1934).

—— *Last Cage Down* (1935; Lawrence and Wishart, 1984).

Hilton, Jack, *Caliban Shrieks* (Cobden-Sanderson, 1935).

—— *Champion* (Jonathan Cape, 1938).

Hines, Barry, *A Kestrel for a Knave* (1968; Penguin, 1983).

—— *The Price of Coal* (1979; Penguin, 1982).

—— *Looks and Smiles* (1981; Penguin, 1983).

Jones, Lewis, *Cwmardy* (1937; Lawrence and Wishart, 1986).

—— *We Live* (1939; Lawrence and Wishart, 1988).

Keating, Peter, *Working Class Stories of the 1890s* (Routledge and Kegan Paul, 1971).

Kelman, James, *Greyhound for Breakfast* (1987; Picador, 1988).

—— *The Busconductor Hines* (1984; Dent, 1987).

—— *How late it was, how late* (1994; Minerva, 1995).

Klaus, Gustav (ed.), *Tramps, Workmates and Revolutionaries: Working-class Stories of the 1920s* (Journeyman, 1993).

Lawrence, D. H., *Sons and Lovers* (1913; Penguin, 1974).

MacGill, Patrick, *Children of the Dead End: The Autobiography of a Navvy* (Herbert Jenkins, 1914).

171

McIlvanney, William, *Docherty* (1975; Sceptre, 1993).

—— *The Big Man* (1985; Sceptre, 1992).

Michael, Livi, *Under a Thin Moon* (Secker and Warburg, 1992).

—— *Their Angel Reach* (Secker and Warburg, 1994).

—— *All the Dark Air* (Secker and Warburg, 1997).

Morrison, Arthur, *Tales of Mean Streets* (1894; Boydell and Brewer, 1983).

Naughton, Bill, *Alfie* (Panther Books, 1966).

Owens, Agnes, *A Working Mother* (Bloomsbury, 1994).

—— *People Like That* (1996; Bloomsbury, 1997).

Phelan, Jim, *Lifer* (Peter Davies, 1938).

—— *Tramp at Anchor* (George C. Harrap, 1954).

Sandford, Jeremy, *Cathy Come Home* (Pan, 1967).

Selvon, Sam, *The Lonely Londoners* (1956; Longman, 1987).

—— *Ways of Sunlight* (1957; Longman, 1987).

Sillitoe, Alan, *Saturday Night and Sunday Morning* (1958; Pan, 1960).

—— *The Loneliness of the Long Distance Runner* (1959; Grafton, 1986).

—— *Key to the Door* (1961; Pan, 1963).

—— *The Ragman's Daughter* (1963; Pan, 1972).

Smith, Herbert, *A Field of Folk* (Lawrence and Wishart, 1957).

—— *A Morning to Remember* (Lawrence and Wishart, 1962).

Sommerfield, John, *May Day* (1936; Lawrence and Wishart, 1984).

Storey, David, *This Sporting Life* (1960; Penguin, 1965).

—— *Flight Into Camden* (1961: Penguin, 1972).

—— *Radcliffe* (1963; Penguin, 1965).

—— *Pasmore* (1972; Penguin, 1980).

—— *Saville* (1976; Penguin, 1978).

—— *A Prodigal Child* (1982; Penguin, 1984).

Tilsley, Frank, *The Plebeian's Progress* (Gollancz, 1933).

Torrington, Jeff, *Swing Hammer Swing!* (1992; Minerva, 1993).

Tressell, Robert, *The Ragged Trousered Philanthropists* (1914; restored text first published in 1955; Grafton, 1988).

Warner, Alan, *Morvern Callar* (Jonathan Cape, 1995).

Waterhouse, Keith, *Billy Liar* (1959; Penguin, 1988).

Welsh, Irvine, *Trainspotting* (1993; Minerva, 1997).

Welsh, James, *The Underworld* (Herbert Jenkins, 1920).

—— *The Morlocks* (Herbert Jenkins, 1924).

Wheeler, Thomas Martin, *Sunshine and Shadow* (1849–50).

Wilkinson, Ellen, *Clash* (1929; Virago, 1989).

Williams, Raymond, *Border Country* (1960; Hogarth, 1988).

—— *Second Generation* (1964; Hogarth, 1988).

Winterson, Jeanette, *Orange are not the only fruit* (1985; Pandora, 1989).

BIOGRAPHICAL AND CRITICAL STUDIES

Abrams, Mark, *The Teenage Consumer* (London Press Exchange, 1959).

Ashraf, Mary, *Introduction to Working-Class Literature in Britain*, Part 2, *Prose* (Berlin, 1979).

Ball, F. C., *One of the Damned: The Life and Times of Robert Tressell* (Weidenfeld and Nicolson, 1973).

Batsleer, Janet, Tony Davies, Rebecca O'Rourke and Chris Weedon, *Rewriting English: The Cultural Politics of Gender and Class* (Methuen, 1985).

Bell, Daniel, *The End of Ideology* (Illinois: The Free Press of Glencoe, 1960).

Blatchford, Robert, *Merrie England* (1892–3; Journeyman Press, 1976).

Booker, Christopher, *The Neophiliacs: A Study of the revolution in English life in the fifties and sixties* (1969; Fontana, 1970).

Campbell, Beatrix, *Wigan Pier Revisited: Poverty and Politics in the 80s* (Virago, 1984).

Carey, John, *The Intellectuals and the Masses* (Faber, 1991).

Carmichael, Stokely, 'Black Power', in David Cooper (ed.), *The Dialectics of Liberation* (Penguin, 1968).

Coates, Ken, and Richard Silburn, *Poverty: the Forgotten Englishmen* (Penguin, 1970).

Constantine, Stephen, '*Love on the Dole* and its reception in the 1930s', *Literature and History*, Autumn 1982.

Craig, David, 'David Storey's Vision of the Working Class', in Douglas Jefferson and Graham Martin (eds.), *The Uses of Fiction: Essays on the Modern Novel in Honour of Arnold Kettle* (Milton Keynes: Open University Press, 1982).

Croft, Andy, *Red Letter Days: British Fiction of the 1930s* (Lawrence and Wishart, 1990).

Crosland, C. A. R., *The Future of Socialism* (1956; Jonathan Cape, 1957).

Cunningham, Valentine, *British Writers of the Thirties* (Oxford: Oxford University Press, 1988).

De la Motte, Brunkild, 'Radicalism, feminism, socialism: women novelists', in Gustav Klaus (ed.), *The Rise of Socialist Fiction 1880–1914* (Brighton: Harvester, 1987).

Dennis, Norman, Fernando Henriques and Clifford Slaughter, *Coal is Our Life: An Analysis of a Yorkshire Mining Community* (1956; Tavistock Publications, 1976).

Fox, Pamela, *Class Fictions: Shame and Resistance in the Working-Class Novel, 1890–1945* (North Carolina: Duke University Press, 1994).

Fox, Ralph, *The Novel and the People* (1937; Lawrence and Wishart, 1979).

Frow, Ruth, and Edmund Frow, 'Ethel Carnie, feminist and socialist in

Gustav Klaus (ed.), *The Rise of Socialist Fiction 1880–1914* (Brighton: Harvester, 1987).

Goldthorpe, John H., David Lockwood, Frank Bechhofer and Jennifer Platt, *The Affluent Worker in the Class Structure* (Cambridge: Cambridge University Press, 1969).

Hennessy, Peter, *Never Again: Britain 1945–1951* (1992; Vintage, 1993).

Hewison, Robert, *In Anger: Culture in the Cold War 1945–1960* (1981; Methuen, 1988).

Hobsbawm, Eric, 'The Formation of British Working-Class Culture', in *Worlds of Labour: Further Studies in the History of Labour* (Weidenfeld and Nicolson, 1984).

Hoggart, Richard, *The Uses of Literacy* (1957; Penguin, 1958).

Holderness, Graham, 'Miners and the Novel: From Bourgeoisie to Proletarian', in Jeremy Hawthorn (ed.), *The British Working Class Novel in the Twentieth Century* (Edward Arnold, 1984).

Hopkins, Eric, *The Rise and Decline of the English Working Classes 1918–1990; A Social History* (Weidenfeld and Nicolson, 1991).

Hutt, Allen, *The Postwar History of the British Working Class* (Left Book Club, 1937).

James, Louis, *Fiction for the Working Man 1830–1850* (1963; Penguin University Books, 1974).

Jameson, Fredric, *Postmodernism, or The Cultural Logic of Late Capitalism* (Verso, 1991).

Johnson, Roy, 'The Proletarian Novel', *Literature and History*, Autumn 1975.

Keating, Peter, *The Haunted Study: A Social History of the English Novel 1875–1914* (1989; Fontana, 1991).

Klaus, Gustav, *The Literature of Labour: Two Hundred Years of Working-Class Writing* (Brighton: Harvester, 1985).

Laing, Stuart, 'The Morality of Affluence: John Braine's *Room at the Top*', in Chris Pawling (ed.), *Popular Fiction and Social Change* (Macmillan, 1984).

—— *Representations of Working-Class Life 1957–1964* (Macmillan, 1986).

Lassell, Margaret, *Wellington Road* (1962; Penguin, 1966).

Lehmann, John, *The Whispering Gallery* (Longman, Green and Co., 1955).

Lukács, George, *History and Class Consciousness* (1920; Merlin, 1971).

Marcuse, Herbert, *An Essay on Liberation* (1969; Penguin, 1972).

—— 'Liberation from Affluent Society', in David Cooper (ed.), *The Dialectics of Liberation* (Penguin, 1968).

Marwick, Arthur, *British Society Since 1945* (Penguin, 1982).

Maschler, Tom (ed.), *Declaration* (MacGibbon and Kee, 1957).

Mitchell, Jack B., *Robert Tressell and the Ragged Trousered Philanthropists* (Lawrence and Wishart, 1969).

—— 'Aesthetic Problems of the Development of the Proletarian-

Revolutionary Novel in Nineteenth-Century Britain', in David Craig (ed.), *Marxists on Literature* (Penguin, 1975).

—— 'Early Harvest: Three Anti-Capitalist Novels Published in 1914', in Gustav Klaus (ed.), *The Socialist Novel in Britain: Towards the Recovery of a Tradition* (Brighton: Harvester, 1982).

Morley, Dave, and Ken Worpole, *The Republic of Letters: Working Class Writing and Local Publishing* (Comedia, 1982).

Morris, Margaret, *The General Strike* (Journeyman, 1976).

Neetens, Wim, *Writing and Democracy: Literature, Politics and Culture* (Brighton: Harvester, 1991).

Pierce, David, and Mary Eagleton, *Attitudes to Class in the English Novel* (Thames and Hudson, 1979).

Richardson, Sarah (ed.), *Writing on the Line: 20th Century Working-Class Women Writers* (Working Press, 1996).

Ritchie, Harry, *Success Stories: Literature and the Media in England, 1950–1959* (Faber and Faber, 1988).

Russell Taylor, John, *Anger and After: A Guide to the New British Drama* (1962; Penguin, 1968).

Salveson, Paul, 'Allen Clarke and the Lancashire School of Novelists 1890–1914', in Gustav Klaus (ed.), *The Rise of Socialist Fiction 1880–1914* (Brighton: Harvester, 1987).

Samuel, Raphael, Ewan MacColl and Stuart Cosgrave, *Theatres of the Left 1880–1935: Workers' Theatre Movements in Britain and America* (Routledge and Kegan Paul, 1985).

Seabrook, Jeremy, *Working Class Childhood* (Gollancz, 1982).

—— *Landscapes of Poverty* (Oxford: Basil Blackwell, 1985).

—— and Trevor Blackwell, *A World Still to Win: The Reconstruction of the Postwar Working Class* (Faber and Faber, 1985).

Sigal, Clancy, *Weekend in Dinlock* (1960; Penguin, 1962).

Sinfield, Alan, *Literature, Politics and Culture in Postwar Britain* (Oxford: Basil Blackwell, 1989).

Sissons, Michael, and Peter French (eds), *Age of Austerity 1945–1951* (1963; Penguin, 1964).

Snee, Carole, 'Working Class Literature or Proletarian Writing?', in John Clarke (ed.), *Culture and Crisis in Britain in the Thirties* (Lawrence and Wishart, 1978).

Stedman-Jones, Gareth, *Languages of Class* (Cambridge: Cambridge University Press, 1983).

Steedman, Carolyn, *Landscape for a Good Woman: A Story of Two Lives* (1986; Virago, 1989).

Thompson, E. P., *The Making of the English Working Class* (1963; Penguin, 1977).

Vicinus, Martha, *The Industrial Muse: A Study of Nineteenth Century British Working Class Literature* (Croom Helm, 1974).

——— 'Chartist Fiction and the Development of Class-based Literature', in Gustav Klaus (ed.), *The Socialist Novel in Britain: Towards the Recovery of a Tradition* (Brighton: Harvester, 1982).

Von Rosenberg, Ingrid, 'Militancy, Anger and Resignation: Alternative Moods in the Working-Class Novel of the 1950s and 1960s', in Gustav Klaus (ed.), *The Socialist Novel in Britain: Towards the Recovery of a Tradition* (Brighton: Harvester, 1982).

Wallace, Gavin, and Randall Stevenson (eds), *The Scottish Novel Since the Seventies* (Edinburgh: Edinburgh University Press, 1993).

Wandor, Micheline, *Look Back in Gender* (Methuen, 1987).

Warner, Rex, 'Education', in C. Day Lewis (ed.), *The Mind in Chains: Socialism and the Cultural Revolution* (Frederick Muller, 1937).

Webster, Roger, '*Love on the Dole* and the aesthetics of contradiction', in Jeremy Hawthorn (ed.), *The British Working Class Novel in the Twentieth Century* (Edward Arnold, 1984).

Williams, Raymond, *Culture and Society 1790–1950* (1958; Penguin, 1979).

——— *The Long Revolution* (1960; Penguin, 1965).

——— (ed.), *May Day Manifesto 1968* (Penguin, 1968).

——— 'The Welsh Industrial Novel', in *Problems in Materialism and Culture* (Verso, 1980).

——— 'The Ragged Arsed Philanthropists', in *Writing in Society* (Verso, 1982).

Worpole, Ken, *Dockers and Detectives: Popular Reading, Popular Writing* (Verso, 1983).

Index